John White

THE SHIP, THE LADY AND THE LAKE

To the memory of my late parents
Wyatt and Billy Larken

The Ship, the Lady and the Lake

THE EXTRAORDINARY LIFE AND RESCUE
OF A VICTORIAN STEAMSHIP IN THE ANDES

MERIEL LARKEN

The Ship, The Lady and The Lake
First published in 2012 by
Bene Factum Publishing Ltd
PO Box 58122
London
SW8 5WZ

Email: inquiries@bene-factum.co.uk
www.bene-factum.co.uk

ISBN: 978-1-903071-42-7

A CIP catalogue record of this is available from the British Library

Cover and book design by Mousemat Design Ltd.

Printed in Malta on behalf of Latitude Press Ltd.

Contents

Illustration acknowledgements

The following illustrations and exerts are reproduced by kind permission of:

Endpapers illustration by John White – marine artist
Archivos Regional Tacna. Peru. p.145, p.151
Birmingham City Archives and Heritage Boulton & Watt Collection p. 41, p.103, p.105, p.141-143 (**MS 3147/3/234**), p.154 (**MS 3147/12/57**);
Centro de Estudios Histórico-Militares – various quotes
Instituto de Estudios Histórico-Marítimos del Perú. p.161
Ministerio de la Marina. Museo Naval del Perú p.57, p.133
National Historic Ships UK p.x-xi
Royal Geographical Society + IBG. p.171

EVER SINCE I FOUND THE HULK of the *Yavarí* on Lake Titicaca in 1983 and subsequently rescued her, people have marvelled at her extraordinary story and urged me to write a book about it. I have tried to do that, but because the project to restore the vessel to an operational standard has taken up so much of my life, our two lives – the *Yavarí*'s and mine – have become fused. This then is the story of my self-imposed task of bringing her back to life, of the many generous people who have helped me along the way with money, expertise or just encouragement, and of Peru.

Peru is an amazing country for its remarkable beauty, history and culture, and I have found it hard to resist including what might appear to be irrelevancies with no bearing on the *Yavarí*, and also some of my own experiences, yet I hope they add something extra to 'our' story.

The happiness for me is that this book also gives me an opportunity to acknowledge those people who have supported me and The Yavarí Project from the day I first clambered aboard the *Yavarí*. If at times I have sounded judgemental, I should explain that it is born of my customary frustration with officialdom, a streak of impatience, and the challenges of a culture different from my own. I certainly would not want to upset anyone, least of all my Peruvian 'hosts' who have taught me so much and with whom I have enjoyed many of the most amusing times of my life.

The *Yavarí* has charmed a great many visitors since I have known her. I hope this tale does her justice.

Foreword

by HRH The Duke of Edinburgh KG KT

BUCKINGHAM PALACE

This book tells a quite remarkable story. The subject is a steam ship called 'Yavari' and how she was built in Britain, taken out to Peru, carried up to Lake Titicaca in pieces and re-assembled. It so happens that I heard this story when I crossed Lake Titicaca by ship during a visit to Peru in 1962. The remains of 'Yavari' were pointed out to me as we left Puno.

I was naturally intrigued when the author got in touch with me about her project to acquire and restore the ship, although I was less than convinced that she had any real chance of success. In the end her project was a triumph, although the outcome may not have been quite what she originally had in mind.

This lively account of the origin of her interest in the ship, and the subsequent frustrations and triumphs in the course of acquiring and restoring her makes a very good read.

NATIONAL HISTORIC SHIPS COMMITTEE

Meriel Larken

16 September 2003

Dear Meriel

MN YAVARI – NHSC ASSESSMENT

My apologies for taking so long with this – we have had a busy summer with an unusually high number of new registrations and some movement at last from the UK Government concerning national policy for historic ships.

As I intimated in my email the Technical Committee looked at YAVARI and were very impressed. There is no doubt that had she been a UK resident they would have strongly recommended her for inclusion on the NHSC Core Collection of historic vessels. Her attributes place her in the same league, as transport craft here like the CUTTY SARK, GLENLEE or GREAT BRITAIN. Below is an outline of the committee's thoughts and how they came to this judgement. This might be of some value in terms of ascertaining insured values. We have some detail of insurance values for other CC vessels but to be honest it is so variable and the logic adopted appears to differ so much from one ship to another that we are not at all sure a comparison helps very much. It is also the case that a lot of the marine insurance we see is tied up with grant applications and is mainly about protecting the investment of public money not intrinsic value.

As you know our present remit only covers vessels that are based or operating in UK waters and therefore our priorities are directed very much to the preservation of historic ships in this country. However if there is anything we can do to help your project or if there are particular needs where our advice or experience might help you you only have to ask. We are recommending very strongly for the UK Core Collection that conservation and business plans should be articulated for all the vessels and have started to accumulate some good frameworks of best practice and experience in these areas – again if this was ever of use to you we would gladly offer help.

Yours ever

John.

CHAIRMAN Admiral of the Fleet Sir Julian Oswald GCB, National Maritime Museum, Greenwich, London, SE10 9NF Telephone 020 8312 6514 Fax 020 8312 6526
SECRETARY J Paton, 98 The Hornet, Chichester, PO19 4JR Telephone/Fax 01243 784873 E-Mail john.paton@thehornet.freeserve.co.uk
NRHV CO-ORDINATOR Paula Austin, National Maritime Museum, Greenwich, London, SE10 9NF Telephone 020 8312 6514 Fax 020 8312 6526 E-Mail nrhv@nmm.ac.uk

The assessment of the *Yavarí* by the National Historic Ships Committee which was succeeded in 2006 by the Advisory Committee on National Historic Ships which in turn has been succeeded by National Histioric Ships UK.

NHSC ASSESSMENT

Our thoughts on YAVARI based on the information you provided and the criteria in our scoring system are:

As one of the earliest iron passenger/cargo carriers constructed in kit form and running on lama dung she scores highly. The jumboization and lifting screw are also noteworthy.

YAVARI has an exemplary status in terms of type and function - small iron plates, lake based and an early example. Her lines have aesthetic appeal, as does much of her original material.

The vessel obviously scores highly in terms of historical association because she has an international flavour and has clearly played an important role in the life of Lake Titicaca. Things like the connections with the Pacific War add to this value.

Originality looks high – the figure of 85% is exemplary – many of the UK Core Collection have much lower percentages. Her condition also looks very stable – cold fresh water and high altitudes sound an excellent environment. Her age makes her collectable; increasingly more value is being attributed to vessels of this age. She is obviously unique as a type of vessel.

The committee were impressed with the outline of the preservation strategy – it would be interesting to identify income streams and get an assessment of the visitor attraction viability. In UK visitor attraction never provides the complete answer – the really successful CC ships have other incomes either through grant-aid, benevolent donors or high income activities like corporate entertainment. They also have strong friend or volunteer inputs, which provide maintenance or visitor guide assets. It also sounds as though considerable professional consultancy and work has been deployed on the project, which to us always augurs well.

All of this supports a view that YAVARI is of considerable international importance, has a very high historical significance and is of pre-eminent national importance. As such, if resident in UK, she would merit a high priority for long-term preservation and would attract a considerable degree of support.

Prologue

IN FACT, IT ALL BEGAN ONE day in London in July 1975. I was late for a party. I hurried along Westminster Pier and up the gangplank of the *Princess Adelaide* just as the deckhands were casting off. As the boat nosed her way into the mainstream of the River Thames, it never occurred to me that this voyage would one day turn my entire life upside down!

The occasion was a family outing in honour of our illustrious ancestor, Sir Alfred Fernandez Yarrow, founder of Yarrow & Co. Shipbuilders and a man universally recognised for his contribution to marine engineering. He was born in very modest circumstances in 1842 in London's East End, to a British father and a Spanish Sephardi Jewish mother. At the age of eight he already showed promise when he invented his first 'machine', an automatic wool-winder for his aunt. He and a school chum erected London's first overhead electric telegraph, and at twenty he and a partner, James Hilditch, designed a steam plough, the success of which – together with a little help from another aunt – enabled them to set up a workshop. In 1875, Alfred opened his own shipyard, Yarrow & Co., and built innovative ships for the Royal and foreign navies but specialised in shallow draught steam launches. He built the 55-foot *Ilala* for the David Livingstone Mission to intercept the slave dhows on Lake Nyasa (Malawi). It was carried in sections 1,400 miles overland and was the first steamer to be launched on an African lake. He also built *Le Stanley* for Henry Morton Stanley to explore the Congo. He was deeply involved in advising the government on rescuing General Gordon from Khartoum, though delays in decision-making meant that his steam gunboats *Lotus* and *Waterlily* arrived too late. After designing the Royal Navy's first two destroyers, *Havock* and *Hornet*, Yarrows became one of the Admiralty's principal shipbuilders. The yard moved to Scotland's river Clyde where Yarrows continued to build warships for the Admiralty throughout the Great War, and 'knock-down' boats for inland waterways. Great-grandfather Alfred was knighted in 1916. Today he is best remembered for the 'Yarrow type water-tube boiler' and for his philanthropy towards several educational, medical and care institutions.

He was also known in the family for his eccentricities. For example, in old age, he took up residence in a distinguished London hotel but couldn't sleep in their distinguished bed until he had installed a motor under it to replicate the motion of a train, the only place in which he could sleep.

We, the descendants of four of his six children, were on a pilgrimage to the Isle of Dogs, the site of his first shipyard where it had all begun in 1865.

The shipboard party was a merry and noisy affair as family members caught up with one another's news, and we were well past the Tower of London before I found myself next to our host, my cousin Eric, Alfred's grandson, and, at that time, chairman of Yarrow Shipbuilders. I just had time to tell him that I was off to South America when he was called away but, as we parted, he stopped, turned back with an afterthought, and added, 'Well, in that case, don't forget to look up our old ship.'

It was this throwaway line that changed my life.

'Old ship?' I questioned. 'What old ship?'

'Why, the one built by your great-grandfather, Alfred. It's on Lake Titicaca'.

Vivid memories of my school days flooded back, and of learning about the far-reaching effects of the Industrial Revolution. I could hear our history mistress explaining that, with the introduction of iron in shipbuilding, vessels could be prefabricated in kit form and carried overland to anywhere in the world, '...for example, to the headwaters of the Nile,' she said, 'or Lake Tanganyika, and even up the Andes to the highest navigable lake in the world, Lake Titicaca!'

Could 'our old ship' be the very one she meant?

I was excited by the thought that such a remarkable achievement might be a family legacy. When I got home that night I added yet another X to my map of South America, already dotted with other Xs indicating the places I was hoping to visit.

This last X was on Lake Titicaca.

CHAPTER 1

My Introduction to Peru

AT THE TIME I WAS TAKING a year out to backpack round South America. Having danced round the ballrooms of London as a debutante, which for a shy, slightly plump teenager was as terrifying and character-forming as it was fun, I had left home to travel and work abroad, in Malta, Australia and Italy. I was now thirty-two, but still had not been to South America and longed to go there.

In the 1970s, before the gap year was invented, South America was not commonly visited by European travellers, who tended to head off to India and the Far East. In Britain, the continent did not feature in the school curriculum and, although it attracted a few enterprising banks and businesses, little was known about it and people looked askance, or merely blank, when I mentioned it. With the exception of the British and French Guyanas and Dutch Suriname, as they were then called, the continent had been colonised by Spain and Portugal and divided between them by Pope Alexander IV; this division was amended by the Treaty of Tordesillas in 1494. Before 1810 the Spanish colonies were closed to foreigners, so the British knew little about them. Even today, I have been asked where Peru is in relation to Nigeria.

I talked a lot about going there, driving myself and everyone else mad with procrastinations, until I realised that I would never be able to settle down until I had got it out of my system. The man who made the thought of 'settling down' seem attractive flattered me by saying he would miss me while I was away, and implied that he would be waiting for me when I got back. His reward was being allowed to inspect the contents of my rucksack.

'Well, you won't want that, or that!' he exclaimed with disdain, tossing out more and more items of clothing. As my rucksack was actually too heavy to lift, I was secretly rather relieved that he was making these decisions for me. 'And certainly not *that*!' he declared, flinging a long green and white Ban-Lon evening dress to the floor. Ban-Lon, a slinky synthetic fabric, was considered the latest thing then, and had the added advantage of packing down to almost nothing without creasing.

I dug my toes in over that dress. 'I might be invited to a smart party,' I said defensively. 'And what a shame to have to refuse just because I didn't have something appropriate to wear.'

Living in London as I did, I was lucky enough to have good friends who did know South America, and they introduced me to a circle of anthropologists, scientists and explorers who spoke of little else. With their help, I soon sketched out a route that would take me beyond the tourist trail to meet remote, sometimes eccentric, people doing exotic things in unmarked places.

The same friends also knew a young and vivacious redhead called Conca who shared my ambitions. Within moments of meeting we had decided to travel together. We must have looked an odd couple. I was five feet seven, while Conca was so petite that her rucksack all but hid her from view. Height, though, was not the issue as we landed in Venezuela, our entry point to the South American continent. Our challenges were those which confronted any budget traveller to what was known then as the Third World – pickpockets and crooked money dealers by day, bed bugs and cold water by night, not to mention poking live electric wires into sockets dangling crazily from the ceiling, and the omnipresent smell of urine.

After several days we moved on to Colombia, congratulating ourselves that we had survived our initiation into Latin America's urban experience. However, we were much less confident about how we would cope with the rudimentary basics of jungle life. An old Dakota flew us deep into the Amazon rainforest, and dropped us in a small jungle township by the river Vaupés, where we hung our hammocks in a hut on stilts reserved for travelling salesmen, and looked for river transport.

A week later, a Hungarian baron heading upstream to check on his chocolate plantations offered to take us with him. His two dugout canoes, known locally as *peke-pekes* on account of the noise of their outboard motors, were already loaded down with equipment, food, gifts for the

South America showing Lake Titicaca

Indians, ammunition and his team of workers. We squeezed in amongst them and over several days travelled many miles up the muddy Vaupés, between a wall of trees hung with trailing vines and climbers dotted with brightly-coloured flowers and, at the river's edge, exposed roots and fallen branches. One of the team sat in the bow looking out for floating vegetation and sand banks and a *motorista* operated the outboard and its six-foot prop-shaft and propeller designed to be easily lifted to avoid

3

hazards. Occasionally an exotic bird flew over the river, and egrets stood out like white flags against the forest foliage. Intermittently we passed clearings opening onto settlements of wooden huts on stilts where children were playing and women in faded cotton dresses washed clothes in the river. We slept in a different community each night, Conca and I hanging our hammocks in the guests' hut or, on one occasion, in the chief's hut. He had vacated it but he wanted us to know that his father would be with us – he was buried in the earth floor beneath our hammocks. We ate round the campfire and washed in the river where we saw flights of little yellow sulphur butterflies extracting minerals from the mud. We later learned that this is called 'puddling'.

In a few days, we came to a site of four huts nestling in an orchard of tropical fruit trees, palms and cassava plants. The baron told us it was unlikely that any western woman had ever set foot here before. We felt most intrepid. The two families who lived there welcomed us warmly. We were just getting accustomed to the daily routine when the baron's factotum, a young Colombian who had been acting oddly towards us since the start, suddenly pulled a revolver on us and waved it in our faces, while shouting at the baron that from here on it was him or us.

So we had to be 'evacuated' more or less back the way we had come but on foot through the forest, not relaxing in a dugout canoe. It was a very different story. It is dark under the forest canopy, and the trails we followed were narrow and lined with potentially hostile, even poisonous, undergrowth. There was no knowing what reaction we might get from being scratched or stung, and underfoot it was like walking on leaf mould, soft and often boggy. At intervals, we had to slither along a fallen branch over one of the many little streams. We were accompanied by a guide, Ernesto, and three porters, all appointed by the baron. At dusk we hung our hammocks between trees recommended by Ernesto and were thankful that our companions did not have their transistor radios with them as they had on the river journey, so we could hear the jungle's night noises and the cacophony of the dawn chorus.

The mosquitoes were awful and I itched all over. One late afternoon I went off to get some relief in a waterhole roughly the size of half a tennis court but well hidden by overhanging trees and lianas. I was in my bra and pants and revelling in the cool water when I looked up and, to my astonishment, saw a jaguar emerge from the forest heading for the same waterhole. It was one end and I was the other. When it saw me it was probably as surprised as I was to see it. It turned its head to look straight at me, paused, blinked slowly, just like pussy does, and then padded slowly on its way over a tree trunk that had fallen across the pool, and gracefully disappeared into the forest. It was big – had it been right beside me, it would have stood almost as high as my waist – heavily built, spotted and magnificent. It was such a privilege for me. The jaguar is the third largest cat after the tiger and lion and the largest feline in the western hemisphere. It is shy and rarely seen by the locals, and sometimes shot if it is, and almost never by visitors. I was so thrilled I forgot to be afraid, only faintly worried that he might smell my clothes on the bank and ravage or run off with them. When I told Ernesto he said I had been incredibly lucky and that it had probably been a young and curious male.

As it turned out, it was just the first of many South American adventures for both Conca and me. However, we had already decided that each would travel better alone, but that before splitting up we should visit the Galapagos Islands together. Access was not as straightforward as it is today and required research and planning. We happened to be visiting the British Air Attaché in his office when his telephone rang. The two Ecuadorian generals who were due to fly to the islands that afternoon as his guests could no longer do so. Suddenly two seats had become available, and that afternoon we were in them. After a fortnight, we returned to the mainland and, with no hard feelings, said our farewells, and went our separate ways.

* * *

I headed south to Peru where I paused to explore archaeological sites which opened my eyes to the age and sophistication of the civilisations which preceded the Incas but which, until recently, received only modest recognition. I ate *cuy* (guinea pig), considered precious fare in those days and served only to important guests, and I walked the foothills of Mount Huascarán, Peru's highest mountain at 22,200 feet. It has since been made famous by Joe Simpson's book *Touching the Void*, and the gripping film made from it.

The *conquistador* Francisco Pizarro called Lima the City of Kings, because he arrived there on Epiphany Sunday in 1535. It became the seat of the Spanish viceroy for most of Hispanic South America, and the richest and most important city on the continent. Traces of grandeur still remain in Peru's capital city, but its fluctuating fortunes since Independence have taken their toll.

I continued south on the coastal road until I came to Nazca. In the desert outside the small town, curious lines known as geoglyphs have been drawn in the desert (400BC–650AD). Dr Maria Reiche, the German mathematician who spent a lifetime trying to interpret them, very seldom came into town from her campsite in the desert so I recognised my luck when I spotted her coming towards me down the dusty main thoroughfare. Being the only foreigners in town, we greeted one another. She said she would like to practice her English and asked if I should like to see 'her' lines.

'Love to,' said I, so away we went to spend the day in the desert. The lines, on closer inspection, proved to be furrows created by sweeping aside the dark top sand to reveal the pale earth beneath. The extent and detail of the designs can really only be seen from above. We climbed a ladder to a wooden platform and looked down on what then became clearly a monkey, a spider and a humming bird among many other figures and lines. Speculation abounds as to who, how and why, but Maria Reiche's theory was based on the relationship between the lines and the solar system. She surmised that the whole formed an intricate calendar enabling the Nazca people to be alert to the onset of the rainy season in the *sierra* in time to prepare their irrigation canals. The area that the lines cover is 190 square miles, and Dr Reiche knew every inch of them and believed it was her destiny to spend her life trying to decipher their meaning. I was sorry that she refused to return to the town and accept my invitation to supper but, as she explained, she far preferred to sleep in the *pampa* in her sleeping bag beneath the stars.

As I rang the bell of my third-rate hostel and headed down a narrow passage to my windowless room, I envied her.

* * *

Eventually, I went east and up the southern Andes of Peru and it was there that I experienced a strange sensation. I was in Pisac, a small town just 20 miles north of the old Inca capital of Cuzco, and making my way down the 'Sacred Valley' to the Inca citadel of Machu Picchu. Pisac, which throbs with life on market day but appears deserted on a weekday when its residents go off to work in their fields, is overlooked by an Inca site.

Being Inca, it is situated in a good vantage position commanding magnificent panoramic views over the Urubamba river and beyond. Being Inca it is also up a steep and exhausting climb, which I managed to do before collapsing on a rock to study my guidebook. It said: '*Remember that there are three hill fortifications but the third is the fortress proper which you can just see right above you…*'

I looked up and blanched. It was, indeed, hundreds of feet further on – and up. Galvanising myself for the ascent I was suddenly struck by an overwhelming premonition. I am not given to extrasensory perception, but the feeling was so strong that I had to sit down again to see if it would go away, but it persisted. Was this Divine intervention? I don't know, but the message, which was unmistakable, was that I shouldn't worry about struggling on because I would come back here one day.

I was so thankful. No more climbing! Glory be! My journey up to that moment had been so rewarding that I was delighted with the thought of coming back one day. With a renewed spring in my step I headed back down the hill to continue on my way towards Lake Titicaca.

* * *

Peru had far exceeded my expectations. I, like most Britons, hadn't realised how very different the thirteen South American countries are one from another. Each one can be identified by its geography, indigenous tribes, culture, dress, music, food and customs. The languages also vary. French, English or Dutch are spoken in the Guyanas depending on their colonists' mother tongue, Portuguese in Brazil and Spanish in the nine remaining countries, but the characteristic common to all is the warmth of the local people and their response to the often inadequate attempts we foreigners make to cross the cultural divide. When Edward Whymper, the first European mountaineer to climb the Andes, was travelling around in the 1870s, he observed that '*a jest may conquer where force will fail*' and that '*a bon-môt is often better than a passport*'[1]. A hundred years later, I would say that patience was more effective than a jest and the best *bon-môts* were 'Bobby Charlton' and 'the Beatles' (pronounced *Beatlés*). The fact that I came from the birthplace of these icons was certainly more useful than any passport. Every door was opened to me, although at first I found being stared at, especially by the children, quite disconcerting. I would look down to see scores of small faces gazing up at me, eyes wide in wonderment. Then I learned why. They had never seen blue eyes before, and mine are bright blue.

Equipped with these keys to friendship and the cheerful conviction that this was likely to be only the first of many subsequent visits to Peru,

Llama; South American camelid; beast of burden related to the guanaco, alpaca and vicuña.

I took the train from Cuzco across the roof of the world, one of the most spectacular train rides on the planet. Between small adobe hamlets and against a backdrop of Andean mountaintops, we travelled through the barren wastes of the *altiplano* (high plateau) inhabited only by herds of llamas and alpacas. Indian herdswomen, who spun wool as they walked, dressed in shocking pinks and psychedelic greens, topped off by a bowler hat, stood out as eye-catching splashes of colour on an otherwise yellow-brown canvas. Little did I think then that I too would one day be just such a splash in a similar landscape.

The train stopped at many sparse communities to be invaded by Indian women and children competing fiercely to sell their wares. Each community boasted a speciality – home-grown, home-made or bought in for the purpose – a cheese, roast pork, biscuits, bananas or roasted peanuts, or knitted bonnets and sweaters. With only two trains passing each day, they had to make the most of the fifteen-minute stop. The roast pork was a particular favourite. Broad-shouldered, sturdy Indian women carrying large baking trays boarded the train crying out, '*Chancho, chancho!*' ('Pork, pork!'), and forced their way along the crowded aisles tearing off hunks of roast pork to hand out in scraps of brown paper to hungry and impatient passengers.

I was the only foreigner in the tightly packed carriage. My travelling companions were all Indians, mostly women clad in cardigans, voluminous many-coloured knee-length skirts or *polleras*, thick woollen socks and a blanket around the shoulders held in place with a nappy pin. Known colloquially as *cholas*, their faces were round, ruddy and weather beaten and their build stocky, but their deportment so ram-rod straight that, however jauntily worn, the ubiquitous bowler hat never fell off. Each wore her hair, black as a raven's wing and as shiny, in long plaits set off with gold or silver drop earrings. Some carried babies on their backs and some bundles, but because their many skirts made it difficult for them to fit onto the narrow banquettes, immense bundles of gaily-coloured weavings were offloaded into the aisle, which quickly blocked it entirely.

These women, whose bustling walk in sandals made of old car tyres makes you think of Beatrix Potter's Mrs Tiggywinkle, are the matriarchs who run Indian society. But treat them like Mrs Tiggywinkle, and you do so at your peril; they can bowl a good potato, particularly at intrusive holiday snappers.

Because the track was uneven, the train clunked and clattered along at barely more than walking speed blowing its whistle frequently to alert pedestrians and livestock to move out of its way. It suited me well because I was in no hurry and there was so much to see. There was also time to catch up on a few facts from the (then) traveller's only bible, *The South American Handbook*.

I learned that, at 12,500 feet above sea level, Lake Titicaca is the largest high-altitude lake in the world and the largest inland waterway in South America. It was left behind after the last Ice Age and lies within a basin between the eastern and western *cordilleras* of the Andean range, which stretches from Colombia to Chile thereby making it the longest mountain range in the world. The lake, which is over 100 miles long, is divided 60/40 between Peru and Bolivia and overlooked by the snow peaks of the Cordillera Real. It is a spectacular setting. The sun blazes

The Cathedral of San Carlos Borromeo, Puno, built in 1757 by the Jesuits and one of several fine Andean Baroque churches in the Lake Titicaca region.

through the rarefied atmosphere, sharpening shapes and brightening colours, and the clouds above seem as close as their shimmering reflections in the blue-black waters of the lake.

Titicaca is known as *el Lago Sagrado,* the Sacred Lake, because popular legend has it that the Incas' creator god, Viracocha, chose it as the birthplace of the first Incas, Manco Capac and his sister Mama Ocllo. It is said that after the great flood, and from a sacred rock on what is now called the *Isla del Sol* or Island of the Sun, Viracocha created light in the form of the Sun and the Moon. When the Inca tribe was in the ascendant, Manco Capac and Mama Ocllo spun the tale that they were that Sun and that Moon. Long before the Incas the lake was considered sacred due to its microclimate. There is evidence of human occupation in the area from as far back as 10,000-8,000 BC but more visible today are the stone foundations and burial towers of the Collas and Lupakas who settled around the lake's northern and southern shores. These two tribes evolved following the collapse of the Tiwanaku culture and immediately preceded the Incas who overwhelmed and subjugated them.

The Tiwanaku, who built beside and were dependent upon Lake Titicaca, formed arguably one of South America's most influential civilisations. The culture evolved from 1600 BC, but had collapsed by 1000 AD. It is suggested that there was a great drought so that their crops failed and the level of the lake dropped away. It is thought that the site was originally built beside the lake, but it is now twelve miles from it, which would lend credence to these theories. Today the complex is a UNESCO World Heritage site and is recognised by its iconic Gateway of the Sun, which stands nine feet high, its lintel 13 feet across, the whole weighing ten tons and carved from a single block of granite. The lintel is elaborately carved with effigies facing what some call the Sun God in the centre, but this is still only speculation. Monolithic pillars, walls, platforms, terraces, sacrificial sites and ceremonial mounds provide evidence of the site's significance and, some say, a population of up to 30,000 people, although the surrounding region could have supported as many as a million.

On the other hand, my destination – Puno – is today an unprepossessing little town on the north-west shore of the lake. It was founded in 1668 due to the importance of the silver mines close by at Salcedo. Sad to tell, such was the success of the mines, the battles that were fought over them and the envy they aroused, that their owner, Sr

Jose Salcedo, paid the ultimate price when he was summoned to Lima, tried on a trumped-up charge, found guilty and duly executed.

When the lake steamers plied between Peru and Bolivia, Puno, as Peru's principal lakeside town, was an important port. Since the road was built between the two countries in the sixties, the town has turned its back on the lake, preferring to focus its attentions on its shopping centre of narrow and overcrowded streets, its contraband market and its football stadium.

There have been many changes to Puno over the years I have been visiting it. The huge piles of rubbish scattered by scavenging dogs, pigs and sometimes children have gone, but so have many of the colonial adobe and thatch houses with their handsome stone doorways and the wooden balconies from which the bourgeoisie watched the processions, festivals and each other. They've made way for concrete constructions, shops, offices and houses of questionable architectural merit whose metal window frames seldom fit and therefore provide no protection from the bitter cold winds. Since my first visit a truly awful 'carbuncle' has appeared in the once-elegant seventeenth-century Plaza de Armas, which is dominated by its eighteenth-century cathedral. Formerly the Plaza Mayor, the square's name changed when it became the place for defeated royalists to surrender their arms in the war for independence. The classical symmetry of its architecture, repeated in all Peruvian towns, is – or was – typical of the main square in almost every small town in Spain. But in the early 1990s, to celebrate the defeat of the *Sendero Luminoso* (Shining Path) terrorists, and to restore confidence and self-esteem amongst the communities that had suffered most from the atrocities, the government allocated funds to provincial municipalities with which to build new town halls. Alas, they seldom conform to the traditional norms.

The town, of a little over 100,000 souls, bustles all day and never more so than when the schools, colleges and Peru's most populous university disgorge their students. It is said that half of Peru's 29 million inhabitants are under the age of twenty-five. As well as through natural reproduction, the population grows irrepressibly as *campesinos* (peasants) migrate to the town in search of a better life.

Like the houses that have been 'modernised', so has the people's everyday dress. For centuries, the Indian women of the *sierra* could be identified down to the smallest community, and their status within that community, by their dress. The pattern of the weave, the colours, the numbers of skirts, the shape and material of the hat, the adornments on the hat, all were symbols proudly worn every day and elaborated upon for *fiestas*. As for the Puneñas (women of Puno), each year I notice that more have forsaken their long black plaits in favour of a short crinkly perm, and their traditional brightly coloured *polleras* and *wachala* (carrying cloth), that I had so enjoyed on the train, for the drab uniformity of the western wardrobe.

Likewise, on my first visit, the men, though less flamboyant, were unmistakably *serranos* (highland Indians). Alas, many have now foresworn the traditional woven belt called a *chumpi*, the *chu'spa* (a woven bag for carrying coca leaves) and the *poncho*, and now sport leather bomber jackets, football shirts, denims, trainers and – horrors – baseball caps. Today the traditional weavings, many of whose designs are incomparably intricate and steeped in symbolism and tradition, are on sale to the discerning tourist. Indeed, before the authorities prohibited the export of any textile over a hundred years old, pantechnicons loaded with the most antique of the weavings left the country. Thankfully, efforts are now being made to resuscitate the craft and the use of natural dyes before the ancient skill, once passed from generation to generation, is irretrievably lost. Similarly, the languages of Quechua and Aymara are heard less and less except in remote areas, but while Spanish has become the lingua franca efforts are being made to give young people at least a grounding in their ethnic tongue. It is sad that tribal languages, like traditional everyday dress, are today considered unsophisticated and homespun, and that people want to look and behave like characters in an American soap opera.

Over the years I have come to know these people a little (only a few foreigners could claim to know them well), and to respect them a lot. Their lives are hard, and it's small wonder that they look for opportunities to change them. Change is inevitable, and desirable if it improves their standard of living, but the transition is uncomfortable to watch. The Indians' psyche and sense of identity must be in turmoil if their aspirations are driven by the more brazen elements of western society. I was disturbed once to see a calendar advertising a company that sold spare truck parts hanging in an adobe shack in the remotest of highland communities. Was the white blonde pin-up girl posing seductively in her perilously skimpy bikini really the best image our 'more advanced' culture had to offer them?

Happily, these changes apply much less to music, dance and traditional costume at *fiesta* time, and in the *sierra* there is a *fiesta* somewhere every day of the year. Puno's main claim to fame these days is as the folklore capital of Peru and the region boasts some four hundred different traditional dances. But the *Fiesta de la Virgen de la Candelaria,* similar to the better known *La Diablada* (The Dance of the Devils) of Ururo in Bolivia, is less about haunting pre-Colombian Andean pipe music and more about the rumbustuous brass tubas and trumpets which came with the Spanish.

When I first arrived in Puno it was Michaelmas, February 1976, and *La Candelaria* was in full swing. The smell of alcohol pervaded the air and the streets were gridlocked with demons and devils, the Archangel Michael, African slaves, condors, bears, Incas and Spanish *conquistadores* leaping and twirling in procession. Every year, this once-pagan festival acts out the themes of good overcoming evil, the Saints versus Satan, and a parody of the Conquest. The costumes, each worth more than a family's entire wardrobe, are fabulous, and the exotic, gruesome and absolutely resplendent masks are the work of highly revered hereditary craftsmen and worth practically a year's salary. The dancers and bandsmen, *a.k.a* the bank manager, the pharmacist and the post office clerk, dance and drink themselves into a trance commemorating the Spanish Conquest and the subsequent cruelty and oppression suffered by the indigenous people and slaves, thousands of whom died down the mines. Typical of most religious festivals in Peru, it is a fusion of Indian paganism and – since the seventeenth century – Spanish Christianity, and opens with a statue of the Virgin, in this case *de la Candelaria,* being processed round the town. Then the action begins. Over fifty teams of dancers and brass bands, most of them commercially or individually sponsored, compete. For the first week at least, the dance steps are choreographed and co-ordinated. By the second week, the sweat-inducing masks, the hired high-heeled boots and the beer have taken their toll and the bandsmen, by now capable of playing only three discordant bars of their music, do so repeatedly until they can no longer muster the breath. By the last day, exhaustion and insensibility have set in and all ends in disarray.

On that first occasion I was reluctant to tear myself away. However, remembering my mission, I elbowed my way out of the crowd and made off towards the port. It was clearly not the most auspicious moment to be looking for an historic ship, particularly as I later learned that none of the ships left on Lake Titicaca was any longer of the slightest interest to the local people. I did find a handful of boatmen around the jetty but they were definitely in *fiesta* mood. The combination of my lamentable Spanish and the effects on them of their local brew led me nowhere. I returned the next day but again the search for information proved fruitless. So while the town danced on, I moved on and, resolving to improve my Spanish and glean more information on the old ship, I headed off towards Bolivia and continued my journey.

* * *

Many months later I had come full circle and was back in Venezuela, where my trip ended. It had been a thrilling adventure, and an education. I had met an extraordinary cross-section of people, some so poor but always generous, some so rich they hardly knew that the poor existed. I had seen parrots and penguins, anteaters and alpacas. I had ridden with *gauchos*, and scaled the heights of Conan Doyle's *Lost World* of Roraima; I had eaten Welsh black bread in Patagonia, many plates of rice, egg and banana, and, most reluctantly, one plate of monkey. In the village where I had landed up there was much rejoicing when a hapless capuchin monkey was carried in by one of a small band of hunters. It was dead. Considered a rich reward for a day's hunting in the rainforest, it was skinned, barbecued and carefully portioned out to the expectant onlookers. It looked to me exactly like a barbecued baby and, though I feigned delight, I would gladly have given my portion away.

I had *not* found the family ship but I *had* worn the Ban-Lon dress. I had been a house guest on an *estancia* outside Buenos Aires, where glistening Hereford cattle grazed their way through rich grasslands stretching to the horizon. After a day of tennis and polo, dinner was a black tie affair. Four courses were served and accompanying wines were poured by white-gloved waiters. It was 1976, but no-one witnessing this show of extravagance could possibly have guessed that Argentina's economy was in dire melt-down and that, while the poor protested in Buenos Aires and we sipped one of our four wines, the president, Isabel Perón, President Perón's third wife and widow, was attempting to flee the country and impeachment for blatant corruption. It was surreal, but not once was the crisis referred to.

By this time, I was eager to get home. I knew that the man who had been privileged to vet my rucksack, and whose letters I had been picking up from British Embassies on my way round, would be at the airport to meet me. But the moment I saw him I knew that things had changed. He told me that recently he had been seduced (implying innocence on his part) but that it was just 'a passing affair'. I thought he showed a poor sense of timing.

The next day I signed up for Spanish evening classes, and began keeping my ears open for opportunities that would take me back to Peru.

CHAPTER 2

Getting to Know Peru

Eighteen months later, in 1978, I was incredibly lucky to be interviewed in Birmingham by Dr Ann Kendall, an archaeologist who was launching a major Anglo-Peruvian dig very close to Machu Picchu. Excavation permits were rarely granted to foreigners by the Peruvian authorities, but on meeting Ann Kendall I quite understood how she had won them round. She was beguiling and her project inspiring. I had volunteered as a digger but three hours into the interview I had become the project Administrator. In her soft, almost wistful manner, which I later learned belied an obsessive single-mindedness, Ann told me that the Cusichaca Project was to be a five-year programme to excavate the pre-Inca and, more importantly, the Inca occupation of a site which, given the number of buildings, amounted to a microcosm of the Inca Empire.

It was obvious, she explained, from the canals and terracing, now in disrepair, that Cusichaca had once been a fertile agricultural site for supplying all the pre-Colombian crops, and in particular the Incas' staple diet, maize, to Machu Picchu. She was especially interested in the historic agricultural methods for their academic value, but she believed too that their resuscitation could be of great benefit to the *campesino* community.

When the Spanish conquered Peru they banned all indigenous crops (especially quinoa because of its brain-nourishing properties) in favour of European grains. Ann was keen to encourage the local community to re-introduce the more nutritious crops appropriate to the high-altitude terrain. Later, I was to witness the subtle way in which she planted this idea in the minds of the chief and his community, whose land she was focused on revitalising, so that they believed it to be their own. The result, five years on, was an entirely rehabilitated complex of canals and an abundance of Inca crops.

I liked this altruistic concept; in fact, the entire project so attracted me that when she told me she had signed an undertaking with the Peruvian authorities to start the following May and dig through the dry season till October, I had mentally already packed my bag. But there was more.

Ann gave me the breakdown of the Anglo-Peruvian team of scientists and diggers and pinpointed on the map the bank of the Urubamba river where we would camp. She also told me how to liaise with our sponsors, the airline British Caledonian, and the ten-man team of Army volunteers who would be exchanging their logistics expertise for the opportunity of trekking in the Andes.

Then I learned that my job would also entail raising money and finding sponsors for the equipment. Manufacturers were generous, and before long my small London flat was stacked high with four tons of kit, from trowels and wheelbarrows to lavatory paper (264 rolls of Andrex was the carefully calculated number required), and quantities of comfort foods like Marmite, Mars bars and beer kits.

All of this, and the British Army team's equipment, was consigned to our other devoted sponsor, Pacific Steam Navigation Company. PSNC was the first shipping line to serve the west coast of South America, which it did from 1808 until the 1990s when, alas, it was absorbed by a global operator.

Two days before my departure, at seven in the morning, the telephone rang. It was my mother. 'Darling, I really don't think you should go', I waited for more; she was not one to panic. 'Haven't you heard?' she continued. 'There's been a revolution in Peru! Things sound very bad indeed.' My dear mother, in the depths of rural England, had been listening to the BBC World Service and was way ahead with the international news. 'There are tanks in the streets of Lima and water cannon and riots,' she went on, clearly agitated. 'And they've had to impose a curfew. They've declared a State of Emergency.'

At the earliest opportunity, I rang the Peru Desk at the Foreign Office in London.

'What revolution?' was the reply. 'We don't know about any revolution. Give me half an hour and I'll get back to you.'

Mum was right. There *had* been riots, there *were* tanks in the streets and a curfew *had* been imposed. Indeed, we were advised that the sudden arrival of ten British soldiers might be misinterpreted.

In the event, I flew out a week later with the soldiers' commanding officer, and they followed. I next saw our container of equipment on the dockside in Lima's port of Callao. Its journey from there to the bank of the Urubamba was beset by threatened theft, delays and abandonment, all of which was, for me, a baptism of fire. And that was just the start. From then on, *every* day held a new challenge.

I learned so much. I learned that Peru's long history is complicated by the many cultures that rose and fell on the coast and in the *sierra*. Of these, most is known about the Incas because they were dominant at the time of the Spanish Conquest. They were impressive as engineers, and built a mighty empire stretching from Chile to Colombia which they ran with ruthless efficiency for a hundred years. However, there were many other cultures, both along the coast and in the highlands, which preceded them and which were invariably more artistic and creative, that deserve similar recognition.

Of more relevance, as it turned out, I also learned a great deal about man (under stress) management, temperamental experts, how to eke out a tiny budget and the discomforts of camping and extremes of climate at 7,500 feet.

The anxieties caused by the logistics of keeping up to 50 people sheltered and fed on a shoestring remain unforgettable, but happily they have been outweighed by the memories of my surroundings. When I woke each morning it was to see the sun breaking over the snow peak of Mount Veronica, turning it first to orange as though on fire, then to a dark pink which lost its intensity as it crept down the mountain side until the scrubby lower slopes were aglow in soft salmon pink. Then the valley, in deep shadow and cold until then, quickly lit and warmed up as the sun's rays burst upon it bringing out the pungent scent of the *ratama* (gorse) blossom. At the end of the day, being so close to the Equator, dusk came early to the sounds of the birds' evensong, the shadows quickly lengthened, and the tropical night fell as abruptly as the dawn had broken.

More important, however, was the invaluable introduction which the experience gave me to the Peruvian *modus operandi*, an experience which would prove invaluable over the years. Half the fun of travelling and working abroad is to see how other people do things, but it is a great mistake to think that one's own way of getting things done is best – it isn't; it's just different.

Victualling in Cuzco for the Cusichaca team was a good example of a cross-cultural scenario which tried my patience to the limit. I tried to find it amusing but seldom could, because I was always in a hurry to catch the evening train back to camp.

In a shop I always waited my turn. Queuing is not a Peruvian custom, but I found it difficult not to; the habit is ingrained. How absurd it must have looked to the locals and yet, quite irrationally, it infuriated me when they didn't conform.

When I got up to the counter, this is how the charade would play itself out:

'Good day, *Señora*,' I would say. 'Please may I have some sugar?'

'Sugar, you say, *Señorita*?' The affirmation seemed unnecessary but perhaps my accent wasn't clear. 'What colour, white or brown?'

'White, please, *Señora*.'

'White, you said? And how much?'

'Just four kilos please.'

Then, just when I thought I had the shopkeeper's undivided attention, a local Indian housewife in bowler hat and with bundle would push past me, march up to the counter, exchange a *Buenas dias* with the *Señora* behind the counter, and place her order. From one moment to the next I had been sidelined, forgotten. When the interloper had completed her shopping and left, the *Señora* would again turn to me but had long ago lost track of where we had got to.

'The sugar, *Señora*,' I would say by way of a reminder.

'Ah yes, *Señorita*, how much sugar would you like?'

'Just four kilos please.' I would be getting a little bit tetchy by now.

'Of brown, did you say?'

'No, white, *Señora*, please,' I would riposte, firmer and sterner.

'Ah, four kilos of white sugar, is it, *Señorita*?' A pause, and then, '*Blanca, no hay*,' meaning there is no white sugar.

'In that case, I'll take brown.'

'How much?'

'Four kilos, please, *Señora*.'

'*No hay* four kilos; I only have two.'

'Well, please give me two then,' I would say through tight lips, trying to keep the exasperation out of my voice, all the time knowing that I would have to go through the whole *divertissement* all over again in the next shop.

I thought it must be because I was a foreigner until I saw them doing it to one another. I could have played the same game and barged to the front, knocking locals out of my way, but it would be unseemly. Instead, I churned and chuntered, and tried to keep calm by reciting Rudyard Kipling's *If* to myself – *'If you can wait and not be tired of waiting...'*

* * *

I realise now how fortunate I was to do my pupillage under Ann Kendall. She appeared to understand the people and was well liked, but she never took it for granted. The Peruvian character is a joy to anthropologists because it is so complex and, probably as a result of their history, their attitude towards foreigners working in their country is even more so. I watched Ann carefully and after a couple of digging seasons began to think, probably misguidedly, that I just might have grasped an inkling of understanding, but I can't boast that it was any more than that.

I was lucky that an opportunity to test my new 'cultural understanding' came after my second field season at Cusichaca, though it was delayed while the Falklands War intervened. I had made a proposal to a BBC TV team to film the last chapter of Dr John Hemming's book, *The Conquest of the Incas*, and to my surprise and delight they had accepted. It tells the story of the desperate attempts made by the Spanish to find and flush out the Incas from their last refuge to which they had fled in 1539. Known today as Espiritu Pampa, it was (and still is) hidden deep in the *semi-selva* (half jungle) of Vilcabamba, down the sacred Urubamba valley past Machu Picchu and over the Andes. Eventually, in 1572, the Spaniards succeeded and the last Inca, Tupac Amaru, was put to death most horribly in Cuzco's main square, marking the culmination of the Conquest.

The first foreigner to discover the site of Espiritu Pampa was the American academic and explorer Hiram Bingham in 1911, but because it was obscured by vegetation he failed to recognise its significance and continued to refer to Machu Picchu, which, with the help of the locals, he also discovered that year, as 'the last city of the Incas'. It wasn't until another American explorer, Gene Savoy, investigated the area more thoroughly in 1965 that the size and importance of the town were established. He found no fewer than 300 buildings spreading over a vast area, almost entirely overgrown by jungle. Even in the 1980s it was still barely known and rarely visited.

As soon as the dust had settled following the war of *las Islas Malvinas*, as they are known in South America, and notwithstanding warnings from the British Embassy that the *Sendero Luminoso* terrorists had recently been active in the area, we set out from Cuzco down the Urubamba valley.

There were six in the television team, innumerable metal cases of expensive camera kit, our camping equipment and food, myself, Washington our *arriero* (muleteer), his three assistants and 21 pack-mules. Washington was taller than the average Indian and wore a trilby hat that added to his air of authority. I accompanied him and his mules readily and while the TV crew discussed and chose their subjects and deliberated on their camera angles he and I travelled ahead to establish the next campsite and pitch the tents.

Loading the mules each morning took at least an hour. They waited patiently to be blindfolded and stood stock-still while knotted rope panniers or woven wool shawls filled with awkward cases and cargo were lashed to their backs. Only when the *arriero* had tightened the girth by placing his sandalled foot firmly against the beast's ribcage and heaving with all his weight, would the blindfold be removed.

The going was certainly tough but worth the pain for the panorama. With raptors circling overhead we zigzagged up the side of the valley on what seemed no more than a ledge cut into the mountainside. Across the valley were more crumpled mountain slopes and ravines covered in dense greenery as far as the eye could see and, when I dared to look down, I could see the Urubamba threading its way along the valley floor far below. It looked harmlessly gentle from our raptor's-eye view but it was, in fact, tumbling and roaring its way down to the Amazon.

We came across Inca roads and mountain passes marked by cairns of stones added to by travelling Indians as a tribute to the *Apus* (mountain gods) and occasionally we met other mule trains. Until we descended into the *semi-selva*, the peaks of the Andes were always in the background.

The experience not only stood me in very good stead later on, but also remains one of my most treasured memories. Nothing could match the silence and tranquillity broken only by a hoof hitting a stone, the squawk of a surprised bird or the intermittent tinkling of a stream. Otherwise, the only sounds were the tread of the mules nearest to me and the distant jongle of the bell around the neck of the lead mule, the pace setter. Washington often had to wait for me, but he never made me feel the lesser for that. I imagined that the special sense of companionship that I felt with him might have been the same as that felt by the intrepid Victorian female travellers such as Jane Digby, Mary Kingsley or Isabella Bird, with their guides. It is a relationship entirely predicated on trust. The lone lady traveller depends on her guide to take her where she wants to go, and back again, in safety, and not to cheat, molest or abandon her. Equally, she is 'the boss', and the guide trusts her to pay him as agreed.

One of the few early women travellers to write about Peru was the feminist socialist Flora Tristan. In her autobiography *Peregrinations of a Pariah*, written in 1838, she writes about her journey from Islay (on the coast) to Arequipa which in those days was intrepid.

> '*We climbed the last mountain, and when we reached the summit, the vast chain of the Cordilleras and the three giant volcanoes of Arequipa spread before us. At the sight of this magnificent spectacle I forgot my sufferings and lived only to admire. I let my gaze wander over the bright billowing sand to the point where it met the azure heavens, then upon the lofty mountains which stretched like an endless ladder to the skies, their thousand snow-capped peaks...*' Then, '*At about eight in the morning we reached the Quebradas, mountains renowned throughout the country for the difficulties they present to travellers. As we climbed the peaks which stretched before us on our way, I lay down upon my mule and trusted to the mercy of Providence, but as we descended it was impossible to do this, as the path was fraught with dangers, and although my mule was very sure footed, I was still forced to take the greatest care. We had to make our animals jump across crevasses, climb huge rocks and sometimes follow narrow tracks where the sand crumbled beneath their feet and we risked falling into the fearsome precipice which ran alongside the mountain. Don Balthazar always went ahead to show us the way.*'

I certainly felt the same sense of adventure and awe as the early explorers must have felt. I also felt akin to them as we approached any settlement. Communities of *serranos* who have invaded the lowlands are protective of their new terrain and not always welcoming to strangers. In the days of *Sendero Luminoso* it was impossible to distinguish an innocent peasant from a terrorist, which was why I felt a certain frisson when coming to signs of habitation, particularly at dusk. We relied heavily on Washington's antennae, behaved with decorum and passed through unharmed.

The journey through the steaming rainforest and its mosquitoes was challenging, and even if it hadn't already proved unforgettable it certainly became so when I ended up with life-threatening septicaemia. I am told I all but expired, but the small town where our journey ended had a doctor. All I remember, as I drifted in and out of consciousness, was this doctor jabbing blunt and probably much-used needles into my veins and what sounded like someone cutting the lawn outside my window with nail scissors. I never did find out what the noise was.

The team went on and I survived. As soon as I was strong enough I made tracks towards Puno.

CHAPTER 3

First Sighting of the Yavari

THE WELCOME I RECEIVED AT THE naval base in Puno was not a warm one. It was 1983, and the Falklands War was still a sensitive memory and my British passport a reminder of it. Early one August morning I found myself knocking at a closed door set in the high wall surrounding the base. When a small grille slid open and a man's eye appeared I held up my passport and asked if I could come in, but before I had a chance to explain why he said, 'No', and the grille slammed shut.

I returned the next day, and got the same reception. At least this time I was allowed to explain that I was a harmless researcher, but the answer was still 'No'.

However, I have learned that most often a Peruvian 'no' to a request seldom means 'no' and is worth working on because it is likely to end up as a 'yes', whereas a straight 'yes' could be problematic. Worse than that is 'yes, in a minute,' or *un rato*, or still worse, *un ratito*, meaning 'in a little minute,' implying immediately. This almost certainly will mean a long wait and finally a 'no'. A yet more hopeless reply is 'yes, in the tiniest of minutes,' *un ratatito*, or worst of all, *un ratatitito* – 'in the tiniest of tiny minutes, maybe only seconds!'

It is endearing because it is said to please, because supposedly that is what you would like to hear. Or, maybe it is said as a ploy to confuse the *gringo*, to appear helpful while retaining the upper hand and so keep us in our place.

When I've made this observation to Peruvian friends, far from denying it, they say with a charming smile, 'But this is Peru!' as if that explains everything. Cynics would probably say, 'But you're so naïve; "No" means

"Pass me the brown envelope".' Maybe, but alas, no project I've ever worked on could even rise to a brown envelope, let alone anything to put inside it.

So I persevered at the naval base, and finally, after several more attempts, the duty officer relented. I imagine he thought I was a spy, but after I had reiterated many times my claim to be on a family quest and researching events of the nineteenth century, he at last received orders from on high to unlock the door and let me in. I was fully expecting to be kept waiting, then frisked and minutely interrogated, but I was instead taken completely off guard by the immediacy and warmth of the welcome extended to me by the port captain. Not for the first time, it occurred to me that in spite of all that I had learned during my time at Cusichaca about the Peruvian culture and character I was still repeatedly taken by surprise. As an Anglo-Saxon used to a structured, predictable existence, I was obviously going to have to learn to be more flexible and to expect the unexpected at all times. 'Si, no,' I can hear a Peruvian say to this, meaning they are in agreement, but it's the idiosyncratic expression which I love.

Having chatted amicably about my great-grandfather Alfred, the port captain sent for *Técnico* Julian González to accompany me down to the port. Walking along the jetty I saw six ships in all, two of which

The sorry state of the *Yavarí* in the port of Puno as I first saw her in 1983.

obviously belonged to the navy, and of these it was the old hulk in the corner that caught my eye. She was a tragic sight. Her hull was dented and scratched, patches of black glared through where the battleship-grey paint was chipped, she had no masts, her wooden superstructure and wheelhouse were rotting away and she was listing badly. Clearly she had been driven into the corner and left to die, or, as I was later told, to be scrapped. Waterweed had engulfed her bow but on her stern I could just read the name *Chucuito*. She was truly pitiful to behold, stern-on to the lake as though she had turned her back on life. Yet she had a certain dignity, and, more importantly, she was afloat.

Técnico González, who was something of a historian himself, confirmed my suspicions that this was, indeed, the little steamship which had been built in England and carried up the Andes to the lake. Furthermore, he had read in a naval journal that both this ship and her sister ship had been commissioned in 1861 by the then president of Peru, *Marascal* (Field Marshal) Ramon Castilla, and had been transported up to the lake on mule-back in 2,766 pieces, while Indians carried the two propeller shafts on their shoulders.

'The journey took them six years,' he told me. 'The *Chucuito* was the first of the two ships to be reassembled. And she was the first to be laid up in the 1950s. But what you should also know...' he paused so I could catch up with my note-taking, '...is that *Chucuito* was not her original name. When the fleet was nationalised in 1972 and handed over to the navy five years later, we renamed both ships. We called the *Yavarí* the *Chucuito* after a neighbouring village, so that is the *Yavarí* you are looking at.' Then he pointed to the other ship. 'You see the letters BAP? They stand for *Buque Armada Peruana*, so she is a warship. Her name is now *Puno,* but she was the *Yapurá*.'

Técnico González glanced down at my notebook to check that I had jotted down the names correctly. 'The *Puno* is still in commission,' he continued. 'But the *Chucuito* we only use as a place to dump our spent cartridges and as an overnight detention centre for wayward sailors.'

Although the *Chucuito* had been decommissioned, her commissioning number had only been partly obscured by a thin layer of paint. It was still possible to make out the number 19 on her bow.

I could hardly believe this incredible story, nor that I had at last found the very ship I first heard of at school so long ago.

'Do you know who built these ships?' I asked *el Técnico*, hardly daring to hear the answer.

'No, but I do know they were built in England.'

So it was still possible that these were the Yarrow ships.

We boarded the *Chucuito*, some 150 feet long, and immediately I fell victim to her charm. She just reeked of nostalgia. I ran my fingers over the rivets holding her iron plates together and thought, each one of these rivets was made in England, on the other side of the world, travelled the high seas and found its way up the Andes to the lake over a hundred years ago, and is still here today.

I was captivated by this little piece of Victoriana, which quite probably had been built by my great-grandfather. As I stood on the *Chucuito's* antique and decaying deck, a germ of an idea crept into my mind.

Oddly enough, my family is predisposed towards ships, and particularly ships in obscure places, so I blame my genes entirely for this infatuation. First my paternal great-grandfather, Lieutenant Wyatt Rawson, sailed to the Arctic in the tenth HMS *Discovery,* on Captain George Nares' expedition of 1875 which reached 83° 20'26'N, the northernmost latitude yet achieved by any expedition. Then some years later, in 1901, my maternal great-uncle, Charles Royds – later to become Vice-Admiral Sir Charles William Rawson Royds, KBE, CMG, FRGS – sailed to the Antarctic as First Lieutenant on RRS (Royal Research Ship) *Discovery*, the eleventh ship of that name, as number two to Captain Robert Falcon Scott. While I like to blame these antecedents for my susceptibility to the little old ship's charms, I wish I had also inherited some technical knowledge of ships. Coming from a long naval line, my father did teach me at an early age about the sea; as Naval Attaché in Stockholm soon after World War II, he was the happy recipient of one of the Folkboats confiscated from the German navy which, with my mother and friends, he loved to sail around the Baltic. The Baltic was black and frightening to a little girl looking down from the deck of a yacht but, with the best intentions, to teach me how to swim my father would tie ropes around me and our beloved Lakeland terrier, Minnie, and lower us both into it so we could doggie-paddle together. Needless to say, Minnie was a lot better at it than I was. As a result of this rugged introduction I've been a retarded swimmer ever since. In due course, my father also taught me how to sail but, not surprisingly, never touched on naval engineering.

* * *

Técnico González took me below, where there were remnants of past occupation wherever you looked; cabins vandalised, holds littered with bits of old iron and spent gun cartridges, and the anchor locker brimming with detritus. There was general rubbish everywhere, and I felt the insult to this grand old lady of the lake.

We continued our tour into the engine room. Here, taking up virtually the entire space, stood a leviathan of an engine. Four colossal grey cylinders stood eight feet tall, dwarfing us as we gazed up at their gunmetal grey steel heads shaped like bowler hats.

'This replaced the original steam engine,' explained *el Técnico*. 'But it hasn't run for a little while.' I imagined it couldn't anyway as much of the copper piping had been sawn off and I noticed several of the bronze taps and valves were also missing. Miraculously, though, it still bore the maker's plaque, which read 'Bolinder's Rundlÿfs Patent Crude-Oil-Engine, Stockholm - Sweden, 320 B.HP. Rev. P.R. M. 225. No.8213/16.'

Then I spotted another engine beyond, almost hidden by this behemoth, a generator bearing the name Petter, made in Yeovil, England.

Besides these, there were fuel tanks in several sizes fixed to the sides of the hull, a few outsized spanners in a rack, a couple of empty jerry cans and various lengths of plastic hosing hanging on hooks, but the general

Plaque of the *Yavarí*'s single-phase Petter generator custom-built in 1927.

scene was one of abandonment.

For the most part, the *Chucuito* had been plundered of her treasures. On the bridge the wheel, binnacle and telegraph were all missing. All that remained were the standing parts of the simple steering gear, a drum on an axle in an iron frame. *El Técnico* explained how there should have been a chain running the length of the deck from the ship's rudder aft to this drum which was then turned by the missing wheel.

'Unfortunately, the chain has been stolen,' he said. 'But the good news is that the wheel and other treasures were removed by the navy before they disappeared and are now in a museum.'

We climbed back down to the main deck. I was feeling quite emotional. Here lay a monument to a time when Britannia ruled the waves, the period of our history which, whatever mistakes we might have made, put the Great into Britain. I felt an overwhelming sense of pride to think that my family had most probably built her and realised that the germ which had bothered me earlier had now become a positive idea. I knew, at that moment, that this ship had to be rescued and brought back to life. I thought, too, of how richly she deserved to be resurrected, and what an asset she could be, providing jobs and attracting tourism to the poorest region of Peru. Compelling visions flooded into my mind of launching an Anglo-Peruvian restoration programme along the lines of the Cusichaca Project, involving young people of both nations, the local community and expert marine engineers who would, of course, come on a voluntary basis. We would also establish links with the various children's homes in Puno where young British volunteers could combine work on the *Yavarí* (I had already mentally reverted to the ship's given name) with time spent with the children. There was so much potential for making a social contribution with this Victorian jewel as the pivotal centre. The world's media would hurry over, lured by her story, so funds would soon flow in from East and West and all points between. *Yavarí* was, after all, only a small ship and the technical work would not take long, so the budget would be modest. Then, as smart as a sailor's salute, she would sail anew, making money out of tourism to finance educational trips related to conservation for local students and international scientists. There was no question – the old lady had to be saved from the breaker's yard.

As we walked away, I turned to take a photograph but *Técnico* González put out his arm to stop me. 'This is a military establishment,' he said. 'And I'm afraid taking pictures is prohibited.'

By the time we had returned to the naval base I had resolved to examine the *Yavarí's* construction drawings, but perhaps that too might be prohibited. No, not at all, on the contrary – and here again was this element of surprise – the drawings were spread out for me to study under a notice which declared that *The success of the Peruvian Navy depends on discretion at all times, especially when in company with foreigners.*

It was obvious that the drawings were not the originals, but nevertheless I was somewhat disconcerted to see the name Cammell Laird in one corner. Where was the Yarrow name? There was no mention of it anywhere. Had it been wishful thinking after all that great-grandfather Alfred had built the *Yavarí?* What if he had had nothing whatever to do with it – how much would I mind? Would I persevere with the idea of restoring the vessel?

All these questions spun round in my head as I tried to weigh up the points in favour and those against. On the one hand, if there were no family link, it would be a serious disappointment and definitely make the fund-raising more difficult. On the other hand, I felt that I had discovered a rare item of historic value, and doing nothing about it would be irresponsible. It was something of a moral obligation, and it would also serve the community well. I reasoned that although finding the money for the Cusichaca Project had been a real challenge, if the *Yavarí* could earn *cause célèbre* status, offers of sponsorship and voluntary help would surely follow.

The more I thought about it, the more I wanted the *Yavarí* to have been built by Yarrows, but I also realised that regardless of from which shipyard she had begun her epic voyage, she had to be saved, if at all feasible. Next question – how could I find out if it was a feasible proposition? I knew that the answer was to commission a survey. So I headed off to Lima.

Through the Anglican church in Lima I had met a number of expatriates who had come to Peru to work as engineers for the Peruvian Corporation and who had stayed on after the Corporation was nationalised in 1972. One such was Fred Parker, who ran his own firm of marine surveyors. I found him in his office, which gleamed with brass nauticalia. He looked prosperous as he strutted over to shake my hand.

I began my tale, but Fred interrupted me. 'Yes, yes, I know the *Yavarí* well,' he said. 'I've sailed in her and in all the lake ships. Yes, we were mighty proud of our lake fleet. It was a wonderful sight to see all five of the ships in the black, white, red and green livery of *La Peruvian*, as it was known, navigating to and fro between Peru and Bolivia, and I have to say...' as if it was all down to him, '...neither they nor the trains have ever run as punctually as they did then. *La hora inglesa* means "on the dot" and those ships and trains ran *a la hora inglesa!*'

Indeed, the Corporation's reputation for efficiency and faultless timekeeping is now enshrined in Peruvian folklore. Those were the days...

I asked Fred about *La Peruvian*.

'*La Peruvian*,' he explained, as he lowered himself into his captain's swivel chair, 'was incorporated to rescue Peru from bankruptcy following the disastrous War of the Pacific when, as you know, Peru was soundly beaten by the Chileans who they've never really forgiven. At the time – and I'm talking about 1887 – most of Peru's foreign creditors were railway bondholders so, as a rescue plan, it was agreed that the Corporation would pick up the country's external debt in exchange for certain concessions of which one was the running of the lake fleet and the railways. They did this for sixty years from London, and very successfully.'

Because it played such an important part in Peru's post-colonial history, I was curious to know more about *La Peruvian*. It was, in fact, masterminded by an Irishman called Michael Grace. Michael left Ireland to follow his father and his brother William to Peru in the late 1850s by which time William had become a partner in a successful ship chandlery. At the time, shipping was a lucrative business with which to be associated. According to the contemporary *Illustrated London News*, the guano fertiliser trade alone accounted for six hundred and twenty ships a year calling at Peru and the list was long of other exports and imports. To save the merchantmen wasting time docking, and expensive port taxes having to be paid, William and Michael loaded their chandlery onto a ship and anchored off Callao. The partnership thrived, and in 1865 William emigrated to New York and founded W.R. Grace & Co. in order to import guano while, in Peru, Michael set up Grace Brothers & Co. to import rail track iron. The company monopolised the business during the railway building boom and, when the War of the Pacific with Chile broke out in 1879, took control of the supply of munitions and ships to Peru. The war, which lasted four years, cost Peru dearly but Michael Grace saved the day. He and another Irishman, the fifth Earl of Donoughmore, took over the country's national debt. They bought all the English and American bonds and in 1890 incorporated the Corporation of Foreign

Bondholders, which became known as The Peruvian Corporation. In addition to the concessions referred to by Fred, they also took control of the guano business, important oil and mineral rights, and millions of acres of forest.

Looking then to Chile, the Grace brothers could see opportunities for making money in nitrates, cotton and sugar and built on their success by opening offices throughout the rest of South America. In 1880 they launched a steamship company which later became the Grace Shipping Line. From these beginnings W.R. Grace and Company grew to become a multinational company. Of the two brothers, William later became Mayor of New York and received the Statue of Liberty (transported in 350 individual pieces) from the French nation; and it was Michael, based in London, whose company shipped the *Yavarí*'s Bolinder engine from Stockholm. Today chemicals have taken over from its fertiliser and shipping interests.

As for the War of the Pacific, it was also essentially about guano and nitrates, although it broke out as a result of Bolivia imposing restrictive export taxes at her ports, which were used by Chile. Chile waged war in order to appropriate those ports and Bolivia's coastline. Peru then sided with Bolivia, which gave Chile the excuse it needed to invade Peru and, encouraged by British investors, to annex the fabulously rich nitrate fields of Tarapacá, much of the country's guano deposits and some five hundred miles of Peru's coastline. It ended in a terrible defeat for both Peru and Bolivia, so it is hardly surprising that the subject is still a sensitive one today. It's no surprise either that, like Grace Brothers & Co., the British played a lively part in the war, first selling ships and arms to both sides and then 'policing' the war to see fair play.

But Fred Parker's office was not the place or the moment to go into all that. I needed a Lloyds Condition Survey of the *Yavarí* and Fred assured me that when his surveyor, *Ingeniero* Manuel Suarez, was next in Puno, he would carry one out and send it to me.

As I got up to go, Fred took me unawares by saying, 'By the way, I do congratulate you if you manage to pull this off. It's a great idea and it makes me quite nostalgic to be talking about Puno again. I spent many happy months up there sailing on the lake. They called me the Wind God, because compared with their lugsail boats my dinghy could point up much closer to the wind and they just couldn't work out how I did it! Yes...' his voice trailed off. 'They were happy days...' and on that note I left him.

CHAPTER 4

Establishing the Yavarí's True Value

BACK IN ENGLAND, MY MOST URGENT task was to find a naval architect who could interpret the survey report. All lines of enquiry led me to one man.

Martin Parr, C.Eng. MRINA, known to everyone as Tim, is one of the United Kingdom's leading experts on veteran ships but, most important, he is an enthusiast. When the survey report arrived I invited him to lunch, and I blush now to remember that it was to a humble pizzeria, but that didn't seem to dampen his enthusiasm in the least. Tim turned out to be a good-looking man, well over six feet, wearing an immaculate blue pinstripe suit and a beaming smile. He was enthralled by the story of the Yavarí, and so positive about the report that I immediately began to see my vision of rescuing the ship becoming a reality.

'A wrought iron hull in this kind of condition,' he said, stabbing the report with his finger, 'at that altitude and in fresh water – it could be good for another hundred years at least.'

And how long did Tim think it would take to restore her to full working order?

'Well, she's only little as ships go,' he said, and thought for a moment. 'I should think about three years. Certainly not more than four.'

I was airborne, and impatient to get going immediately. So I thanked Tim profusely and was only too delighted to pay his professional consulting fee – the cost of one pizza.

* * *

The next thing I had to establish was the provenance of the *Yavarí*, and whether she definitely was a Yarrow ship.

My cousin Eric Yarrow invited me to breakfast at the Dorchester Hotel (more generous than I with Tim), and over coffee and a croissant I brought him up to date. He was less enthusiastic about the *Yavarí* than before because, since our river trip to Alfred's first shipyard, Yarrow Shipbuilders had been nationalised and stripped of all its links with the past, leaving Eric with something of a broken heart. He had left shipping and struck off into a different sphere altogether. That morning, I was still hopeful that the date 1861, given me by *Técnico* Julian González as the year when the *Yavarí* was commissioned, might not have been spot on. Historic records can vary in the detail, and after all, it had been Eric who had made the claim that she was a Yarrow ship and he should know. Eric, however, was a realist, and could be quite blunt.

'Grandfather Alfred took his first order in 1865,' he pointed out, 'so it seems unlikely that he built the *Yavarí* in 1861.'

My shattered hopes were obviously plain to see because he then suggested that I should check with his former secretary who could photocopy Yarrows' yard list for me, and that I should talk to the Glasgow University Library who now hold all Yarrows' archives.

When I got home, I opened great-grandfather Alfred's biography, and looked again at the photograph that had given rise to Cousin Eric's claim that Yarrows had built the *Yavarí*. It shows convicts carrying a paddle-shaft 'over the Andes'. Although the caption says, 'in the rear there are ten *Colombian* soldiers', I had taken that to be just an inaccuracy. What I should have noticed, though, was that the part of the ship being carried was a 'paddle-shaft', not a 'propeller-shaft', and the *Yavarí* was never a paddle steamer.

I knew that the photocopy of the yard list would provide conclusive evidence one way or the other and, sure enough, I could find no mention of any ship or boat being built prior to 1865. After that date, boats were sent to the Yangtse-Kiang, the Irrawaddy, the Mekong delta and even the Amazon, but I could see nothing about Lake Titicaca.

This disappointing discovery was confirmed by a letter from the Glasgow University Library dated April 1983. They wrote that the *Yavarí* and the *Yapurá* could not have been built by Yarrows because of the dates, but went on to say, '*As yet, we do not know whether these vessels were built by A & J Inglis... we are hopeful that there may be some information pertaining to them in the Archives of Anthony Gibbs and Son, which are held in the Guildhall Library in London'*, and that they were awaiting a reply to their enquiry on my behalf. A fortnight later they wrote again, *'to acquaint you with the information gleaned, as promised'*, which was that *'a long search might be required'* to find out who built the ships and that regrettably they could not take that on.

'Unfortunately' they went on to say, they *'cannot suggest any other way of tracing the details of the Yavarí and the Yapurá, as to my knowledge there were no shipping journals in existence in the early 1860s.'*

There were the facts. The *Yavarí* had not been built by great-grandfather Alfred after all. There was categorically no family connection with the ship, no link, no association, no legacy. It was a cruel moment of realisation. The dreams were dashed, the delusion over. The truth was in front of me in black and white. I couldn't disguise it; the *Yavarí* and I were not related in any way.

And yet... could I leave the old lady to be scrapped? Could I simply put the survey in a bottom drawer and walk away? I knew in my heart of hearts that I could not, nor could I shake off the vision I had had of the entire project. The concept of saving and restoring the ship was as romantic as it was a duty. Even knowing the truth, I wouldn't give up. I would carry on and meet the challenge. Besides, what is four years out of a lifetime? I made my resolve. I would first find out who had built the ship, then prepare a strategy, get a costing, find the money, recruit the experts and young volunteers, and go to work.

I convinced myself that, within the prescribed time, the *Yavarí* would be motoring around the lake, restored to her original glory.

* * *

With Yarrows conclusively out of the running, I looked again at an article I had been sent in *Cammell Laird News*, dated February 1971. *'100 – And Still At Work'* was the headline and, underneath a photograph of the *Yapurá*, it said, *'A ship built by the Company 100 years ago is still in service on Lake Titicaca, in Bolivia* [and] *Peru – probably a record in the annals of world shipping. This is revealed in a letter which the Company received from Señor Ernesto de Losada, Managing Director of the Peruvian Corporation Ltd. of Lima...'*

It was possible that John Laird had built the *Yapurá* before he merged his business with Johnson Cammell & Co. in 1903, in which case he would have built the *Yavarí* as well. Remembering that I had seen Cammell Laird's name on the drawings in Puno and on correspondence dated 1934 from the Peruvian Corporation, I hurried up to Birkenhead to examine their yard list with Frank Lindstrom of the Ship Design department acting as company archivist. But there was no mention of the two lake steamers. Frank was surprised, but convinced me that there must have been some mistake.

I wanted to agree with him, so I went looking for evidence in Birkenhead's Town Library and the Liverpool Maritime Museum where I reeled through thousands of yards of microfiche, looking at contemporary newspapers. I fully expected to find reports of the building and dispatching of two steamers to the highest lake in the world. My belief only wavered when I read of the high level of local interest in the American Civil War because in 1862 Lairds were actually building the notorious blockade-running Monitor *Alabama* for the Confederate army. Perhaps this news might have overshadowed that of the two little steamers destined for South America.

I asked Frank where else I might find Laird memorabilia. He directed me to the two Miss Lairds, direct descendants of the yard's founder William Laird, father of John. The sisters, who lived in North Wales, were country ladies in tweeds and sensible shoes, who gave me a warm welcome and a cup of tea. We compared notes about springer spaniels, but they could throw no light on the mystery of the lake steamboats.

I began to think I was chasing a red herring and the awful thought occurred to me that I would have to examine the yard lists of every single Victorian shipyard. The task itself didn't daunt me, but the time it would take did. I had assumed that whichever shipyard built the *Yavarí*, be it Yarrows or Lairds, would hold the greater part of the background history, and the rest I would track down in Peru. As for the engine, its history would be easy to find in Sweden, or so I thought. However, if I didn't even know the name of the shipyard, the research alone was going to take four years. There had to be a better way.

* * *

I went to the National Maritime Museum to look at the Lloyds Register of Shipping, but amongst the hundreds of ships being built at the time there was no mention of the *Yavarí*. I read stories similar to the *Yavarí's* – such as that of the *Chauncy Maples,* which, like Yarrow's *Ilala* twenty years before, was transported piecemeal overland to Lake Nyasa (Malawi) in 1898 by 450 Ngoni tribesmen and their oxen, and which is now being restored – but not a single reference to the *Yavarí*. No-one could tell me why, and no-one could tell me where I should look next. For several months my search took me from the City of London's Guildhall Library to Glasgow, and back to the City of London, to maritime libraries, to steamship associations, ship trusts, institutes of engineers and naval architects. I sifted through newspaper archives and pored over the *Illustrated London News*. I was gratified to come across several references to the *Yavarí* but they all differed in the detail; and if they attributed her construction to anyone, it was always to Lairds.

However, although I was coming up with little about the *Yavarí* herself, I was learning a great deal about the Victorian shipbuilding industry. In 1861, as a result of the Industrial Revolution, the British Empire was at its zenith. Indeed, all manufacturing industries had been revolutionised but, arguably, nowhere was this more apparent than in modes of transport, whether by road, rail or sea. As for shipbuilding, it is now incredible to think that in the peak years, including artisan slipways up river creeks building small craft for home waters, some three thousand shipyards were in operation in Great Britain. Every day, tens of thousands of shipping tonnage was being dispatched from Britain all around the world. As I read on, I began to realise the actual importance and rarity value of the *Yavarí*. She is one of very few extant examples of the most significant breakthroughs in shipbuilding technology which evolved at this time, and which led to the industry's boom. She and her sister ship, *Yapurá,* might even be the only surviving examples to combine all significant features in each vessel.

There are four main reasons why the *Yavarí* is so important in the history of shipbuilding.

First, she was built as a steam sailing ship. Steam! The very word evokes the excitement of a Golden Age. The discovery of how to harness its power was truly one of those 'giant steps for mankind'. James Watt is always given the credit for it, but I feel sorry for Thomas Newcomen who actually led the way. Some fifty years ahead of Watt, Newcomen designed an entirely novel steam pump with which to drain Cornish tin mines. James

Watt then developed the idea and, in 1769, was perspicacious enough to patent it. This alerted the world to the glowing opportunities it presented and sent engineers and inventors hurrying back to their workshops to devise ways of applying it. Experiments succeeded and failed. Engineers either died penniless or became knights of the realm. Patents proliferated and patrons pounced hungrily on marketable prototypes.

Every sphere of industry was ripe for change, and especially shipping. Ships that hitherto had been dependent on the wind could, with steam power, propel themselves anywhere and in any weather. They could manoeuvre in sheltered waters, sail faster in open waters and keep to a timetable. Crossing the Atlantic, which used to take four to six weeks, under steam propulsion took ten days.

The competition became fierce between the Americans, the French and the British to design the first commercial steamship. Each shrouded their progress in secrecy because no-one was above industrial espionage if it would win them the race. In the end there was no outright winner because so much depended on the exact definition of a 'steamship', whose account you read and the nature of the race, be it to cross the English Channel or cross the Atlantic or to be the first up New York's Hudson River. Several claims were made and several claims justified.

In sharp contrast to the mercantile sector in which engineers, merchants and shipping lines were pressing the frontiers of science, the Admiralty was dogged in its resistance to change. Their attitude was that so long as Britannia ruled the waves as she did, why bother with new-fangled inventions? When a young Scottish engineer, Henry Bell, presented himself to the Admiralty as early as 1800 to draw their attention to the concept of steam propulsion their response was that it was 'of no value in trans-marine navigation.' Only the lone voice of Admiral Lord Nelson was heard to protest, 'My Lords and gentlemen, if you do not adopt Mr. Bell's scheme other nations will, and in the end vex every vein of the Empire.'

Their approach to the second of the features that make the *Yavarí* so rare today was exactly the same. Her hull is built of iron. The idea of building a ship of iron was met with incredulity. Wood floats, iron does not.

The transition from building in wood to iron was not straightforward and, unlike the introduction of steam power, even the mercantile sector was sceptical.

To the proponents, the advantages were obvious. Iron ships would not break up so easily on impact, which meant fewer shipwrecks. There would be less labour and strain, less likelihood of leaking or of backs breaking in big seas, and iron hulls could be driven into head seas more safely. These were a few of the points in favour, but the strongest argument of all was the urgent need for larger ships with larger cargo holds. The maximum length for a timber-built vessel was 300 feet. Ship owners, ambitious for more space, were easily swayed from their initial scepticism. For obvious reasons, traditional boat builders were bitterly opposed. And more than anyone, mariners were wary, unconvinced that an iron ship would float, and would not sag, corrode or deflect the magnetic compass. Regardless of such doubts, ship owners were commercially driven and motivated to exploit the benefits. Larger ships with larger bunkers and more space for cargo and passengers meant larger profits.

Iron also enabled smaller ships or boats to be either 'pin-built', piecemeal in kit form, or 'knock-down' in sections, then crated up and dispatched for delivery and re-assembly on any inland waterway anywhere in the world. The scope was limitless.

As with the innovation of steam propulsion, the Royal Navy was obdurate in refusing to accept change. Unfounded fears were deep-seated and only allayed when the first ships built of wood but *clad* in iron proved to be seaworthy. When the French navy launched *La Gloire,* the world's first ironclad battleship (5,630 tons and 255 feet long), in 1859, it was proof enough. Reassured, the Admiralty's answer to that was to build HMS *Warrior,* also an ironclad but, at 9,210 tons and 418 feet, she was not only larger but one knot faster than *La Gloire* and, at the time, the largest warship in the world. She is now moored in Portsmouth Harbour.

Inevitably chisel and adze had to make way for steam punch and rivet gun until, in the words of Rudyard Kipling, the hammers of Britain's shipyards were '*Clanging from the Severn to the Tyne*'[2] and beyond.

There was nothing new about iron; it was the ability to produce it in sheets either by hammering or rolling that developed with the Industrial Revolution, but in the early days the quality varied depending on the level of impurities. According to the *Yavarí*'s Specification dated 1861, which I later unearthed, the iron was '*to be of the best hammered scrap...*' When we later came to survey the thickness of the hull with an ultrasonic meter it was the scrap's impurities, or 'slag', which utterly bamboozled the meter. Its eccentric readings perplexed us utterly until, in reply to our frantic e-mails to Tim Parr, we learned about slag.

SPECIFICATION
of an
Iron Screw Steam Gun Boat.

Dimensions	Feet. In.
Length Between Perpendiculars	100. —
Breadth extreme	17. —
Depth to top of Keel	10. —
Burthen. 158 $\frac{4}{94}$ Tons B.M.	

Keel.
To be of Bar Iron 5 × 3/4 inches.

Stem.
To be of Bar Iron 5 × 3/4 inches
tapering to 3 ins × 5/8 in at top.

Stern Frame
To be of best hammered scrap iron
5 ins broad by 2 in thick with 3 Gudgeons
forged on the same to receive Rudder
with suitable Inner Post for Screw.

Frames
To be of angle iron 2½ × 2 × 5/16 in
placed at a distance of 18 ins
apart throughout.

Reverse Frames
To be of angle iron 2 × 2 × 5/16 in
on every frame along top of floors
to the turn of bilge; on every
other Frame to be continued up
to Gunwale.

(1)

The first page of *Yavarí's* Specification prepared by James Watt & Co. (1861).

In an effort to reduce the slag content, foundries added more alloys to the iron to produce a more superior material, the result of which was steel. Within the comparatively brief period of forty years, steel had largely replaced iron in ship construction, which is why the *Yavarí* is one of very few iron ships afloat in the world today.

Thirdly, the *Yavarí* was prefabricated. An iron ship or boat could either be built in watertight sections, known as 'knock-down', which could be unbolted for portage around cataracts, or 'pin built' in hundreds of individual parts for transportation in kit form, as was the case with the *Yavarí*.

Great Britain cornered the market in 'pin built' construction. The concept was brilliant and clearly the forerunner of Meccano, invented in 1898, and later of Airfix, perhaps even of the flat-pack. Prior to its dispatch, the ship or boat (the former being bigger than the latter but no-one seems to know the significant size at which one becomes the other) was tacked together in the shipyard, as a seamstress might tack a garment. The iron hull frames, bulkheads, deck beams and plates were drilled with rivet holes but, at this 'tacking' stage, bolted rather than riveted in place. The funnel, ventilators, davits, hatches, pipes, valves etc. were manufactured and installed in the British yard. It was sometimes the custom to construct an iron framework for the bridge, superstructure and decks prior to dispatch, sometimes not. With or without a prefabricated framework, the type and quantities of wood required for the superstructure and the decks as detailed in the Specification would be bought in the country to which the vessel was being dispatched. The ship was then 'disassembled' under the scrutiny of the Chief Engineer, or 'Engine Erector' as he was called, who would ultimately be responsible for putting the whole thing back together again at its destination. Every part was numbered, if necessary painted red for port or green for starboard, then meticulously inventoried in neat copperplate columns, and crated up; then the crates were also inventoried before dispatch. I've even seen detailed specifications of the wooden crates as well. Nothing was left to chance. The steam engines were dealt with in a similar way. They were assembled and fired up in the workshop, before being stripped down and packed ready for shipment. The kit-built and knock-down craft became best sellers. Thousands of pre-fabricated vessels, shallow-draught riverboats, dredgers, steamers, gunboats, hospital ships and luxury launches custom-built for maharajahs, viceroys, sultans and princes, were dispatched on a daily basis to far-flung river estuaries, lakes, tributaries and creeks. Every gulf and river from the Euphrates to the Amazon boasted a British-built craft.

It is easy to take for granted ships on Lakes Victoria, Malawi, Tanganyika, Baikal and Titicaca, but the human effort required in getting them there was prodigious. Lake Victoria, for example, is five hundred miles inland from Mombasa. When the 200-ton *Kenya* was commissioned for the lake in 1898 – it took 3,500 caravan trains of native porters and Chinese coolies to carry her piece by piece on their heads, from the coast to Port Victoria (losing a serious number of plates and parts in the long grass on the way). No corner of the world was too remote for coolie, native porter, ox, bullock, camel, yak or, in the *Yavarí's* case, mule, to deliver a ship.

I knew that the *Yavarí* and her sister ship together amounted to 2,766 component parts, including two boilers of fifteen tons each, condensers of five tons each, crankshafts, iron lifeboats and anchors, but at this stage of my research I had yet to learn how great was the achievement of getting every part up the Andes to Lake Titicaca. Presumably, as was the custom for getting the 'boat-in-a-box' to its destination and reassembled, the responsibility was that of the Engine Erector and he, in my opinion, was an unsung hero.

In Victorian England, plenty was known of foreign shores. The ports around the British coast must have hummed with sailors' tales of exotic landfalls, but little was known of the hinterlands beyond. The Engine Erector and a small team of shipwrights, a boilerman and a carpenter, would be sent for years at a time to the most outlandish corners of the globe of which they probably knew virtually nothing about the geography, language, culture, diet, poisonous flora, dangerous fauna, climate or deadly health hazards. Nor would the Erector know in advance who and how to recruit and train a reliable work force. I read the account of one Engine Erector who commented that within his team he was dealing with fifteen different languages. Like so many Victorians who made the Empire what it was, he must have been a truly intrepid and resourceful leader of men.

With this in mind, it came as a surprise that, search as I might in the news coverage of the *Yavarí's* launch which I later found in Peru, I could see no mention whatsoever of any British involvement.

As her fourth innovative feature, the *Yavarí* was designed with a single screw propeller. The first steamships were propelled either by a paddle wheel each side of the vessel or by one at the stern. The idea of an underwater screw propeller to make the vessel more streamlined and manoeuvrable and less noisy challenged engineers for years. Then a farmer from Middlesex, one Francis Smith, came up with a device which left the greatest Victorian shipbuilder, Isambard Kingdom Brunel, in no doubt that he should alter the design for his SS *Great Britain*, the largest ship ever built in the world at that time, from paddle wheel to single screw propeller. That was in 1843, so the *Yavarí* was an early example of this innovation and bridged the transition between sail and steam. In the early days, the cry from the bridge of 'Down funnel, up screw' required block and tackle and a full crew of strong men to lift the propeller out of the water. By the time of the *Yavarí* the crew of strong men had been superseded by the invention of an elliptical well to house the propeller inside the hull and a clever device detailed in the *Yavarí's* Spec:

> '*A Screw of Brass about 6 ft diameter and about 7ft 6 pitch, fitted with bearings of wood, with bolts & nuts, screw frame Cross Bar Hook for blocks, guides for lifting it on deck when under sail alone.*'

This well still exists on the *Yavarí* and greatly excites veteran ship enthusiasts because it is one of very few remaining in the world. Moreover, for a hull of one hundred feet, a 'Screw of Brass' measuring six feet is considerable and would have been heavy to lift manually.

Thanks to the ingenuity of Victorian shipbuilders and their innovations, in just forty years the movement of people and merchandise around the world was revolutionised. Trade and travel took on a whole new dimension and the *Yavarí* remains today as a rare showcase of the most significant advances that brought it about.

Whereas I had previously been driven purely by sentiment, the *Yavarí's* maritime significance now strengthened my resolve to save the Old Lady of the Lake, and it became a matter of urgency. What if someone else realised the same and got there first?

CHAPTER 5

Trying to Buy the Yavari

A S QUICKLY AS POSSIBLE I RETURNED to Peru. I needed to see the Peruvian equivalent of our First Sea Lord who was a *Contralmirante* but took the title of Minister of the Navy. But how? The only possible way of getting an appointment would be by personal introduction. Who did I know?

I had contacts relating to the Cusichaca Project, and as chairman of the Anglo-Peruvian Society Appeals Committee I knew lots of people associated with the many social projects up and down the length of Peru to which we had given money. My address book was full of names but they were not the right names. I was bemoaning this fact to my hostess, Teresa Quesada, who was a concert pianist and the most unlikely person to have military connections, whereupon she picked up the telephone, saying, 'Let's just see if my cousin, Marcela, can help. I think her son-in-law's mother's brother is something to do with the navy. I'll ring her.'

She did and within half an hour had spoken to her cousin's son-in-law's mother's brother and it turned out that he was an Admiral. That is how it's done. It is who you know that makes things happen. Not so long ago, an oligarchy reputedly made up of eight Spanish and other European families ran Peru. Between them they owned the banks, the land and the mines, and ran the institutions. Before the Agrarian Reform in 1969[3], they were also the *haciendados* who owned highly productive sugar and cotton plantations on the coast and hundreds of square miles in the highlands for breeding and running sheep and alpaca. The Reform wrought dramatic changes and although their lands were drastically redistributed, leaving them with estates of hundreds as opposed to thousands of hectares, the *haciendados* maintained their position in the social hierarchy. Post-colonial immigrants who came to do business aspired to be included in this elite class as do today's newly rich entrepreneurs and drug barons. To some extent, the newly rich have elbowed the eight families to one side. Happily for me when I was looking for the Minister of the Navy, the oligarchs still held sway and, although hesitant at first, I soon learned to take full advantage. The power base in Latin America is the family, and as all families are extended the result is an abundance of uncles, aunts and cousins, or *tios, tias* and *primos/as*. If you know one, that is enough for you to be introduced to any of the others who might have connections with the people of influence who can open any door.

In the case of the navy, I was extremely lucky. Officers of the armed forces tend to keep themselves a little aloof from civilian society and, by and large, are not members of the oligarchy, but they maintain a respectful regard for it, as the oligarchy does for them.

That one telephone call by my hostess Teresa was, by chance, the masterstroke for which I shall always be grateful. Not only was 'our' new contact an Admiral, he was also friendly with the Minister of the Navy. I wondered what I had done to deserve such good fortune, because compared with the Royal Navy the Peruvian navy is rich in admirals but not every one is on Christian name terms with the Minister. I knew that the link would guarantee me an appointment and, sure enough, just days later the telephone rang and it was a member of the Minister's staff offering me a day and a time to see his boss. I was not in fact given a choice, but thought better of saying, 'Actually Tuesday would suit me much better…'

On the appointed day, and with hours to spare, I presented myself at the Naval Headquarters in Lima and this time, unlike my experience in Puno, there was no delay. Even the officious guard on the gate appeared impressed by the importance of the person I had come to see. The duty officer escorted me across the parade ground and my heart gave a little flutter of recognition. Not since my salad days in Malta, as an 18-year-old working for the local radio and television station, had I been inside a naval establishment and suddenly seeing the anchors, the cross-trees flag pole and, of course, the uniform brought it all back. I smiled at the happy memories.

Quietly humming *Every nice girl loves a sailor*, I climbed the broad sweep of steps to the porticoed entrance to the officers' HQ and was signalled through various checkpoints to the room where I was to wait to be summoned. I sat down under the penetrating stare of Admiral Miguel Seminario Grau, who vies as Peru's top hero with General José de San Martín who led Peru to victory in the country's fight for independence. As my eyes met Admiral Grau's, I didn't fully realise how deeply he is venerated. He was a commander in the War of the Pacific, but although he was a wily strategist, the odds were stacked against him. His flagship, the 200-foot Monitor *Huascar,* built by Lairds of Birkenhead and crewed by Peruvian sailors and English mercenaries, was already obsolete and no match for the Chileans' firepower. His fleet, outdated, outnumbered and outgunned, was all but lost even before the final engagement on 8 October 1879. Yet even so, the Peruvian navy fought with skill and daring under Grau's fearless command.

The distinguished geographer and writer Sir Clements Markham, Secretary (later President) of the Royal Geographical Society (1893-1905)[4], gives a most moving account in his *History of Peru* of the last sea battle, fought off Punta Angamos in Bolivia (at that time), which finally brought defeat to the Peruvian navy.

The '*brilliant Admiral Grau, seeing that escape was impossible, resolved to make a bold dash at his enemies, and fight his way through, or perish in the attempt.*' Alas for Peru, the Admiral '*was blown to atoms*'. Notwithstanding his demise, his ship's company kept up the fight, but though '*heroic*' and '*glorious*' they stood no chance. '*At 11 a.m., one hour and a half after the commencement of the action, the flag of the Huascar was at length hauled down.*'

The date, 8 October, has been commemorated ever since. Commander Grau was posthumously promoted to Admiral, and at ceremonial wardroom dinners, a place is always laid for him in his honour and each course duly served and cleared away (and later enjoyed by the galley crew).

Chile captured the *Huascar* and, to the ongoing anguish of the Peruvians, she is today cherished as a floating museum in Chilean waters at Talcahuano. Two brass plaques on the deck mark the spots where the two countries' most renowned naval heroes fell. The first to fall was the gallant Chilean Commander Arturo Prat, who was cut down when he jumped aboard the *Huascar* which had rammed his ship, the *Esmeraldas.* Five months later it was the fate of Commander Miguel Grau to fall on the very same deck.

However, I knew nothing of the admiral's heroic reputation as I sat waiting and running over in my mind what I was going to say, in my best Spanish which wasn't – and still isn't – especially fluent. I was startled out of rehearsing my subjunctives when the Flag Lieutenant appeared and invited me to follow him. He opened a door and there, behind a desk the size of two billiard tables beyond a couple of hectares of carpet, sat the Minister of the Navy. He got up and, with hand outstretched, strode out to meet me. He was a couple of inches taller than me, slim, probably in his late fifties, but although his hair was already grey his eyebrows were still ebony brown; they met in the middle, and reminded me of a child's sketch of a seagull in flight. Like most Limeños in summer time – a brief three-month respite from the overcast and misty norm – he had obviously spent time on the beach and was well bronzed. We shook hands as he greeted me with a softly spoken 'Buenas dias, Señorita Larken'. I noted, though, as I met his penetrating almost-black eyes, that they were anything but soft.

He was impeccably turned out, plenty of gold braid on his uniform attesting to his rank. I was glad that I had put on my one and only 'best outfit' for the occasion, and only wished that the steamy heat of a humid summer had not crimped my hair and made my face shine.

A commander, the flag lieutenant, a junior officer and an NCO, who later took notes, stood flanking the admiral's desk. I sat primly on the edge of a chair. A cup of coffee, borne on a silver tray by a white-gloved steward, suddenly appeared by my side. I tried to look cool and composed, praying that the nervous tremor in my arm wouldn't make the cup rattle on its saucer as I lifted it off the tray.

When thanks from me and courtesies from him had been dispensed with, the Minister opened a file on his desk and earnestly leant forward to say, 'As I understand it, Señorita, you are interested in buying the BAP...' He looked down at the file marked Chucuito, then looked across at his commander to check that he'd got the name right, for which I was thankful. It would have been awkward if we'd got the wrong ship. I couldn't afford a destroyer, and what would I do with it anyway? 'Yes, the Chucuito in Puno,' he re-confirmed. 'Now do tell me, Señorita – why?'

A foreigner and a woman interested in buying a navy ship, albeit an abused and abandoned one, was sure to meet with curiosity, if not suspicion. I tried to imagine what would happen if a Peruvian woman turned up at the Admiralty in London to buy HMS Belfast. The idea was preposterous. The Minister had every right to quiz me closely. As his questions were predictable I had taken good advice as to how to answer them. I didn't want to emphasise the historical importance of the *Yavarí* too strongly in case he thought her too rare and valuable to sell. It might also influence his decision as to price. On the other hand, if I showed indifference to her intrinsic value, he would wonder why I wanted to buy a load of old junk and suspect there was some more sinister motive for my wanting her. My answer had to be delicately balanced between the two.

Straight off, I told him of my long naval lineage and what a pleasure it was to be a guest of the Peruvian navy. I thought this was a good strategy because the Royal Navy, on which the Peruvian navy is modelled, is mightily respected and Admiral Lord Nelson venerated almost as highly as Admiral Seminario Grau. Then I told him of my long association with Peru and that I had been decorated by the Peruvian Government with the *Orden al Mérito por Servicios Distinguidos* for the work that I, as chairman of the tirelessly energetic charity committee of the Anglo-Peruvian Society, had done to help the needy. Well, this wasn't the moment to hold back, was it?

I wished I had achieved more at my Spanish courses and evening classes. I don't have a gift for languages and it upsets me when people put on a perplexed frown when I speak Spanish so I was greatly relieved that the Admiral was obviously too polite to. In fact, he appeared to approve of what I was saying so I carried on. I spoke about the ship being a symbol of the historic and amicable ties between his country and mine, its value as Peru's patrimony, and its potential for offering employment and training to the local community and attracting tourism and revenue to one of the poorest regions in Peru. I then added a little, but really only a little, about involving young volunteers and ploughing any profits from the ship's operations back into the community. I was afraid that the concept of 'volunteering' or 'ploughing back profits' would raise an eyebrow or two so I thought it best to play safe. Twenty-five years ago the concept of doing anything which was not for personal financial gain was either derided or deemed to be a cover for illicit trafficking or some other covert activity. I wasn't going to press the point; my noble ideals probably sounded absurd anyway, but I felt it was important to be as transparent as possible to avoid any misunderstandings later.

He asked me how I would fund the project, about the timing, and how much work I thought would be necessary to restore the *Chucuito*.

With the aid of photographs, I showed him what a dilapidated state the ship was in. He studied them before passing them on to his commander and flag lieutenant. There was a pause. Then he said, 'I understand what you are wanting to do.' I was so glad. 'But,' he went on, 'why do you want to *buy* the ship? Why don't you rent her from the navy, do all you want to her, and then hand her back?'

Whoops, this could be a tricky one. My advisors had covered a variety of responses but not this one. Without causing offence, I had somehow to tell him that such an idea was absolutely out of the question.

The Admiral seemed to have understood. 'If you are so determined to buy the ship then,' he said, 'what do you think she is worth?'

This one I had been prepared for. I had been told her approximate scrap metal value and I knew that the navy had no further use for her, that she could only be a drain on their resources and that by taking her off their hands, I would be sparing them the expense and trouble of breaking her up.

Pausing a moment before making *más o menos* – more or less – signals with my hands, I said, 'I am advised that her value is between 3,500 and 4,500 US dollars.'

He wrote the figures down on his pad and looked across at his commander. 'I see,' he said, keeping me in suspense. 'Well, my experts tell me that a more accurate figure would be between 4,500 and 6,000 dollars.'

I looked crestfallen. '*Señor Almirante*,' I said pathetically, 'I'm afraid I just can't afford 6,000 dollars.'

I was speaking for no formal body or charity at this stage. The money I had set aside for the purpose was my own.

The Admiral consulted with his commander again and I got the distinct impression that he didn't want to spend a lot of time haggling. We were dealing with a hulk of scrap iron somewhere up in the *sierra* and he had a navy to run, so after a *sotto voce* discussion, he turned back to me.

'*Señorita*,' he said leaning back in his chair and narrowing his eyes slightly. 'I think we may be able to come to a compromise. Suppose we say 5,000 dollars, on condition that you pay the money within ninety days. How does that sound?'

I hesitated, not wanting to show my delight. That was exactly the figure I had been told to aim for. I looked down at the papers on my lap

The author, aged 5, takes an early interest in ships.

On the plain below Mount Roraima (Venezuela 1976).

A first for the author – fried guinea pig (Peru 1976).

The Urubamba
Valley taken
from above
Cusichaca, Peru
*(photo by Dr
Ann Kendall).*

Dr Ann Kendall supervising the dig at Cusichaca (1978).

Loading the BBC TV's 'Chronicle' film equipment (Peru 1983).

Sir Alfred Yarrow – the author's great-grandfather who inspired her search for the origins of the *Yavarí*.

Yapurá and a barge under construction 1871.

The Thames Ironworks and Shipbuilding Company's charter currently hanging in the bar at West Ham United FC's Boleyn Ground.

British and Peruvian shipbuilders, Puno 1870s.

Early 20th century - mules delivering cargo to the steamers.

The *Yavarí* in Puno port 1985, two years after she was first sighted by the author, waiting to start her new life.

Below decks: a cabin in equally dilapidated condition.

Julian González and John Kusner.

David Henshall with ultrasonic meter measuring the thickness of the hull.

Tim Parr and Ing. Pedro
Vasquez.

Los Uros floating islands
outside Puno bay where
everything from homes to
boats are made of *totora*
reed.

Two Uros *señoras* competing for Captain Carlos' affections.

Responsibilities start young! Supervising fish drying on Los Uros.

The author's mother in Pisac market – 1990.

Early days with Captain Carlos – 1993.

British Ambassador John Illman inaugurating Peru's first floating museum 1998. Central figures l to r: Author, Mrs Marjorie Michell, Mrs John Illman.

Captain Carlos on a 'Run Ashore' at fiesta time.

Máximo proudly showing off
'his' engine to his mother.

Teodocio.

Antonia.

Young children visit the *Yavarí* and learn about its history.

In 1999, mules being scarce, we trekked with llamas in the foothills outside Tacna.

Another sleepless night at 14,500 ft. but putting a brave face on it.

Campesinos on the *altiplano* met on the 1999 trek.

and, for good measure, scribbled a few calculations, which I studied thoughtfully for a moment, feigning a little frown. Then I looked up and nodded slowly. 'Yes, Admiral,' I said. 'I agree to 5,000 dollars, and thank you'.

Without further ado, the Admiral charged his commander with getting a sale contract prepared immediately, informed me that the matter would now pass to *Abastecimiento* or Naval Stores Department, and gave me the name of the admiral in charge. The meeting was now over. He emerged once more from behind his desk and, showing me the decorum appropriate to someone who had just bought one of his warships, wished me every success with the project and farewell.

I left his office very happy indeed, and skipped down the broad sweep of steps thinking what fun it would have been to dance down like Ginger Rogers. The meeting had gone much, much better than I had ever dared to dream it would, and we had settled on a price I had been told was the scrap metal value of the *Yavarí*. This was a highly satisfactory outcome, which could only bode well for the project; I felt I was already half way there. Little did I know how ludicrous this was.

* * *

I needed to return straight away to the naval base on the lake to prepare for the handover. I was uneasy about the whereabouts of all the documentation relating to the *Yavarí*, which I had never seen again after my very first visit. When I got to Puno I found that the *Fiesta de la Candelaria* had come round again but that this was to be no ordinary *fiesta*.

The newly-elected President Alan Garcia was to attend the opening in the stadium. I bought a ticket for a seat in the Press and Foreigners' Stand which was next to the President's.

What we were about to see was *Strictly Come Dancing* for groups. Fifty-plus dance groups from throughout the *altiplano,* including Bolivia, were to dance the traditional dances of their region, competing all the while for Best Choreography, Best Music and Best Costume prizes.

The stadium quickly filled with dancers, musicians and spectators. Tens of thousands of Puneños had come to see their new President. He had campaigned energetically in the region and, to a man, they had voted for him. He was now returning to thank them. At thirty-seven he was also the second youngest president ever to be elected in Peru. He had been heralded as the JF Kennedy of Latin America, born to return Peru to her world standing, born to give the Indians back their dignity, born to quell the rising threat of terrorism. In short, he was the great hope for the future. The atmosphere was electric with anticipation, the tension palpable.

While we sat waiting, I got chatting with my neighbour who became tremendously excited about my plans to restore the *Yavarí*. 'The President should be told about this,' she insisted.

I could see it would be a shrewd move, but wondered how on earth I would get the news to him.

'Why – write to him, of course!' she expostulated. 'Write him a note and give it to him!'

'What, right here, do you mean?'

'*Por supuesto,* of course! Right here and now – why not?'

'Oh, no,' I demurred, shy of the attention it would attract. 'I really can't do that. You can't just write notes to presidents.'

'Oh yes, you can!' said she, having by this time broadcast to everyone within earshot what I was doing and what was being proposed.

'Oh yes, you can!' echoed the pantomime chorus. 'Write him a note and pass it along to his box.' They were insistent and produced a little scrap of paper to encourage me.

I deliberated for a moment, then the idea caught hold. What on earth could I lose? I smoothed out the crumpled piece of paper, no bigger than a lottery ticket. With a noisy input from my supporters' club, I wrote five lines to explain that I was English, a fan of Peru and dedicated to saving and restoring the *Yavarí* for the good of all.

I folded the scrap and wrote 'El Presidente, Sr. Alan Garcia' on it and asked my neighbour to pass it along the row of spectators. I watched it travel along until it came to the President's box. Progress from there was slow because each officer, and there were many from the police and special branch, the army, navy and town hall, felt it his duty to read it.

Then, to a roar as tumultuous as the one that greeted the post-wedding appearance of Prince Charles and Princess Diana on the balcony of Buckingham Palace, the long-awaited messiah entered. We, foreigners and press, all clapped and roared too. Alan Garcia had electrified everyone on his election campaign. At well over six feet, which is unusually tall for a Peruvian, he towered over the stocky Indians in his entourage. He was broad-shouldered and strikingly good-looking, and his powers of oratory had left no-one unmoved. Moreover, his policies sounded sane and his message convincing.

He climbed to his box and acknowledged the welcome with a wave. The band struck up the national anthem and we all stood to attention, right hands on hearts, sharing with the Puneños their dreams, their optimism and the faith they had in this man. As the last note died away, he raised his hand and, with a Caesar's wave, gave the signal for the contest to commence. It was just at that moment that an aide handed him my note. I and all my supporters watched anxiously as he unfolded the paper and peered at the carefully scripted message. Minutes of suspense passed before, lifting the note to the sky, he turned in our direction and shouted out, 'Who has written me this note? Please come forward!'

It was an imperial summons. Was the President cross? Insulted? Curious? There was absolutely no means of telling. I didn't know what to expect, but lots of urgent nudges and shoves from the pantomime chorus urged me to get going. I edged along the row, conscious that everyone was enthralled to know who would 'come forward'. When I reached his box, he leant over to shake my hand.

'May I congratulate you, *Señorita*?' he shouted against the music and the blaring loudspeakers. 'This sounds like an excellent project. How can I help you?'

I told him that if the *Yavarí's* file containing the ship's plans and provenance, now in the naval base in Puno, could be sent down to Lima as quickly as possible, we could get on with the transfer of ownership. In fact, I'd been told that it was the new port captain himself who was obstructing the file's movement, and he was at that moment within earshot. I wondered what would happen.

'Of course,' declared the President. 'I shall give orders to the port captain here to give you all the support you need. And be sure to let me know at the Palace if I can be of any further help in the future.'

Shaking my hand again, he indicated that I was now dismissed and turned back to watch the dancing while I struggled back to my seat along the same row of spectators I had squeezed past before, all of whom now wanted to pat me on the back and congratulate me. I felt most embarrassed; I might have won a Bafta award for all the adulation. Anyway, when I reached my new best friend who had instigated the plot in the first place, I gave her a big hug and thanked her warmly for her spirited support.

When I got back to Lima, I called the Admiral of *Abastecimiento* whose name the Minister had given me and, to my immense surprise, learned that apparently the President had let it be known that he was enthusiastic about the project and that his admirals were to give it a fair wind. I asked whether the *Yavari*'s file had arrived from Puno yet.

'No, no, I've seen no file.' The Admiral was dismissive. 'But we don't need it anyway. Everything is very straightforward. I can't see why there should be any delay. The sale contract *esta en mis manos* – it's in my hands. You will have it very, very soon.'

In my naivety, I took that to mean that any day now the contract would pass from his hands to mine and that the sale would be completed forthwith. Now I smile wryly when I remember my optimism then and so many times since. I waited expectantly, but there was no word, no sign.

Whatever the President may have said, I had no illusions whatsoever as to the insignificance of my project, still less the file, to the top brass of the navy. I counted for nothing, so clearly I needed to enhance my status. The only way to do that would be to bring the weight of the British Embassy to bear on the situation.

I had no reason to presume that I would get any support at all from the Embassy, so I was thrilled when – spotting a challenge – the Naval Attaché Captain George Hogg RN agreed to take part. He, tall and bearded, upright and impressive in all his naval finery, and I descended on the naval base in search of the elusive file. A great deal of saluting ensued as we were escorted to the relevant Admiral's office. He gave us, or to be exact, he gave Captain Hogg, a warm welcome followed by repeated assurances that a thorough search would be made for the said file, last seen in Puno, which contained the *Yavari*'s original drawings, registration and historic documentation. However, though I asked for news of the file several times after that, it has never ever been seen again, but in 2004 the *Yavari* was officially re-registered as Vessel No. PU-021 926-ML.

In Lima, waiting for the contract to be finalised, I had time to begin researching the *Yavari*'s origins in the Peruvian naval and military archives. There I found Peru's entire colonial and post-colonial history stowed away in boxes and bundles, indexed to varying degrees of classification, the most elementary being dates from/to on a box. Inside one such box dated 1860–1865 lay folders containing memoranda from Lima directed to the prefects, municipalities and mayors of each of Peru's twenty-four political departments. Happily, the folders were separated into departments, so I had only the southern ones of Tacna, Mochegua and Puno to search through. Nonetheless it was a challenge. There were literally hundreds of memos, some written in a bold and flamboyant hand with extravagant curlicues to every word, others, now faded to almost illegibility, in a more conservative copperplate. All of them bore rubber-stamped escutcheons of authority and a flourish of signatures, and covered everything from the smallest details of a pending visit by a functionary to strategic advice on suppressing an Indian uprising.

Rather endearingly, the two ships destined for Lake Titicaca were referred to as '*los vaporcitos*' (the little steamers). Knowing that and having familiarised myself with the writing, I was able to chase through the bundles scanning each document for the words *Lago Titicaca*, *vaporcitos*, *Yavarí* and *Yapurá*. It was tempting to read about other matters which caught my eye, but I could only allow myself momentary pauses. When she had time, I sometimes got help from the archivist, Elia Lazarte, who indebted me to her by offering to transcribe the more important memos on her antique Imperial typewriter.

Elia was Chinese. Her great-grandfather had come to Peru in the early 1900s. She was over-qualified and underpaid but the only working member of her family; she also had to look after her mother and a sprinkling of elderly aunts. Her situation is not uncommon in Peru. Had she been able to afford to leave and train for another job or study after work, she could have gone to the top, but she was trapped by her circumstances. She couldn't even afford to travel outside Lima, let alone further afield. Yet she showed no resentment that I was able to fly back and forth to Europe. On the contrary, she was always cheerful, insisting that the only thing she wanted was for me to bring her an Englishman to marry! Alas, I never managed this, but any man fortunate enough to marry Elia would be a lucky man.

Elia's workload was such that she could only type out a few of the memos. The rest she photocopied for me because it was impossible in the time I had to read each one intelligently. My aim was to accumulate as much relevant material as I could to study at a later date. What I did read supported *Técnico* Julian González's summary of the *Yavarí* arriving at the port of Arica in 1862 and subsequently being borne up the Andes to be reassembled and launched on Christmas Day 1870.

One barely legible but particularly valuable memorandum I found, dated 15 July 1862, was sent from London and signed by the Peruvian Admiral Ignacio Mariátegui, who was charged with commissioning the two ships. In it he was reporting to the Ministry of the Navy in Lima that *los vaporcitos* had been consigned to a ship called the *Mayola* which had sailed on 28 June bound for Arica which, prior to the Pacific War, was within Peruvian territory. Unfortunately, the Admiral did not say from which English port the ship had sailed. It was likely to have been Liverpool or London, but it would have been useful to know which.

In between visits to the archives, I was ringing the Admiral responsible for 'my' sale contract to establish progress. If that sounds simple, it was not. Twenty-five years ago, telephoning in Peru could drive one to suicide. The network was totally inadequate so all lines were permanently engaged or out of order. When I eventually got through to a secretary, she would always tell me that her boss was *en una reunión* (in a meeting), *por otra linea* (on the other line), or *fuera de su despacho* (out of the office). Any or all could have been true, the last being the most probable. She would never know when he might be available but she would definitely tell him I had called and he would return my call. 'But when?' I would plaintively ask, because I had no secretary and certainly couldn't wait by the telephone all day. 'As soon as he returns/is free/feels like it.'

It was rare that anyone called back. I never knew whether that was another example of the Peruvian ploy to keep me – *una gringa* – at bay, or if it was the general rule. All I do know is that I absolutely dreaded making those calls. I had to psych myself up to face the horror of ringing from a public telephone in the street. First, it was important to have enough tokens called *rines*. Imagine how stupid I felt when, in my anxiety, I asked in a shop for *riñones*, meaning kidneys! Next, I had to find a public telephone which worked. The bleep-bleep sound that emanated from the handset was the same whether the telephone itself was out of order, the line was jammed or the specific number was engaged. Worse, the telephones were not in a kiosk or box; they were hiding under a hood that was supposed to be soundproof but was as effective as a paper bag. If and when I eventually got through, pitting my Spanish against the traffic noise was like shouting on the start grid of the Monaco Grand Prix. In those days, there was no such thing as an MOT. The silencers on many cars, most buses and all 1950s Chevrolets, Buicks and Packards, which served as 'combi' taxis, had burnt out long ago. Furthermore, Limeños love to blow their horns at no matter what – cars or pedestrians, it makes no difference. The quadraphonic combination drowned out any attempts at a coherent telephone conversation.

Admiral Mariátegui's letter informing the Minister of War and the Navy in Lima that the two little steamers for Lake Titicaca had been dispatched on the *Mayola*, 28 June 1862.

What worried me even more was that I was due to fly home and had naively imagined that the contract would be signed and sealed by then. I postponed my flight, paid the fine and kept ringing. I postponed it again, paid another fine and still kept ringing. It was a humiliating experience of 'the ploy'.

Eventually, I had to go. My last call to the Admiral, who had claimed to have the contract in his hands, was from the airport. Again he wasn't in his office and his secretary couldn't possibly tell me anything about the contract. I had no choice but to leave Peru empty handed.

CHAPTER 6

Fundraising at Home and Away

When I got back to London, frustrated but still undeterred, I applied myself to looking for support and raising money. The first snag was obvious. Having only me as a supporter the cause lacked substantivity, yet I felt shy of courting trustees and setting up a charity until I had actually bought the *Yavari*. Instead I sought endorsements from bodies like the National Maritime Museum and the World Ship Trust to lend credibility to my improbable appeal. Frank Carr, formerly Director of the National Maritime Museum but then Chairman of the World Ship Trust, liked the story of the *Yavari* very much. He said he remembered Prince Philip telling him that he had seen the British ships on Lake Titicaca when he was on a world tour in 1962.

'I'm sure he'd be interested to know what you're up to,' said Frank. 'When I next see him I'll tell him.'

That focused my attention. It was now obviously crucial to have a printed leaflet of some kind. Seed-corn money for any project is notoriously difficult to find but if The Yavari Project was going anywhere it needed publicity material. I begged favours – of marine artist John White, to paint an artist's impression of the restored *Yavari* plying Lake Titicaca, of Christina Sapieha, an artist friend, to transcribe my logo from sketch to drawing, and of John Benn to typeset it and Silverline Press to produce and print the leaflet. The *Yavari* and her story won their hearts; they were inspired by the romantic idea of saving her from the breaker's yard and involving the local community and young people in her restoration.

The publicity leaflet which resulted launched The Yavari Project and fired me up anew. I realised that the *Yavarí* did not have the appeal of a humanitarian project like an orphanage. I had also been made very aware by working on the Cusichaca Project that fundraising for a project outside the British Commonwealth was inherently more difficult. Nonetheless, the enthusiasm and generosity of the people who produced the leaflet convinced me (or, with hindsight, fooled me into thinking), that funds would be forthcoming.

Confident of a sympathetic hearing and fruitful outcome, I drew up a list of companies, organisations and individuals to call on. It started with shipyards. I would invite them to adopt the project and, in exchange for what it offered in PR, lend their expertise and donate materials and, as a long-term investment in their apprentices, use the project as an incentive or leadership training scheme.

When Britain's shipyards were nationalised in 1977 they became owned and managed by the British Shipbuilders Corporation. Although in 1983 they were returned to private ownership the BSC lived on as a quango. Cousin Eric knew the Chairman, whom I rang for an appointment.

'What a charming story!' he said. 'But I have to tell you that this is a very bad time for British shipbuilding.' He emphasised the word 'very', looked grave, and proceeded to tell me why. It was not at all what I wanted to hear.

I went north for better news, to the Lake District to see George Pattinson, founder of the Windermere Steamboat Museum. He was passionate about boating history and, at the time, was restoring the steam launch *Dolly*, built in 1850. If anyone could reassure me of the worth of my mission it would be him. He did do that, but his tales of fundraising did nothing to raise my aspirations.

I went on to Swan Hunters shipyard, and then to many companies with maritime interests in Liverpool and Birkenhead. All resisted my appeal. The next stop was HM Naval Dockyard, Portsmouth, where I was delighted to be offered the navy's traditional hospitality which, misguidedly, I interpreted as a positive sign. The Flag Officer, Portsmouth took me to lunch at Whale Island, base of the Commander-in-Chief, Home Fleet. It brought back many childhood memories of visits to Portsmouth Dockyard when my father was based there, but I had never before travelled in the Admiral's Barge. I love being saluted when boarding a Royal Naval vessel, I love the boathook drill, and that day I loved even more all the saluting that went on from the Home Fleet. All hands on all ships turned to salute the Admiral as we motored passed. It felt propitious.

The lunch was good, I went all-out with my presentation and, as usual, the *Yavari's* story captivated, but the outcome was again a 'no'.

This became the pattern. Wherever I went, I was warmly welcomed and my remarkable tale listened to and applauded, but as for getting involved – no, that would be out of the question. Surely I knew the trouble that British shipbuilding was in.

I made a list of all the companies with shipping interests or who were operating in Peru. Through my work with the Anglo-Peruvian Society I was lucky to have good friends at the Peruvian Embassy and I already knew many companies with Peruvian links. None of them gave me any reason for optimism but as I persevered with my quest I was told repeatedly how Britain's first and last ironclad, HMS *Warrior* built in 1860, had been restored by the Manifold Trust. Inspired by Sir John Smith and at a cost of £7million, the project had involved teams of young people as part of a government initiative called the Youth Training Scheme (YTS). As Cammell Laird ran a course for both apprentice and YTS shipwrights, I put to them the idea of sponsoring a team of both – good for experience, good for international relations and good for publicity and PR.

The idea obviously had its attractions because they invited me to Birkenhead to give a slide talk to the young trainees in question. 'But keep it brief,' they said. 'Some of the lads don't have much of a concentration span.'

I may have roamed South America, but giving a slide talk as a female from the south who 'talked posh' – that was a truly daunting prospect. As I resolutely edited my slides down to a mean fifteen, I could already hear the mimicry and mockery with which I and they would be received.

The emphasis of the talk, timed to be not a second over twenty minutes, was on challenge, job satisfaction and a lot about time off for climbing mountains and trekking in the Andes. I wanted it to sound like an extract from the Victorian Boy's Own Paper, all derring-do and adventure.

But these were not Victorian boys. I finished with 'Any questions?' and held my breath.

A hand went up. I prepared myself with answers to 'When can we start?' and 'How high is the highest mountain?' But no – the first question was about 'facilities', which I gathered meant fish & chip shops, pubs, discos and girls. Then another asked if they would be expected to work the same hours as in the UK, and the third, 'What's the pay?'

Once the room had cleared of lads, I looked ruefully at the training instructor and was dumbfounded when he said, 'That was one of the best talks we've ever heard here. Well done! I really do congratulate you.' I must have looked aghast because he went on, 'Well, you kept them quiet for twenty minutes, they didn't fidget, chatter or throw eggs, *and* they asked questions!'

I laughed with relief, and was deluded into thinking that there was definitely a future in involving young people. At the time I was speaking to two competing television companies, both of which were extremely keen on the idea of northern youths facing the challenges of working on the ship at 12,500 feet. One even proposed dedicating a five-minute slot every week to a personalised update 'to camera' from each of the lads speaking from the world's highest navigable lake.

This was completely in keeping with my vision. I was so enthused, I wrote an article for a magazine calling for volunteer housekeepers, adventure-training instructors, photographers and more or less anyone who would like to work for a unique project in an exotic location. I was inundated with replies, but only then did I discover that, like almost all youth projects in the 1980s, the YTS did not work abroad and certainly not outside the Commonwealth.

Still hopeful, I visited HMS *Warrior* in Portsmouth Dockyard to find out more, and met up with Captain John Wells RN, a member of the project team. He suggested that I approach Sir John Smith, Chairman of the Manifold Trust. I made a mental note to do so as soon as The Yavari Project had been registered as a charity.

As the project was still so much in its infancy, and not yet officially recognised, I was utterly astonished one morning to open my front door and be saluted by a trim and smartly tailored Queen's Messenger. He handed me a thick white vellum envelope which was clearly too wide, too long and much too important to go through my letterbox. It was from Buckingham Palace, a Royal Message from HRH The Duke of Edinburgh.

I was so thrilled I could hardly make any sense. This lifted the project out of obscurity and into the light of Royal recognition. I was quite overcome and, having rung Frank Carr with the news, had five hundred

BUCKINGHAM PALACE

In 1962 I was travelling round South America and one of my most vivid memories was an overnight crossing of Lake Titicaca in an unpressurised passenger ship at 12,500 feet.

As we left Puno my attention was drawn to the remains of another ship of an earlier vintage. As I was told the same story about her having been brought up from the coast in pieces small enough to be carried on the backs of mules, I can only assume that she was the YAVARI. I also gathered that she had been replaced by a more modern ship some years later but in this case the pieces could be somewhat bigger as they were able to be transported up to the lake by the newly constructed railway.

I have therefore a rather personal reason to be interested in the idea of restoring this unique vessel as a touring ship on the lake. I very much hope that The YAVARI Project will attract the necessary support to make it a resounding success.

Philip

1986

HRH The Duke of Edinburgh's 1986 goodwill message.

copies made immediately.

The letter was dated, which for a four-year project was fine. But it was dated 1986, so by the time 1996 came round, and the project seemed hardly to have begun, it would have sent out the wrong message. Of course it would be dreadfully impertinent to ask for the date to be changed, but I had to be impertinent. Prince Philip graciously obliged, but with a note of gentle exclamation over the time the project was taking. When, in 2006, I was subsequently presented to him, he laughed out loud just at the mention of Lake Titicaca and the *Yavarí*. What was I to interpret from that?

I was so sorry that my father never knew of this recognition by a member of the Royal family, and one whom he so highly regarded. He would have been proud, but tragically he died the previous year, 1985, too young and much missed. I should also love to have been able to report on my encounters with the Peruvian navy although I couldn't swear that he would have approved of the project. He followed my initial trek around South America in minute detail, marking my every move on his Reader's Digest World Atlas which was his way of showing approval but, since his naval career had been spent in the Far East, on the Arctic convoys and in the Mediterranean, Latin America was *terra incognita*. I don't think he ever understood what drew me to Peru, but I suspect that had he witnessed the project dragging on, he, like so many of my good friends, would have encouraged me to let it go and move on.

Proud and buoyed by Prince Philip's support I set about the fundraising with renewed energy and optimism, but first I needed to know more about the *Yavarí's* origins.

I referred again to the Lloyds Shipping List for the 1860s and HM Customs' contemporary ledgers. Sure enough, there was an entry for the *Mayola*, a 400-foot three-masted barque belonging to a Liverpudlian called W. Porter and skippered by a Mr Quircy, which sailed from London Docks bound for Arica on 28 June 1862. She was carrying a cargo valued at £19,000 (equivalent to £820,000 today[5]).

There was another entry, dated 30 June, signifying that the *Mayola* had cleared Gravesend and was heading south towards Cape Horn. I saw from the Shipping List of 23 December that, having rounded the Horn, the vessel arrived in Arica, then in Peru, on 15 October 1862. Antony Gibbs & Sons were the handling agents who took receipt of the cargo.

Antony Gibbs & Sons were still trading from the City of London in the

London Customs' List of Actual Exports for 27 June 1862. The Gibbs & Sons entry for Arica is near the top (fifth down) of the third column and shows the cargo values at £19,000 (the value of two gunboats, tools and spares).

1980s. Before visiting them I researched their history. At our meeting I wanted to talk about the firm's past links with South America, and was surprised that they appeared not to be interested. It became obvious why when, shortly after my visit, they were absorbed by HSBC and their archives, uncatalogued, shipped off to the Guildhall Library. They had shelved their past.

What I did learn about Antony Gibbs & Sons was probably typical of a Victorian enterprise and not dissimilar from the story of the Grace brothers who succeeded them. In the early nineteenth century, wool merchant Antony Gibbs established an import/export business in Spain from where, in due course, his sons George and William set sail for South America where they arrived at exactly the right time. William sailed on to Chile and made a fortune from the nitrate business while George remained in Peru and made a fortune out of guano.

Peru had recently become a republic and those early years were turbulent. In all the Hispanic colonies which had fought bravely for and won their freedom from Spain there was instability, but nowhere more so than in Peru. Independence was declared on 28 July 1821, but then came adjustment to the complexities of self-governance. For three centuries, as the Spanish Viceroyalty, the country had known protected trade, wealth, glamour and power. Suddenly, with freedom, came autonomy, free trade and competition. Conspiracies, rivalries and personal ambitions prevailed among the *caudillos* (military strongmen) who, with no experience of running a country, jostled and fought for political supremacy, while Europeans and Americans, aware of the country's wealth of natural resources, eagerly hurried in to take advantage.

George Gibbs was among them. He was there in 1840 when the first consignment of guano was dispatched to England.

Guano, the Quechua word for 'excrement of seabirds', is exactly that – the accumulated excreta of seabirds which, over countless millennia, has become compacted into mountains and cliffs. The richest concentrations are found on the Chincha Islands, 13 miles offshore, about 150 miles south of Lima. Most seabirds excrete in flight but cormorants, pelicans and boobies excrete mainly on land and on islands like the Chinchas, which are free from predators. It is these birds, together with seals, sea lions and various skeletal remains, that are responsible for these deposits of putrefied gold. Since the beginning of time seabirds have inhabited southern Peru and northern Chile where the Humboldt Current provides the world's greatest diversity of marine life and most prolific fishing grounds. The Incas, and the cultures preceding them, prized the excreta as a fertiliser and harvested it for their agricultural terraces in the Andes. The sixteenth-century Spanish Jesuit missionary, José de Acosta, wrote of it, '... *in some llands and headlands, which are joyning to the coast of Peru, wee see the toppes of the Mountaines all white, and to sight, you would take it for Snow, or some white land, but they are heapes of dung of Sea fowls which goe continually thither... this dung is so commodious and profitable, as it makes the earth yeelde great aboundance of fruite...They call this dung Guano.*[6]

However, it was not exploited by the Spanish and neither did the young republican government appreciate its true worth. Anxious to make a quick return in a desperate attempt to slow the country's decline into bankruptcy, they undersold a six-year export concession. The first shipment was to England, where it was hailed by farmers as being thirty times more effective than standard farmyard manure because of its high nitrogen content, and they wanted more. George Gibbs heard of its outstanding success through the company's London office and moved in to negotiate his own contract. There were other merchants, but Antony Gibbs & Sons dominated the export market for the next twenty years. When the family was later granted the Barony of Aldenham, a rude ditty described them as: *'The House of Gibbs, that made their dibs, by selling the turds of foreign birds'*.

The extensive number of ships loading guano around the Chincha Islands in 1863.

The business was a phenomenon. At its peak in the late 1850s, labourers, coolies and convicts, working in the most repugnant of conditions, were digging out enough to load twelve ships per week with the foul-smelling cargo which they had to pack by hand into the ship's hold in temperatures of 120°F, ammonium stinging their eyes and burning their lungs.

William also made a fortune trading nitrate in Chile. A visible legacy of some of the great wealth which both companies accrued is Tyntesfield House, just south of Bristol in Somerset. William built this 'house built on guano' in 1863, but after the death of William's great-grandson George (known as Richard) Gibbs, the second Lord Wraxall, it was bought and is being restored by the National Trust, who describe it as a 'full-blooded

Gothic Revival extravaganza'.

By the time the *Yavari* arrived in 1862, Antony Gibbs & Sons was also well established as the agent for all incoming trade from England.

* * *

My research was slowly turning up the facts of the *Yavari*'s story, but I still didn't know where or in which yard she had been built.

In view of the evidence in HM Customs' contemporary ledger of the *Mayola* and her cargo having sailed from London, I was sceptical about the *Yavari* having been built by Lairds of Birkenhead, a short hop from the port of Liverpool. I hoped my suspicions were unfounded because, by this time, I had propositioned Vickers Shipbuilding and Engineering, or VSEL, who were negotiating the acquisition of Cammell Laird.

While correspondence travelled slowly between them and me, I was being prompted by Tim Parr to find someone to assess the ship's stability by measuring the hydrostatic curves of the hull, known as 'taking off the lines', and carrying out an 'inclining experiment'.

Extraordinarily, a young naval engineer called Steve Pullen came up on my radar. He was working at Southampton University's Wolfson Unit and volunteered to carry out the test and inspection in exchange for his airfare, bed and board. I had no legal charge on the *Yavari* but, forever the optimist, I drove Steve to the airport, having set up a chain of complicated arrangements and interpreters in order for him to be met, looked after and, through the Peruvian Naval Attaché, given access to the ship.

Three days later, the telephone rang. It was Steve. He had been barred from boarding the ship. I might have guessed. It was a conspiracy between the port captain I had offended at the *fiesta* in front of President Alan Garcia and the notoriously disagreeable civilian port manager. My position was parlous. Even if I could get through on the telephone, I was sure that neither of these gentlemen would take my call. Telex was the only other option, but would get me nowhere. As Steve only had a fortnight to spare, time was critical. I had no choice but to go back to the Peruvian Naval Attaché in London. Signals flashed to and fro, no doubt to the irritation of the port captain, but the next thing I knew, Steve was on board. He did all he could, given that the port was flooded and the *Yavari*'s jetty submerged. This was because of El Niño, an abnormal warming of the surface waters of the Pacific Ocean that can cause both severe flooding and droughts. It occurs roughly every five years and Peru and Ecuador are particularly vulnerable. Fishermen named it 'the Christ Child' because it usually coincides with Christmas.

I can only assume that the barrage of signals from the Naval Attaché jogged someone's memory to excavate the *Yavarí*'s file from a drawer because not long after that I got a letter through the Diplomatic Bag. The letter informed me officially that my offer to buy the *Yavarí* for 5,000 dollars had been accepted and that the sale contract would be drawn up forthwith. Clearly it had never been in the Admiral's hands at all.

I was becoming wary of Peruvian 'forthwiths', so to fill the unforgiving minute I accepted an invitation to go to Mystic, Connecticut, to give a slide talk at the Seaport Museum.

This was definitely a more serious undertaking than giving a twenty-minute talk to my previous audience of shipyard trainees. I rehearsed a couple of times and, although I blethered between 'ums' and 'ahs', I felt sure it would all come together on the night. What folly! To anyone so deluded, here's a word of advice. Like Winston Churchill's 'spontaneous' speeches, a slick slide talk needs an inordinate amount of rehearsing, preferably in front of a mirror. I gave my first dry-run talk to good friends who, unbeknownst to me, had also invited a number of their intellectual friends amongst whom was an eminent literary editor. My performance was risible and my *amour propre* still quakes at the memory of the beating it suffered that day.

In advance of my arrival, Nigel Kenyon, my dapper English host in New York, had written on my behalf to several potential backers, from Donald Trump to the Smithsonian Museum. Once in New York, and between interviews, the slide talk was further tweaked by him and rehearsed by me. By the time I got to Mystic it was, in Nigel's words, 'tight, evocative and amusing'. I milked the involvement of Prince Philip and somehow worked it in that Queen Victoria was my grandmother's godmother, but I might as well not have bothered. They told me the talk was 'cute' and the project was 'cute' and wished me every success, but I came away without a dime.

I suppose I shouldn't have been surprised that neither the talk nor the interviews resulted in anything, because North Americans share no affinity with their Latin American neighbours. Indeed, if pressed, some would admit to having certain misgivings about native Indians, hallucinogenic drugs, altitude and Latin volatility. The news which then broke would have done little to change this attitude.

'You're going to like this,' Nigel said one morning with a wicked grin. He had just been out to buy a newspaper. 'Guess what's happened in Peru!'

'There's been an earthquake,' I guessed, thinking it was all a joke. 'Or the President's been shot...'

'Much worse than that.' And Nigel held up the banner headline, which read: *American Tourist Shot On Train To Machu Picchu.*

At the time, 1986, incidents of terrorist activity carried out by *El Sendero Luminoso,* or the Shining Path terrorists, and another sect called Tupac Amaru (the MRTA) were escalating. Every day the terrible atrocities perpetrated on the peasant communities in the *sierra* became more gruesome. In Lima, the blowing-up of power plants, blackouts, bombings outside government offices and popular restaurants, kidnappings and hold-ups were becoming commonplace. Citizens were getting on with life as best they could but had resorted to carrying firearms and building high walls around their houses. The country was under siege and particularly by the Shining Path.

A Maoist guerrilla movement, the Shining Path was founded by 36-year-old Abimael Guzman in 1970. He came from a middle class background but had adopted communism, visited China several times during the Cultural Revolution, and been inspired by Chairman Mao. He became a professor of philosophy at Ayacucho University where he attracted other provincial intellectuals of similar mind and prepared for war on the political and social order. In a chilling speech, on 19 April 1980, he declared that the hour had come, that he was on a '*glorious mission*' to lift up the masses, lift up the peasantry, and he urged the people '*to rise in revolution to put a noose around the neck of imperialism and the reactionaries*', the flesh of whom would, as '*black filth*', sink into the mud. In case anyone was left in any doubt as to his intentions, he concluded with a call to arms: '*The future lies in guns and cannons! The armed revolution has begun! Glory to Marxist-Leninist-Mao-Zedong Thought! Let us initiate the armed struggle.*'

With those words he launched a campaign of brutality, torture, intimidation, destruction and killings that was to last for twelve years.

Within Peruvian society there was some sympathy for the cause. I knew people who readily recognised that the *campesinos* had been abused first by the Incas, then by the Spanish and, in today's Peru, were still sidelined, but no-one could condone the terror tactics. The core activists were left-wing professionals, lawyers, doctors and teachers, but many other ordinary folk were coerced or intimidated into joining. Financed by drug money and armed by foreign agents, the brutalities they inflicted were beyond anything I would want to describe here. Ruthlessly, they targeted community leaders, police, mayors, missionaries, leaders of foreign projects, the military and, confusingly, peasant communities who did not concur. However, curiously, they did not target foreign tourists.

Indeed, it transpired that the shooting on the train reported in the US press had been a terrible mistake and nothing to do with the *Sendero*, but the damage had been done. I was sure that, as far as the Americans were concerned, Peru and the *Yavarí* were condemned.

However, contrary to my worst fears, I was still received and listened to by the *National Geographic*, the Society for the Americas, the Explorers' Club, bankers, friends and top-flight travel agents. The *New Yorker* wrote an evocative piece about the project and I thought I had reached my rainbow's end when the American Express Foundation called me back for a second interview, but in the end I came away with nothing.

Amongst the pile of mail waiting for me when I got home were two letters that more than compensated for the disappointment. The first was from the Peruvian Naval Attaché telling me that the sale contract had arrived and the second, from VSEL, inviting me to visit them to discuss my proposition.

The sale contract turned out to be several pages long and incorporated many conditions, one of them being that the *Yavarí* would always fly the Peruvian flag. I am still not sure whether they were afraid of us running up the Red Ensign or the Bolivian Ensign. Of more immediate concern, however, was the agreement I had made so many months ago that the contract be signed and payment made within ninety days. This was a problem, because I had intended to pay in cash and in person which would mean asking for an extension to the ninety days, and that could well jeopardise my position. I again bothered the Peruvian Naval Attaché who was buying a frigate for his navy at the time, but he was sympathetic and offered to ask for an extension. The signal in reply from Lima said, 'Yes, for a further two months'.

Much cheered, I made my way north to see VSEL and in particular the MD – the propitiously-named Mr Frank Noah. Surely, I mused, God would wish him to launch another vessel.

For VSEL to employ YTS youngsters and do a makeover of the little *Yavarí* would have earned them any amount of kudos for a very modest outlay and, although Mr Noah and his Board gave me a grilling, I could see that they found the idea appealing. So it came as no surprise when they said that before making any commitment they would want to send their surveyor out to inspect the vessel.

I suppressed an overwhelming desire to fling my arms round Mr Noah. It had been my goal to persuade someone to go and actually see the *Yavarí* for themselves, because no-one who visits can resist her charms. I was convinced that VSEL's backing was as good as confirmed.

While Andy the surveyor flew business class on Lufthansa, I flew Economy with the Colombian airline Avianca, and we met in Lima.

Andy was over sixty and winding down to retirement. The last thing in the world he wanted was the inconvenience and upheaval of flying to the other side of the world. I couldn't blame him, particularly as until that moment he had never been further afield than France. His preconceived ideas about the Third World were unflattering and, as we were heading for a fairly primitive corner of it, I was apprehensive.

From the minute we arrived, everything – but *everything* – that could possibly go wrong, did. Due to terrorist activity a curfew had been imposed in Lima. Andy stayed at the downtown Sheraton and I stayed with friends in a suburb five miles away. We were due to fly south the next day to Juliaca in the highlands, Puno's nearest airport, and from there drive the forty minutes to Puno. Not for the first time, the airline's computer was down so they had no record of our booking. We re-applied and were put on the waiting list. In those days, flying internally in Peru was a lottery known as flying Air Chance. It was pure chance that your reservation was respected and pure chance that the plane took off on the right day, if at all. Delays and postponements were the norm but announcements and apologies out of the question. I once totted up the amount of time I had spent in either Lima or Juliaca airport waiting for postponed or cancelled flights. It came to an entire month of my life, and as for my blood pressure, they've yet to produce a monitor capable of taking such apoplectic readings.

That night we dined with *Ingeniero* Manuel Suarez, the surveyor who had carried out the Lloyds Condition Survey, but on account of the curfew we couldn't find a taxi to take either of us home. We stood at the roadside and the minutes ticked by until, at last, a 1958 Volkswagen Beetle limped into view. Its showroom glamour had long since been marred by years of abuse; in fact, it really only amounted to a steering wheel, a gear stick and three pedals hidden in a tangle of electrical wires. The whole was held together in a rusty shell by heavy-duty adhesive tape. It was a toss-up as to whether we would get home before the curfew. 'No hay problema,' said the driver confidently and set off at his maximum speed of 25mph. Andy was not impressed.

The flight we were hopeful of catching left the next day at 5.00 a.m. I ordered a taxi and, because of the curfew, we drove to the airport with the taxi's internal light ablaze to avoid being arrested by the police. At the airport we hurried through the formalities to the departure gate with ten minutes to spare. The only plane we could see out on the apron was alive with mechanics. It was ours. Two and a half hours later, during which we neither saw nor heard a single member of staff, we were suddenly invited to board. We sank into our seats with relief, belted up and took off over the Pacific Ocean. Fifteen minutes later we turned back. Andy was even less impressed.

By mid-morning we were in the air again, heading south towards Arequipa. I did my best to lift Andy's spirits by extolling the beauty of both the 'White City' and the iconic snow-capped volcano El Misti which overlooks it. He peered out of the window only to find that everything below us was hidden in thick fog. I said nothing, knowing how close the mountains are to the runway, but we landed without incident and there we remained. All onward flights to Juliaca had been cancelled.

When we discovered that the bi-weekly train to Puno had left that morning, I began to get worried. Andy only had a week in Peru. I rang the only person I knew in Arequipa, Mrs Marjorie Michell, whose late husband had founded Peru's foremost alpaca wool export company. I didn't know her well, but the situation was so dire that it was important to log on to the Arequipa network, which worked on the same basis as the one in Lima that had proved so useful.

Mrs Michell couldn't help, but she knew exactly who could. The next day at 6.00 a.m. we climbed into a four-wheel-drive Cherokee to travel the 200 miles up to Puno. Even on a good day, this was southern Peru's most atrocious road, but this was the rainy season so we could expect the twelve-hour journey to take at least fifteen. I tried to hide my excitement at the prospect of travelling overland. Andy, on the other hand, was appalled. It was a long slow ascent, bumping in and out of potholes, sidestepping landslides, getting bogged, wet and very weary. But we were well compensated; we should never otherwise have seen the red-legged *puna* plover or the ducks, gulls, geese, flamingos and avocets on the *salinas* lakes. We caught a glimpse of a *viscacha* (a rabbit-like creature with a long tail) and passed many herds of llamas and alpacas. We even saw the shy vicuña apparently posing for us on the *altiplano* against a backdrop of craggy Andean peaks and snowcaps. Our driver, Orlando, pointed out Mount Ambato where, in 1995, they would discover the sacrificial Inca Ice Maiden 'Juanita', at rest in a slope of the volcano. For me the panoramic grandeur and wild beauty of the scenery and the adventure of the unexpected made the journey unforgettable. It was also unforgettable for Andy, but for all the wrong reasons. Clearly he found the ride uncomfortable and the panorama too bleak and hostile.

When we reached Juliaca, I found myself more in sympathy with him. Driving through the town was like driving a gondola through Venice, except that the water sloshing into people's houses and up to our running board felt as though it was sub-zero degrees. The Cherokee stalled often and someone had to get out to dry the points. Whoever's turn it was had to brave the torrent and stand firm against the chunks of glacial ice hurtling by. In the end, because the bonnet could only be opened with a crowbar, Orlando decided to drive with it open. This meant that he couldn't see where he was going so, as it was dark by this time, either Andy or I had to hang out of the window with a torch to illuminate the way.

I was becoming increasingly anxious as to how much the experience would influence the tone of Andy's report and tried to cheer him up with the news that he was staying in Puno's best 4-star hotel where he could expect to be very comfortable and well fed. When we finally got to the hotel we found the central heating had packed up and we were too late for dinner.

The streets of Puno, far from resembling Venetian canals, were more like running drains gushing down to the port where mud, fetid pools of excrement both human and animal, and putrid rubbish tips being excavated by scavenging livestock combined to give Andy the very worst first impression of the town. Things have much improved since then.

In the morning, I went to fetch Andy from his hotel. He was looking pale and puffy on account of general fatigue and the altitude but, to give him his due, he never ever complained. At one point, all he said rather plaintively was, 'The view from my bedroom window reminds me of Cumberland.' He obviously wished it was. I was saddened to think that nothing of the clarity, the light, the dawn, and the very fact that we were on the world's highest navigable lake, which was a lot higher than any lake in Cumberland, had made any favourable impression on him. I put it down to the altitude, which can be debilitating.

But I repeat, Andy never complained. Instead, dressed in an immaculate white boiler suit, he navigated the track of railway sleepers that the navy had laid down to give access to the *Yavarí* and the *Puno*

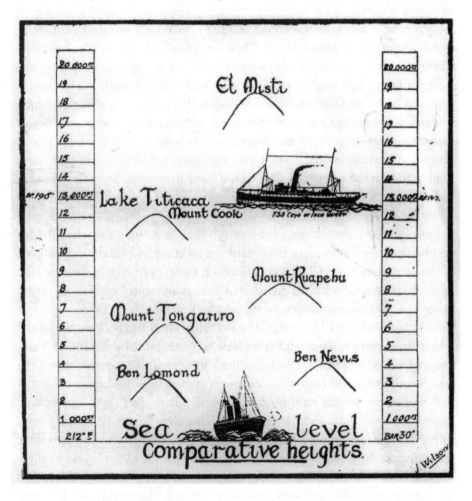

A sketch of mountain heights compared to Lake Titicaca by John Wilson, the Engine Erector charged with reassembling the *Coya* (1893).

beyond, and spent the next days crawling over the *Yavarí* with hammer, measuring tape and notebook. I didn't dare ask him what he thought and he didn't volunteer to tell me except to comment rather darkly that there was 'a lot to be done'.

Once he had finished he said, 'If VSEL are going to do the job, they will want to know what facilities are available to them.' By which, I knew, *he* didn't mean girls and discos – he meant machine shops and chandlers.

Técnico González borrowed the key to the shipyard from the disagreeable port manager and we let ourselves into the machine shop. It was equipped entirely with belt-driven lathes, drills and punches made in Stockton or Leeds which – to me at least – although poorly maintained, had a quality look about them. Then we unlocked the winch shed. The steam winch used to haul ships out of the water onto the slipway was made in Leith, Scotland in 1893. It was, and still is, a collector's piece. It is driven by an equally impressive locomotive boiler of similar age which I was told then came from Swindon although an American boiler enthusiast (yes, for everything there is an enthusiast) told me later that it was an American model. Not to be outdone, a British enthusiast later suggested that the original boiler would have been from Swindon but that it had been replaced by the American one. This seemed to satisfy everyone.

Andy cast a disparaging eye over all that he saw and reached for his notebook. I tried to explain that cranking up these old machines was part of the overall appeal of The Yavari Project. I also pointed out that the lake fleet of six ships had been assembled and maintained over many years using exactly this machinery, so it must be functional.

At that time – 1987 – the lake fleet consisted of the *Yavarí* and the BAP *Puno,* and the *Inca* and the *Ollanta,* both built by Earle's of Hull, one in 1905, the other in 1930, but both piecemeal for reassembly on the lake. By the time the *Inca* arrived a railway had been laid from the coast to Puno, so the weight limitation of the individual pieces was a great deal more generous than for the *Yavarí.* These two steam passenger/cargo ships, of 220 feet and 260 feet respectively, quite dwarfed the two little steamers and looked splendid in the livery of *La Peruvian*, brass fixtures shining in the sun. The *Manco Capac,* a Canadian roll-on-roll-off, joined the fleet in the 1980s and was functional but not glamorous. With regard to the British-built ships, the fleet dated back to the *Yavarí*'s launch in 1870. To me, that said a lot, not only for the prowess of the shipbuilders and the contemporary machinery, but also for the inherent skills and acquired knowledge of the local engineers and shipwrights who had kept these ships afloat for so long.

Sadly, one of the fleet, the 170-foot *Coya*, was sitting in the mud beside the machine shops like a beached whale having suffered a terrible wrong. Built in 1893 by Denny's of Dumbarton, Scotland, she had been arguably the most handsome ship of the fleet, with cabins for forty-five first class passengers, thirty second class and capacious cargo holds. When El Niño hit Puno with a vengeance in 1986, the year of Steve's visit, and floods inundated the region and Lake Titicaca overflowed, the *Coya* was driven inshore and left there. Drought followed, the waters withdrew, and the *Coya* was left high and dry. Within the year she had been pillaged and vandalised down to a hulk.

Some years later, in Puno, I was told that the *Coya* had been clandestinely sold to a scrap metal merchant who, we heard by chance, was in town preparing his oxy-acetylene equipment. I rang the British Embassy to appeal for help to save the old ship but wasn't surprised that no help was forthcoming. Instead we chased the merchant all over town in an effort to stall him and, although we had no money, haggle with him

S.S. *Coya* – two types of boat on Lake Titicaca.

to do a deal. Our efforts were in vain, but at the eleventh hour, a local entrepreneur appeared from nowhere and bought the *Coya* as a hulk. She is now restored to her former glory and, though forever beached, operates as a restaurant.

The *Inca*, on the other hand, was not so lucky. She was first stripped of all her copper piping, bronze portholes, wheel, binnacle, telegraph and any other treasures that might adorn someone's house, and then thoroughly and absolutely scrapped. It was a brutal and short-sighted deed which the authorities responsible have since lived to regret.

At the time of Andy's visit, the *Inca* was still afloat and lay alongside her sister ship the *Ollanta*, a handsome steamship with cabins for seventy-six passengers which was being reassembled at the time of the Royal Princes' visit to Puno in 1930. I knew people who remembered well the progress of the Prince of Wales (later known as the Duke of Windsor) and the Duke of Gloucester, and were only too happy to pass on naughty and indiscreet anecdotes.

Andy wasn't interested in any of the historic or archaeological aspects of the project that I found so irresistible. He was a professional and a practical man and, in his opinion, particularly when taking the state of the workshops into account, if you wanted a ship on Lake Titicaca, it would be much easier to build a new one.

We were lucky to catch one of the irregular flights back to Lima where I delivered Andy to the airport. I could see how relieved he was to be going home and although I felt I might have been unfair to him – because I had enjoyed glimpses of his dry north-country humour – I feared the worst for his report.

CHAPTER 7

Creating La Asociación Yavarí and Buying the Yavarí

T HE PRESSING PRIORITY NOW WAS FOR me to sign the sale contract. I was directed to the Admiral in charge of Naval Stores and made my way to Callao, Lima's port, some seven kilometres north of the capital city. The duty officer on the gate barely disguised his contempt for a civilian female foreigner. I didn't care – I was on my way to clinch the sale of the century. Let him put my passport to one side, let him deal with the four people behind me in the queue, let him waste my time. I was keeping my cool. Eventually he rang through to another naval guard somewhere.

'There is a *señorita inglesa* – Larrr-ken' (unsure of how to pronounce a foreign name, he emphasised the Spanish rolling of the 'r'), 'who says she has an appointment with Admiral X,' he said, implying by his tone the improbability of my claim. Obviously surprised by the response from the other end, he grudgingly handed me a pass and waved me through with the briefest of instructions as to how to find the Admiral's office.

With a bounce in my tread and a song in my heart, and ignoring the stares of the sailors, I navigated my way through the vast establishment, checking every now and again that I was on the right course, until I came to the *Abastecimiento*.

January in the *sierra* is the rainy season. In Lima it is summer and this particular summer was one of the hottest and most humid I can remember. I arrived sticky and steamy at the Admiral's office whereupon I was asked to wait for the prescribed time to demonstrate the insignificance of my visit. It was a long wait, but I was seldom alone.

There was a constant flow of smartly dressed men in white uniforms adorned with varying degrees of gold braid and buttons and shiny black-patent leather (or were they plastic?) shoes passing in and out of what I assumed was the door to the Admiral's office. They all greeted me most politely and because I couldn't tell in a hurry by counting the gold rings on their sleeves how senior each one was, I thought it safest to jump almost to attention every time in case one turned out to be the Admiral. Understandably the steward was a bit surprised when I leapt to my feet with my hand outstretched.

In due course, it was a young lieutenant who came to fetch me. I was shown in and, with a cheery '*Buenas dias, Almirante*,' I again held out my hand in greeting.

The Admiral, a man of medium height with curly dark brown hair, was not smiling. He returned my greeting, asked me to sit down, and then without further ceremony said sternly, 'Look, *Señorita*, I have to tell you that this contract,' and he held it aloft so that there could be no mistake, 'is absolutely null and void. It is worth nothing.' He almost threw it to one side. I felt a gurgle coming up my throat and knew it was a scream making its way to the surface. He went on, 'Yes, I am informed by my legal advisor that it is completely out of order for a foreigner to buy one of our naval vessels.'

I could just choke back the scream but was otherwise poleaxed by this new twist. Of all the possible obstacles for which I had tried to prepare myself, this one came as a sidewinder. As I thought about it, it didn't seem to be so unreasonable, but why had no one raised the issue before? Trying to keep my exasperation and frustration under control, I asked the Admiral – why?

He shrugged. 'I really don't know,' he said. 'But all senior naval personnel have changed since your contract was drawn up and I certainly can't speak for the admirals who agreed to the sale.'

In truth what had happened was political. President Alan Garcia was the leader of the *Alianza Popular Revolucionaria Americana*, known as APRA, and in a successful attempt at political nepotism he had replaced the heads and senior management of every ministry and institution with *Apristas*. In the absence of a civil service, this is easy to do, but it didn't stop there. It opened the floodgates for nepotism on a grand scale, filling all state-run organisations and municipal offices with the families and friends of *Apristas* regardless of their qualifications or whether there were even vacancies. The result, of course, was disastrous. Massive over-employment resulted in ministries being overrun with employees with nothing to do but discuss either football matches or recipes. However, the philosophy proved to be so popular that many of the less principled quickly became *Apristas*.

It was evident from my meeting that in the same vein the *Aprista* officers in the navy had risen swiftly to the top in the biennial promotions because I felt a distinct change of attitude in both the Admiral and the lawyer towards me as a foreigner.

What had happened was absurd, I thought to myself, my disappointment being outweighed by exasperation and indignation. How could a ruling as fundamental as the sale of a naval vessel change with the individual in charge? Surely the navy must have policies and rulebooks by which to govern itself? But this was certainly not the moment to question such inconsistencies. I had to keep the dialogue going until a solution could be found.

Then I had a brainwave. Maybe I could buy the vessel in the name of a Peruvian national, or possibly even two or three nationals?

As it had always been my intention to involve the local Puno community, I wondered whether I should buy the ship in their name, but I didn't wonder for long. It would mean returning to Puno, to form a local committee of people I didn't know and appointing a chairman from amongst them, who I didn't know, and although my knowledge of Puno was scanty, instinct made me wary of what I might be letting myself in for. I had to think up an alternative plan.

However, in an attempt to buy time, and fearful that the Admiral would quickly dismiss my case as hopeless, I mentioned something of this idea to him.

Probably due to my less-than-perfect Spanish, the Admiral understood that I was suggesting setting up an association or foundation, but in Lima. It would never have occurred to him that I might have been thinking of Puno. He would have held the common view that the only people to live in the *sierra* were Indians or terrorists, to neither of whom would he dream of selling a ship.

Why not Lima? It would certainly be a lot easier, but who did I know well enough to ask, and who would be prepared to make such an obscure commitment? I voiced my concern.

The Admiral called in his legal advisor who eyed me like a cat eyes a mouse it intends to tease to its death. The Admiral, buoyed by the possibility of finding a solution which could hasten the meeting's conclusion, sought the lawyer's approval for the idea of an organisation of which the 'Board' would consist of any number of people but the majority would need to be Peruvian nationals. He chose the number seven as an example, counting three foreigners and four Peruvians on his fingers.

The lawyer would have been unwise not to approve of his Admiral's idea, but in order to assert his professional superiority he put forward several plausible objections. The Admiral cut him short and sent me off to find six friends.

My mind was racing as I climbed on the bus to take me back to the centre. By the time I arrived I had the names of six good friends scribbled on the back of an envelope and because they were, indeed, very good friends they gave their consent.

I rang Teddy Ronalds first. Although he was Peruvian, he claimed English ancestry and was more British than the British. He was in tourism, had an encyclopaedic address book and became a mainstay of the project until his early and untimely death. Then I asked Teresa Quesada. Not only an international concert pianist, she had been Cultural Attaché in London, and although neither ships nor lakes fell within her areas of interest, she was a very dear friend. *Ingeniero* Mauricio de Romaña, a zoologist, wildlife conservationist and promoter of sustainable tourism to the Colca canyon – the world's deepest – was next. He in turn recommended *Señor* Victor Salas Bartra, a former mayor of Puno. These were the Peruvian nationals. The two foreigners were an American land developer who subsequently resigned, and Ellie Griffis, a BBC fixer who had also fixed for us in the Cusichaca days. Her mother was British, and her Canadian father owned Peru's only English-language newspaper, the *Lima Times*. In total we were seven *socios* (the nearest equivalent to a trustee).

Within twenty-four hours a constitution was drawn up and legalised, and *La Asociación Yavarí* was born.

I returned to the Admiral and we began all over again. His lawyer, whose smile reminded me of the scary pre-Inca feline carvings which decorate the walls of Chavín de Huántar, looked ominously gleeful when charged with preparing the new contract and I was soon to learn why. He was going to entertain himself at my expense.

As I mentioned, it was a sweltering summer and never more so than when travelling down to Callao which now became a daily event. My journey began on a No.1 bus which dropped me in Javier Prado Oeste, one of the principal thoroughfares linking the south with the north of the capital. Fortunately, Lima teems with buses, so there was never long to wait for my connection. The No.13 which could carry me the nearest to my ultimate goal was articulated but I seldom got a seat. I stood, hanging on for dear life, clutching my papers, as we swerved and swayed around corners. Luckily the windows were large enough that even as a strap-hanger I could see where to get off. The third leg of the journey was in a psychedelic purple and pink Noddy bus being run till it fell apart. Built a long time ago for very short people, its windows were so small and low that I felt like Alice in Wonderland after she had drunk from the bottle that said, 'Drink me!' and became too tall to see down the rabbit hole. Even crouching down, it was impossible for me to look out without falling into someone's lap as we lurched in and out of the traffic. I have never discovered whether Peruvian bus drivers have to pass a driving test, but I feel driving in Lima should be an Olympic sport anyway.

Typical Peruvian street scene captured in the book *El Perú Romantico del Siglio XIX*.

Usually my travelling companions on the psychedelic bus could see my problem and would tell me when to get off but always with warnings about how dangerous the district was and urging me to take special care of my bag. From where I got off (the joy of the buses in Lima is that they stop almost on request), I walked, circumnavigating piles of rubbish, to the naval base. There was a new duty officer every day, so I had always to go through the identity quiz regardless of the fact that I had been there only the day before.

The sailors never got used to the spectacle of me striding along, desperately trying to hold my skirt down from riding up above my knees, steaming from the heat and hair all of a frizz. They made no attempt to disguise their amusement.

The problem I had with the lawyer was that he relished causing me as much anguish as he knew he could. The contract was drafted and my job was to type it up as a clean copy. Easy, you might think; but every time I produced the finished article he would find something wrong with it. Of course I could have made the corrections in his office, but Oh no! I had to make the whole bus journey in reverse back to where I had been lent the corner of an office desk. There I had to wait my turn for the use of a typewriter – not a computer, an electric typewriter – to retype the six-page document. It was a race to get it done between power strikes, and because Tippex strips for making corrections were few and therefore precious it had to be done as accurately as possible. The document then had to be approved by the notary whose office was two blocks away. Invariably there was a queue, but once 'approved', I had then to return to my borrowed office to photocopy the document before taking it back to the notary to be stamped as being an authentic copy of the original.

This revolving door routine was both frustrating and exhausting, but I had to bite my tongue for fear of erupting in front of the lawyer. I would return in the evenings to my wonderful hostess, Teresa, in a state of nervous collapse, tears or both. Her revival remedy – a strong drink and a hilariously droll account of her day – was instantly effective. But I knew that the routine would ultimately break me. I was out of my depth and I needed sound Peruvian advice as to how to proceed.

Emboldened by desperation, I rang Dr Andrés Aramburú who had recently been Peru's Ambassador to the Court of St. James, London. In fact, I knew him quite well as it was he who had honoured me with the Order of Merit. Knowing that 'who you know' was the only way to get things done, I was a fool not to have rung him before, but pride and reticence had blinded me from seeking help. In Peru that is a mistake. If you ignore the network of contacts you could spin in a vacuum till you drop; resort to it and – well, here's an example of what will happen.

Dr Aramburú invited me round to his house immediately, where he welcomed me in his Savile Row pinstripe suit and shoes hand-crafted by Lobbs. Slim, grey-haired and erect, he was a diehard Anglophile. He was also an erudite and distinguished lawyer. His office was lined with learned books and his mantelpiece groaned with photographs of himself shaking hands with important people, including HRH Princess Alexandra. I was instantly reminded of the occasion when it had been taken.

In London, whilst I was chairman of the charity committee of the Anglo-Peruvian Society, we threw a party to raise money for the Hospital del Niño (Children's Hospital) in Lima. Dr Aramburú presided, and our celebrity guests were television presenter Esther Ranzen and her husband Desmond Wilcox who had recently made the top-rating TV documentary *The Boy David*. David was a baby boy from the jungle with noma, a gangrenous fungus caused by malnutrition that eats away the facial flesh. He had no palate to the roof of his mouth and most of his mouth and nose had rotted away. He was horribly disfigured. An aid-worker found him in the rainforest and had him flown to the Hospital del Niño in Lima for medical attention. As luck would have it, David's arrival coincided with the visit of Ian Jackson, an eminent Scottish plastic surgeon on a fortnight's mission of mercy from the States to tend cases like David. He was so appalled by the boy's condition that he applied to adopt him so that he could take him back to the Mayo Clinic in Minnesota and carry out an ongoing 'course' of operations. The bureaucratic red tape that confronted him would have put off a lesser man but he persevered and succeeded, and fifty operations later, David's face is almost normal.

We invited Princess Alexandra and her husband the Hon. Angus Ogilvy to our fundraising party as our Guests of Honour because we knew that she had long cherished a wish to return to Peru after a brief visit there many years before with her mother, HRH Princess Marina, Duchess of Kent. Receiving royalty was a first for the Society, which probably accounted for the flurry of members who appeared from nowhere volunteering to help. Profit from the evening was enough to buy two large crates of medical equipment chosen by the doctors at the Hospital del Niño, which I was subsequently privileged to hand over. I also helped to plan Princess Alexandra's trip to Peru to ensure she visited the *Yavarí* so it was especially sad that, for security reasons, it had to be cancelled.

* * *

That day in Lima the *Yavarí* took priority. When I'd finished recounting my tale of woe, Dr Aramburú said, 'Meriel, you have come to the right person. I am Arbitrator and Legal Consultant to the Peruvian navy. We will visit your Admiral and his lawyer together. Be here tomorrow morning at 9.00 a.m.'

In his chauffeur-driven car, the journey was painless. As we sped past the No.1 and No.13 buses, he told me how, during the Falklands War, he had advised the Foreign Office in London on Britain's position with regard to the 200-mile offshore limit and the sinking of Argentina's cruiser ARA *General Belgrano*. His knowledge of international maritime law was prodigious.

At the gates of the naval base, we paused but a moment for the duty officer to throw a cursory glance over Dr Aramburú's identity card before being waved through.

There was no waiting. We were shown straight into the office where Dr Aramburú was welcomed most cordially by the Admiral, his assistant and the Chavinesque lawyer and invited to sit down. I followed suit although for the next half an hour, while the gentlemen pursued a lively debate on the state of the nation, I might just as well not have been in the room. Then, remembering the point of his mission, Dr Aramburú suddenly brought the debate to an abrupt halt and said, 'Admiral, I understand that *Señorita* Larken has a *lindo proyecto* [literally, a 'beautiful project'] but that there are one or two problems with the contract. Perhaps I can help in some way.'

'Thank you, Doctor. That is most kind of you,' said the Admiral, with a little bow. 'But no, I think the *Comandante* has managed to sort everything out for us.' He turned to the lawyer. 'Haven't you, *Comandante*?'

The lawyer oiled his way over, fairly glowing with the unction of self-righteousness, and said obsequiously, 'Si, *Señor*, everything is in order. It only needs to be signed.'

I glowered in his direction and gladly would have killed him.

'Good, *muy bien,*' said the Admiral. 'So let us do that right away.' With which he moved over to a small conference table, and we all sat down. 'All we need now, of course, is the money,' he said, giving me a graceless smile.

I reached into my bag for my precious money and slowly counted out 5,000 US dollars. The Admiral handed them over to the *Comandante,* who promptly counted them again.

'Excellent!' said the Admiral. 'Now, where is the contract?'

With that, the shameless lawyer produced the cause of all my heartache and placed it before the Admiral who, with about as much ceremony as you would accord the sale of a second-hand pram rather than a warship, still less the oldest ship in Latin America, summarily signed each page and pushed it over to me to do the same.

'Right, that's done. *Señorita,* my secretary will type you out a receipt.'

The job done, I immediately returned to being insignificant. The Admiral turned to Dr Aramburú, thanked him profusely for his visit and so charmingly hoped that there would be another such occasion very soon. Dr Aramburú reciprocated, everyone shook hands, and the meeting was over. Alas, Dr Aramburú has since died, but he took with him my deepest and most heartfelt thanks.

I was well aware that the contract contained many of the original conditions plus a few more, but I would deal with those later. Right then I could only rejoice. The *Yavarí* had been saved and was now in the safe hands of *La Asociación Yavarí* which would bring her back to life and give her the future she deserved.

My mood had rocketed from despair to jubilation. Things were suddenly looking distinctly brighter. Stage One was successfully concluded. No-one could snatch the *Yavarí* from us now. The project was truly underway. It would be easy from now on – or so I, wearing my rose-coloured spectacles, thought. Little did I know...

CHAPTER 8

Willingly Distracted Around Lima

To RESTORE THE *YAVARÍ* TO LIFE, it was important to make friends with Volvo because they had bought up Bolinder, manufacturers of the *Yavarí's* monster engine. At that time, Volvo had the monopoly for supplying Peru's trucks and buses and I spent the next ten years of my life ingratiating myself with them and the Swedish Embassy, while they resisted all appeals. My lucky break came when I was invited to Eskilstuna in Sweden to give a slide talk at the Bolinder Museum. Following my visit, the curator made a telephone call to Volvo's South American HQ in Brazil. They said 'no' to any support, but they did make a call to the Lima office, which reminded the PR manager that, before handing back a video I had left with him, he should perhaps look at it. The next thing I knew, I was holding a cheque payable to *La Asociación Yavarí* for 10,000 US dollars.

In between soliciting support I talked to historians and former employees of *La Peruvian,* and continued my search in the archives to learn more about the *Yavarí* and her background. Somehow the story of the ship's rescue reached Peru's national daily newspapers and, thanks to a short burst of publicity, the *Yavarí* and I became twenty-four-hour celebrities resulting in many interviews which I knew were important for the project, but which I dreaded; I was so self-conscious about my Spanish.

Limeños were astonished that I travelled to Puno. At that time, if they thought of the *sierra* at all they thought of terrorism. As far as the southern *sierra* and Puno were concerned, they shuddered, thinking it was high, cold and suitable only for Indian peasants such as their maid. This attitude was the genesis of *Senderismo*, and *Senderismo* served only to compound it. Any Limeño with money to go on holiday travelled to Miami. To them, Lake Titicaca was just a name, like Atlantis or Planet Mars. I was considered some kind of freak, and pointed out at parties – 'That is the woman who goes to Puno!'

Even I found it difficult to extol the virtues of Puno, though I did try to promote the Indians, Lake Titicaca and the magnificence of the *sierra* and the *altiplano*, but talking to glazed eyes told me that I was on a highway going nowhere. The tyranny of the *Sendero* had confirmed to Limeños that the *sierra* was somewhere dangerous and uncomfortable, and definitely somewhere they would never go. I felt like a voice in the wilderness and that nothing I could say would ever change their view.

The other thing that concerned me, because I had seen it on the Cusichaca Project, was the vulnerability of the young volunteers who I hoped would work on the *Yavarí*. If they mixed with the wrong crowd, they could be talked into doing or trafficking drugs, or drugs could be planted on them. Proving innocence in such cases was unheard of. In order to put the fear of God into them, I needed to have first-hand knowledge of the fate that would await them.

As soon as I had the contract in my hand, I called on the British missionary, John Roberts, who delivered mail and newspapers to the English-speaking inmates of one of the world's toughest jails, the notorious prison at San Juan de Lurigancho, Lima. He agreed to take me with him on his next visit. When we duly presented ourselves at the governor's office, he told us that the Peruvian prisoners were on hunger strike and, in an angry mood, might well take me as a hostage. It would be wiser, he said, for 'our' inmates to be brought to us rather than visiting them in their cells.

The padre and I were led to a safe room across the quadrangle. It meant walking close to one of the wings and I could see hundreds of hands grasping the bars and faces peering through to shout and jeer as we passed. Lurigancho is the overcrowded home to some of Peru's most violent criminals and terrorists. The foreigners were invariably in for drug trafficking and with a little money could buy a bearable existence, but life inside for the Peruvians was then, and probably still is today, quite appalling.

We didn't have to wait long before eight English-speaking prisoners were shown in. The padre handed out the letters and sought a general updating from each one as to their health, their spirits, the fortnight's activities and whether they wanted to send a message to their lawyer, friends or family.

While he engaged the group, one of the prisoners made his way over, and sat down on the bench beside me. I noticed immediately that he had lost his right forearm. He was about twenty-seven, neatly and cleanly dressed in a red short-sleeved shirt and blue jeans. He introduced himself as George. George was South African and charming and, in reply to my question, was happy to tell me his story. He was guilty, no point in denying it, he told me with a serene smile. He'd been trafficking for years, couldn't remember when he last travelled on his own passport, and was by his own admission a complete wrong'un who knew it was only a matter of time before he'd get caught. What annoyed him, though, was *how* he got caught.

'I'd checked in at the airport,' he explained, 'and was walking through to the departure lounge when four armed policemen appeared from nowhere. One of them was pointing a knife at me. Ha ha! I thought, you're going to take a slash at my artificial arm, and you know and I know that you're not going to draw blood, you're going to draw an armful of white powder.' George laughed. 'I lost my arm in a motorbike accident when I was doing a runner from the fuzz some years ago, and ever since then I've used my false one for concealing the goods. It's the ideal place!' He gave me another seraphic smile. 'But those policemen – what annoyed me was that they would never have known I was carrying the stuff if they hadn't had a tip off. And I know exactly who tipped them off. What's more, the guy who did it is a really serious punter. He was checking in behind me, so while they were busy with me, he went through with hundreds of kilos more than I could ever carry.'

This had all happened four years ago after which George had passed through two 'holding prisons' before being locked up in Lurigancho to await sentencing. He was subsequently given eight years; but meanwhile, his passport had expired. His principal problem was that South Africans had no diplomatic representation in Peru. All their affairs were dealt with by the Swiss Embassy who, George suggested, did not consider his release as a priority. What could he do? He desperately needed a new passport for when he was freed, but he could never get hold of his lawyer because he couldn't get money to pay him. His mother was doing all she could but everything had to go via Switzerland to South Africa and back. I asked him if I could help.

'No, thank you,' he said. 'I don't think there's anything anyone can do. But it would be great if you could contact my mother and tell her you've seen me and that I'm doing okay.'

'Of course,' I said. 'It would be a pleasure; where does she live?'

'She lives in England.'

'Well, that's easy. I thought you were going to say South Africa. Whereabouts in England?'

'In London.'

'Where exactly in London?'

'In south west London.'

'This is getting easier and easier,' I said. 'I live in south west London.'

'She's in a suburb called Putney, between...'

'Don't be ridiculous,' I interrupted. 'I live in Putney. Which is her street?'

It turned out that George's mother and I lived only ten minutes apart, so I can tell you the end of his story.

Somehow, with money set aside and surety provided by missionary John, George managed to bribe the judge to release him after seven years but the prison governor would not let him out. I took his mother to see the Peruvian Ambassador to explain the situation, though not about the bribing of course. Within weeks she got a call from George to say that he was free. He told me later that because another parolee stole his money from missionary John's house the judge never did get his bribe.

However, there was more. In Peru, a released foreign prisoner is considered to be on parole for one year during which time he may not work to earn his keep nor leave the country. This did not suit George but to escape he had to have a new passport which was somewhere between South Africa and Switzerland. Thanks to his mother who charmed the Swiss, they sent it to her in London and from there it flew by express courier into George's hand in Lima. The next telephone call his mother received was from George, in Bolivia. He had dealt with the border guard's interrogation as to why there were no stamps in his passport with a couple of bank notes and he was now really and truly free.

Within a few days he was back at Heathrow and guest of honour at a welcome home party in Putney. He gave himself a few days to catch his breath before signing on to do a theology course in order to counsel in London's prisons and to teach.

From all that I saw and heard about Lurigancho, it would be easy to speak with conviction when advising any young person. It is definitely not worth dabbling in drugs if you risk ending up there.

* * *

In more general terms, my time in Lima was always a runaround, contending with the frustrations of trying to make appointments and then attending them looking cool, relaxed and uncrumpled in spite of having been body-pressed in an overcrowded bus. Appearances mean everything in Latin American society and never more so than at a business meeting. That was yet another challenge for me.

At weekends, I sought the haven of a friend's suburban garden to sit by a small pool among the geraniums, bougainvillea and plumbago and listen to the birds. Whenever I hear the gentle cooing of a ringdove, I am immediately transported back to this sanctuary and the balm that it offered.

Another form of escape I enjoyed was to take time off to visit the social projects which the Anglo-Peruvian Society had elected to support, and to evaluate the merits of new ones. I felt more comfortable there than at business meetings and these visits gave me much greater pleasure than chasing after sponsors. They took me to the shanty towns or, as they are known in Peru, *pueblos jovenes* (young towns), which encircle Lima and stretch for miles into the desert with dunes the colour of raw umber on all three sides, the Pacific Ocean forming the fourth. These squats grow daily as more migrants descend from the highlands in search of the streets of the capital which they think are paved with gold. They are not paved with gold; they are mired with sand, poverty and hardship, which defies both survival and our imaginations. The typical migrant family's first home is a 14-foot square box made of reed matting, with no electric light, no water and no sewage disposal system. Lighting is by candle or a fire, which is why the burns unit of any hospital is inundated with children. Water, delivered by tanker, costs more than domestic water in Lima's most fashionable districts. Yet I have seen children on their way to their First Communion emerge from these hovels looking as though they had stepped out of an advertisement for Persil washing powder.

The women are the linchpins of these homes. Their spirit is indomitable. While their male counterparts are often feckless, drunk or promiscuous or all three, the women battle against all odds to bring up the family. Finding a job is a lottery. The lucky ones become maids or cleaners in the city but the journey to and from work can cost them half their meagre wage. Alternatively, they go to market and buy a vegetable, a few oranges or half a dozen bottles of Coca-Cola to sell in their district at a pittance of a profit. It is a subsistence existence.

This side of Lima life was a real eye-opener for me. These were real people tackling life head on. One day I met Ignacio and Carmen, who delivered meals to handicapped children, and they took me to meet Juan. Juan was fifteen but the height of a twelve-year-old. His shack, on the very outskirts of one of the most recent settlements, was new; its reed walls, not yet sapped of colour by the sun, were still yellow and fresh. He and his family had only recently arrived in Lima. Juan had TB, which is all too prevalent amongst the poor, and the reason why his mother had brought him down from the highlands. He was thin, consumptive and crippled, and lay on a makeshift shelf which served as a bed. He was alone all day while his mother went to work and his siblings went to school. He didn't know where his father lived. His eyes were bright and intelligent and he told us that he had loved listening to his radio until someone had stolen it the day after they arrived. Stolen – from this boy! Even though he knew that his mother would never earn enough to be able to replace it, he wasn't complaining; he was just telling me. It was truly humbling and I was overcome with a fierce indignation at life's injustices. The fact that I could replace his radio so easily somehow made it worse, throwing into stark focus the disparity between our two lives.

Another time I went with Margaret Saunderson, a British missionary who has been working in the *pueblos jovenes* for twenty-five years, to see Soila. Margaret was helping her to buy a mobile sweet stall. Soila was Afro-Peruvian and, according to an Afro-Peruvian musician friend, you can't get lower in the social hierarchy than that. Afro-Peruvians, of whom there is a significant population along the coast of Peru, are the descendants of the African slaves shipped over to work the cotton and sugar plantations. They are recognised for their Afro music and dance, which is exotic and sensuous, but otherwise treated with contempt even greater than that reserved for the Indian *campesino* from the *sierra*.

I had invited a friend to come along with me to meet Soila. Marie Christine came from an aristocratic family and, like her peer group, the nearest she had ever been to the shanty towns was driving through them along the Pan-American highway to her beach house. She was clearly apprehensive, even fearful.

Soila's story was not an uncommon one. Her current man had been killed in a brawl, leaving her with three children by two different fathers. Her shack consisted of an iron bedstead and a mattress that even a dog would spurn, which she shared with her three children. She had a three-legged table, a chair, a small kerosene burner, a few burned and battered saucepans, a couple of chipped plates and a few ragged items of clothing hanging on a string across the room. When we walked in, Marie Christine just gasped and burst into tears.

Though she herself was in financial straits by her own standards, Marie Christine had a new mattress, kitchen utensils and the difference needed to buy the mobile stall delivered to Margaret's house the next day.

The situation in the *pueblos jovenes* is bleak, but it would take a lot more to break the spirit of Peruvian women like Soila. They and their kind are inspiring, the backbone of the country. They face their daily grind with resolution, faith and humour, praying and dreaming that one day things will get better. They have no choice. And things do get better. Somehow, often with the help of the older children or the choice of a more ambitious partner, they manage either to move to a better location or to buy a course of bricks, a bag of cement or a couple of sheets of corrugated iron and, over years, improve their first home. Simultaneously but slowly too, the authorities are extending the supplies of water, power and drainage. Some of the new settlements I visited in the eighties could now almost be classified as garden suburbs. Yes, even in that ghastly arid desert often the first thing these house-proud women will do is plant a flower.

In the eighties the poverty was so extreme that the government set up soup kitchens to ensure that the children got a glass of milk and at least one wholesome meal a day. The Anglo-Peruvian Society supported two of these, several homes for handicapped, deaf, abandoned or orphaned children, schools, hospitals, workshops and homes for the elderly and lepers. The amounts we gave were modest but we relied heavily on our good friends, Pacific Steam Navigation Company, who transported the containers of prostheses, crutches, second-hand wheelchairs, medical equipment, toys and clothes that we scrounged around London. On one visit to a *pueblo joven* I was greeted by a man walking proudly towards me on an artificial leg I had last seen in our container in West London. It was the first time he had walked unassisted since his leg had been amputated many, many years before. It was moments like these that gave me one hundred per cent job satisfaction.

At a small clinic in a poor district of Lima, I was allowed to attend the first operation where theatre equipment we had donated was to be used. The plastic surgeon gave a day a week to assist at this clinic and the patients paid what they could afford. This particular clinic was run by a Belgian nun who was simply inspirational, just like the other nuns, missionaries, padres and religious brothers who dedicate their lives to caring for the needy. The children, suffering from noma disease like the boy David, and hoping to be treated, were many. They first visited the clinic to be assessed. The most serious cases were chosen then sent away for a fortnight with a diet sheet of nutritional food to build up strength prior to the operation. The boy undergoing the operation on this occasion had no palate and his upper lip and gum formed part of his nose. His face was horribly distorted and I wasn't surprised to be told that he could only eat liquid food. Where I would have been hollering for a pre-med so as to be as blotto as possible, this gutsy boy, aged ten but little for his age, walked into the operating theatre and climbed onto the table, the table we had donated. He was anaesthetised and the surgeon and assistant went to work, snipping and stitching. Never having been one to see blood without passing out, I had readily accepted a wad of cotton wool soaked in *sal volatile* to keep me upright, but to my astonishment I became so engrossed in the procedure I forgot to faint. The operation took an hour and was one of two. The little boy would return in three weeks' time for the second and would then have an almost normal face and certainly be able to eat solids. The next patient was being shown in as I left.

* * *

Over the years I have seen many changes, the good effects of which must eventually filter down to the shanty towns. For example, it is now compulsory, on pain of heavy fines, for companies and individuals to pay taxes and social security which entitles employees to a modest pension and hospitalisation. Although the black economy is still common practice, it is becoming increasingly difficult to avoid paying one's citizen's dues and, in general, social attitudes are changing. I often wonder how Britain would be today had two world wars not affected the nation's community conscience so profoundly or emboldened the working man to speak his mind.

As an outsider looking in, I would say that the trend to migrate to

Lima and the other coastal towns will surely continue until more visionary ideas and money are invested in the *sierra* to stimulate a more attractive and sustainable existence. Hope comes with the improving standard of education and a growing credence in family planning.

Leaving that side of Peru, I returned to Puno to report the news that the ship had now changed ownership. As I walked up the two railway sleepers which served as a gangway, I stopped, overcome for a moment with the realisation that I was actually boarding the ship which I had bought. In fact, she was not mine, she belonged to *La Asociación*, but that day I felt she was mine. As I stepped onto the deck, I loved that ship, and she so badly needed to be loved. Everywhere I looked I saw abandonment, flaking paint, cracked and rotten skylight frames, yawning gaps between the deck planking and dents and chips to the bulwarks. The main deck was steel which was warped and wavy, and the bridge was empty but for the steering gear frame. On the aft deck there was an iron tender which I could see was the right size to hang from the davits and was, presumably, the lifeboat. I forced open the engine room door and climbed down the companionway. There was the leviathan engine. I walked round it admiringly and noticed water in the bilges, but I knew from the survey that this was only rainwater and nothing to worry about. The hull was completely sound.

There was a great deal to do, I could see that with my amateur eye, but I was blissfully unaware of exactly how much. I was just thrilled to have rescued this incredible relic of a bygone age in what Tim Parr, the veteran-ship expert, had implied was remarkably good condition. The officers' accommodation consisted of six cabins, a saloon, a scruffy little galley and the 'heads'. They were all in a very poor and dirty state, but all except two of the bronze portholes were in place. I chose the only habitable cabin in which to roll out my sleeping bag and, taking advantage of the antique ship's table in the saloon and the only stool, sat down to write my diary and a letter home.

For the first time, I headed the writing paper '*Yavarí*'.

* * *

Four days later, I received a visit from Julian González, the *Técnico* who had first shown me over the *Yavarí*, plus the second-in-command from the naval base.

'*Señorita*,' said the second-in-command. 'I don't wish to alarm you, but I have come on behalf of the port captain to advise you that he would consider it prudent if you were to move ashore.'

I must have looked as amazed and as indignant as I felt. 'Why? What on earth is wrong with my living on board?' Some petty reason, I thought; it can't be serious.

'Because, *Señorita*, since you arrived there have been two men watching you and your movements very closely, and we are afraid for your safety.'

'What two men? What are you talking about?' I had been taken right off my guard. This wasn't at all what I'd been expecting.

'We don't know them, they're not locals, and we don't like the look of them. We believe they may be *Senderistas* and that your life may be in danger. You know, of course, that five people were murdered in Juliaca three weeks ago and – well, it's your decision of course – but these days we don't trust anyone we don't know.'

I didn't, in fact, know about the deaths in Juliaca, just forty minutes away. In those awful black days, such occurrences were so commonplace they often didn't reach the newspapers.

Similarly, crimes of human violation most horrible, murder, kidnappings and firings of whole villages were occurring on a daily basis and instigated by people indistinguishable from the community around them. What the First Lieutenant was suggesting was not unreasonable; however, it seemed to me that I was far safer on board the *Yavarí* with the heavy iron-clad door locked than anywhere else in town. The ship was impregnable.

I said as much to the No 2 and that I was extremely grateful for his warning but, for the time being at least, I would be very careful and watchful, but would much prefer to remain on board.

'Just as you like, *Señorita*,' he replied. 'But I think you're making the wrong decision.'

After they'd gone, I peered surreptitiously through a porthole to see if I could see these two men. There were plenty of men about, but I was too new to know a local from a terrorist. I did wonder whether I'd made the right decision but easily convinced myself that if I was careful to lock the door, I would be fine. However, two days later, Julian González and the First Lieutenant returned.

'*Señorita*,' said the First Lieutenant. 'I am sorry to have to tell you this, but as you chose to ignore our advice to move, I'm afraid that the port captain has no alternative but to order you to move. The two men have continued to keep you under surveillance and we believe you are seriously at risk.'

Well, what could I say to that? A slight shiver ran over me. Either the navy just wanted me out of the way, or I should be taking the threat as seriously as they were. Besides, as the safety of the port and anything therein was the responsibility of the navy I had no choice but to obey orders. I looked helplessly at Julian.

'Don't worry,' he said. 'You can stay with us.'

So I moved in with Julian and his wife Nidia and their daughter Miriam. Whereas the *Yavarí*'s iron hull retains the day's heat for much of the night, I almost froze to death in Julian's concrete house, regardless of the eight blankets he lent me, but a friendship was cemented with the family that later produced for me a Puneña goddaughter – Cinthia – whom we call *La Mascota del Yavarí*.

The 'surveillance' scare was a chastening experience for me, particularly as four weeks later the Mayor of Puno was shot dead.

The *Sendero* stopped at nothing, and indeed a few months later threatened me in London with a note bearing the message *THE POOR DON'T WANT YOUR CHARITY BUT DIGNITY* scrawled across it. It could have been my chairing the Anglo-Latin American *Fiesta* or my work for the Anglo-Peruvian Society which upset them, but either way I was obviously on their contact list. It was somewhat disquieting because the leader of the London cell of *Sendero* terrorists and sympathisers lived only a short ride from my house. For a while I caught myself sneaking a look over my shoulder and at my reflection in shop windows to see if I was being followed. Then I realised how unlikely it was that they would harm me in the sobriety of leafy south-west London, but I did fear for what they might do to the *Yavarí*.

It was their custom to pronounce at the beginning of each year who they would be specifically targeting – for example, local authorities, teachers, priests or missionaries – and it was the year following this incident in Puno that they levelled their gaze at leaders of foreign projects. A German and a Dutchman working on humanitarian projects in the Puno region were both brutally tortured and murdered.

Life was like that then; everyone lived in fear, no-one knew who was who, everybody was under suspicion, and the whole country lived under a dark cloud of desperate despondency, threatened by the terrible menace. And it was yet to get worse, much worse. When I flew home I felt like a deserter, but it never occurred to me not to return to Peru if only to show solidarity. Terrorism, combined with an economy poised to spiral into chaos and inflation racing out of control, was beginning to alienate the country from international funding sources, foreign investors and tourists. The wonderful President Alan Garcia was not performing the miracles he had promised and the people were disillusioned. Uncharacteristically and undeservedly, the country had become a sad place which, for its friends, served only to double our efforts back home in London to rally support and wave the flag.

CHAPTER 9

Registering The Yavari Project

IT WAS ALSO TIME FOR ME to register The Yavari Project as a charity. Repelling the solicitors who wanted to charge hundreds of pounds to prepare a charitable trust deed I found the National Council for Voluntary Organisations who would do it for £25, but I needed four trustees.

Tony Morrison had already given me encouragement and good counsel. As a zoologist-cum-writer and film maker with many successful titles to his name, he had travelled to every corner of Latin America. He and his wife Marion ran Europe's most comprehensive library of South American photographs, and I knew that his experience of the media would be useful. He definitely could not escape becoming a trustee.

Colin Armstrong also agreed to sign on. Having had long associations with South America he became director of an international trading company with outlets throughout the continent and in Peru. With that background and his understanding of doing business in South America he would, I was sure, make a valuable contribution.

Adrian Evans was a banker and, in his spare time, Chairman of Gap Activity Projects for Young People. GAP was the first organisation to offer school leavers work opportunities in social projects overseas in the year between school and university. It was well respected as an NGO (I learned why when I later worked for them as a Project Manager) and I knew that Adrian would give good advice when we came to launch the young volunteers' programme. I was also flattered by his describing the project to the chief executive of one of Britain's leading cruise lines as 'romantic, exciting and extremely worthwhile, an astonishing project.'

That is the sort of man you want as your trustee. He further endeared himself to me by issuing a three-line whip to a young employee in his bank called Simon Cole, who had no choice but to become our diligent and long-suffering Honorary Treasurer.

Dr John Hemming's name was and is synonymous with Peru. He knows the country intimately and has written much about its Inca history. As I mentioned before, his account of the Spanish conquest of Peru is a classic. He was Director and Secretary of the Royal Geographical Society at the time, but he also agreed to put the weight of his knowledge and name behind The Yavari Project.

I felt proud and privileged to have the backing of such a prestigious team and one so well and widely seasoned in South American, and especially Peruvian, matters.

We now became Registered Charity No. 298904 but, to endorse the project further, I also approached other distinguished people to ask if they would be Vice Presidents. I asked Viscount Montgomery of Alamein, in his capacity as consultant on Latin American affairs; Ralph Hammond Innes, author of many novels including *The Wreck of the Mary Deare* (set in South America) and founder member of the World Ship Trust; Sir William Harding, former British Ambassador in Peru; Admiral Sir Frank Twiss, a beloved family friend, one-time Black Rod and, together with Captain John Wells, involved with the restoration of HMS *Warrior*; Dr Alan McGowan of the National Maritime Museum; Peter Stanford of the National Maritime Historical Society of the United States, and my cousin Sir Eric Yarrow. You can imagine how gratified I felt when such an illustrious line-up all accepted. It said a lot for the *Yavari*.

The charity was now well and truly established and, remembering Captain John Wells' advice, I wrote to Sir John Smith of the Manifold Trust as well as a host of other potential sources of funding. Amongst the first donations we received was one from the Duke of Edinburgh's Trust. I was overjoyed, and quite certain that it would *encourager les autres*. Other benefactors would surely follow this example, and fundraising would be easy.

CHAPTER 10

The Origins of the Yavari

WHILE I WAS WAITING FOR REPLIES to my begging letters, I received a fat envelope from Peru. A well-wisher, Rafael Gilardi, had sent me a proof copy of a chapter to be included in the many-volumed *La Historia Maritima del Perú*[7] which he thought I might find interesting. Interesting? It was much more than that.

It recounted the history of the *Yavari*, and it gave the name of her builder – James Watt & Co. of Birmingham, the furthest point from the sea it is possible to be in Britain. The name wasn't even on my list of contemporary shipbuilders, so I might never have found that out.

I made my way straight to Birmingham City Archives and, after a couple of days' searching through uncatalogued papers, found a file of correspondence. Amongst a lot of other contemporary documents, I suddenly came across *the* contractual letter dated 10 October 1861. It was from James Watt & Co. and was addressed to the Peruvian government's agents, Antony Gibbs & Sons. At that moment I knew what Howard Carter felt when he discovered Tutankhamun's tomb. Elation! This is what it said:

> *Dear Sirs,*
> *With reference to the conversation which we had the honour to have this morning at your office with his Excellency the Peruvian Minister in which it was arranged that we should undertake the construction of two gunboats for the Peruvian Government intended for the lake Titicaca we have the pleasure to state that having carefully considered the question we shall be*

The Letter of Agreement to build two Gun Boats from James Watt & Co. to Messrs A. Gibbs & Sons dated 10 October 1861 which was so exciting for me to find in the Birmingham City Archives.

ready to supply the Boats and Machinery in accordance with the following general description.

The vessels to be built of iron having a length of 100 feet and depth 10 feet, and breadth 17 feet, the draft of water 6 feet, the engines to be of the collective power of 60 horses.

These boats will have a speed in smooth water of about 9 knots and will carry two pivot guns (Armstrong 24-pounders), one in the Bow and the other in the Stern: the screw will be capable of being lifted on Deck if the Boats are to be navigated under sail. The whole of the materials will be sent out in pieces, or boxes, the weight of any one piece not to exceed 3 and a half to 4 cwt.

The cost of the vessels and Engines packed as described and delivered alongside a vessel in London will be £8,000.0.0 each (£742,652). It will be necessary to have an establishment consisting of various tools and other machines necessary for putting the Boats and machinery together which will cost a sum

103

not exceeding £3,000.0.0 (£278,494) which will serve for the completion of these two vessels and for any future ones and also for any spares that may be required. A supply also of stores and tools for the engine room and some duplicate articles will be required the cost of which will be about £500.0.0 (£46,415) for each vessel. We may add that there will be good accommodation in cabins fore and aft, for passengers if required.

We shall be able to prepare all materials for these two vessels at our works in four months, the payment to be made to us by instalments as is usual.

We have the honour to remain, Gentlemen, Your Obedient Servants,

James Watt & Co.

I could not believe my good luck. Here, in front of me, were the bones of one of the most unlikely stories in the world. It all began right here. Had I not been in the hallowed and silent City Archives I would have whooped with joy.

The James Watt papers were in some disarray while waiting to be catalogued so it took me several more days to track down the relevant ledgers, letter files and engine specifications for the 'two gunboats' ordered by the Peruvian government. Another copy of the contractual letter stated when the instalments were to be paid, namely '... ⅓ *on receipt of order, ⅓ when the vessels and boilers are plated and cylinders bored and ⅓ when they are ready for delivery at our works packed for shipment.*'

There were countless memos exchanged between the Soho foundry in Birmingham and the firm's London office updating each other and discussing technical points and which engineer they should send to supervise the reassembly. Then there was the list of all the tools and spares and the engine specifications.

In the Order Book the engines were referred to as WI & J and WK & L and the weight requirements were the same. No piece was to weigh more than four hundredweight. This meant that they probably built the crankshafts and propeller shafts in four-foot sections and, from the correspondence, it is obvious that they were concerned about manufacturing the cylinders within the weight allowance and whether a boiler built in parts to be riveted on site would be able to withstand the air pressure it would be required to provide.

(Copy)

London
October. 15th 1861

Messrs. Antony Gibbs & Co.
15 Bishopgate St.

Gentlemen,
(suppose 10th)   With reference to our letter of the
11th inst. We hereby undertake to construct for
you 2 Iron Gun Boats and Engines, intended
for the navigation of the lake Titicaca in Peru
in accordance with the annexed Specification
for the sum of £ 8,000..0..0 for each vessel and
Engines, payable in 3 instalments, viz.
1/3rd on receipt of the order
1/3rd when the vessels and Boiler are plated,
& cylinders Bored.
& 1/3rd when they are ready for delivery at
our works, packed for Shipment.
These vessels and their machinery will be
completed at our works in four months from
the date of order.

We remain Gentlemen,
Your obedt Servts
(Signed) Jas Watt & Co.

The Contractual Letter regarding payment details and annexing the Specification from
James Watt & Co. to Messrs. A. Gibbs & Co., dated 15 October 1861.

W. S. Garland in Birmingham wrote on 9 November 1861 to Mr Langdon in the London office, '*How do you intend to divide the boilers?*' Five days later, '*...you have not answered our question as to how the boilers are to be divided to come within 4 cwt which prevents our proceeding with them...*' Then two days later, from Gilbert Hamilton in Birmingham, '*We note Mr. Langdon's instructions about the boilers going in pieces for these vessels which shall be attended to.*'

It is frustrating that the instructions don't appear to have survived. Nonetheless there were so many relevant documents that I couldn't possibly study them all there and then, so I had them photocopied.

I was irrepressible with excitement. The search was over, but so was any future we might have had with VSEL. I knew I had to ring them, and also to eat humble pie with the National Maritime Museum, who had refuted, though politely, my argument (founded on conjecture only) that Lairds had built the *Yavarí*.

I had heard nothing from VSEL regarding Andy's report so I didn't know where we stood with them. It was with some misgivings that I put a call through to Mr Noah, the CEO. He told me that, contrary to my expectations, Andy's report had not put them off but – he emphasised the 'but' – conditions within the company had changed so they wouldn't be able to take us on either now or in the near future. In the circumstances I was thankful. It would have been an agony for me to have to turn them down.

Then I rang my friend David Lloyd at the National Maritime Museum, whom I had been bothering with my queries.

'You were right after all,' I said. 'I should have believed you. I've just discovered that the *Yavarí* was built by James Watt & Co.'

'Well, that's very interesting,' came the response. 'But James Watt's Foundry didn't build ships; they built the steam engine and supplied all the component parts to the ship, but the actual building of the hull would have been sub-contracted to a shipyard.'

'Oh no!' I cried. 'You mean I've still got to track down the shipbuilder?'

'I'm afraid so,' was the reply I least wanted to hear. So, in spite of the big breakthrough, the search was far from over yet.

* * *

I don't remember Tim Parr having any say in the matter, but thanks to both his knowledge and enthusiasm he became the project's consultant naval architect. By this time it had become important for him to make a site visit but, sensibly, not before we had carried out the 'inclining experiment' and thoroughly surveyed the hull which Steve Pullen had been unable to do. The principle of an 'inclining experiment' is to establish the centre of the ship's point of gravity. This is done by hanging a pendulum from a high point amidships, inclining the ship from side to side and measuring the angle of swing on the pendulum.

A young marine engineer volunteered to do both tasks for us and we flew to Puno together. On the flight out David Henshall outlined the procedure and detailed the equipment he would expect to find in a shipyard.

'First, the ship needs to be emptied of everything extraneous to the basic fixtures,' he said, and my mind raced to the anchor chains, the mounds of spent cartridges, the old iron stove and the ship's twelve-foot iron lifeboat which had been dredged up from the port and was now lying on the deck. 'Then we assemble enough weight in sandbags or use fifty-gallon drums full of water, which the dockside crane can embark for us, and which we then move from port to starboard while we measure the angle of the pendulum.'

I had to break the news to him that, unfortunately, Puno port had none of these facilities and that we would have to improvise. We asked Julian if he could raise a team of naval conscripts to help us empty the ship and then, instead of drums of water or sandbags, to collect enough iron bits and pieces from around the port to make up the required weight, load them on board and stand by to carry them from one side to the other while we took the measurements. I assured him that they would be appropriately rewarded.

At that time, the port was an industrial archaeologist's dream, a junk yard of nineteenth and twentieth century scrap iron from the railway or the fleet, and among it was either the *Yavarí's* or the *Yapurá's* original steam engine. I know this because a steam engine of the appropriate age was identified by an eccentric American engineer living in Puno at the time. I greatly regret now not having taken immediate action to acquire engine WI & J or WK & L. No-one responsible for the yard had any idea what the scraps were nor cared, but I knew that as soon as I showed an interest in buying one of them the local manager would either make off with it believing it to be valuable or refer the matter to the National Railways Board's Head Office, which would involve the inevitable red tape. So I bided my time, thinking that one day, with more time and experience, I would either broach the subject or, more likely, mount a commando raid one night and liberate it. But to my lasting chagrin I missed the boat or, in this case, its engine. In 1990, on the election of the new president, Alberto Fujimori, and the introduction of a raft of 'new broom' policies, ENAFER – *La Empresa Nacional de Ferrocarriles del Perú* (the state-owned railways) – was ordered to clean up its yards. When I next returned to Puno, the steam engine was gone. It had been scrapped, with all the other museum exhibits.

The young ratings recruited to help us incline the *Yavarí* welcomed the change in routine and before long had amassed a mountain of old iron on the quayside, each item having been weighed and marked. We had no paint, but a friend produced a bottle of nail varnish which did the job perfectly. While we weighed and marked, the lads manhandled the lifeboat and all the other detritus ashore and began loading the iron weights onboard. They lined them all up on the starboard side and the *Yavarí* inclined slightly but not enough to take a reading. More parts were scavenged and loaded, and the *Yavarí* inclined a little more, but still not quite enough. We wondered what to do next.

'I know,' said David, his face suddenly lighting up. 'If all the sailors added their body weight, we might just have enough.'

So, with a lot of joshing amongst themselves, each sailor was duly weighed and his weight called out to be added to the whole. It was declared a brainwave. By day's end, David had all the figures he needed for his calculations, the old iron had been returned to the quayside, and the sailors retired to their quarters tired but happy.

Although the experiment was 100 per cent successful, a couple of years later the Peruvian Maritime Authority insisted on sending their own team up from Lima, at our expense, to check our figures. We couldn't see the point until we learned that the commander in charge had a girlfriend in Puno, which of course explained everything.

David was warmly congratulated, not only for his ingenuity but for spending the subsequent week without a break in the *Yavarí's* hold measuring the thickness of the hull i.e. each iron strake at three separate heights within every frame width of approximately one foot. The frames are the ribs of the ship onto which are riveted or bolted (today, welded) the longitudinal iron plates, or strakes, which provide the watertight shell. That meant applying his ultrasonic meter to the hull and recording the reading around an amazing 450 times. It was a remarkable achievement, but it paled beside his achievement at the anniversary dance thrown by the Republican Police Force's 69th Division, Puno Region.

David was of slight build, not at all the drinking type, not fully acclimatised to the altitude and didn't speak any Spanish, but he was afraid to refuse a beer if it was offered for fear they would think he was a stuck-up Englishman. On the contrary, he accepted all offers, remained standing, and by bluff and smoked mirrors became a living legend for not keeling over. Meanwhile, in all modesty, I thought I was out-performing him by winning laurels on the dance floor. There were a lot of policemen and very few girls so I suddenly became *extremely* popular and was barely able to catch my breath between turns of the *huayno*, the local dance, which is essentially skipping and which at 12,500 feet should really carry a health warning. However, out shopping the next day I was put sharply in my place. When I spotted my various partners and waved with a cheery *Hola!*, not one of them recognised me.

I had met the eccentric American engineer quite early on in my visits to Puno, and was glad to know him. John Kusner was working for an American-funded agricultural project on the *altiplano* but devoted much of his spare time to thinking about the *Yavarí*. He had worked in the Historic Engine Department of the Smithsonian Museum in Washington, and so was able to understand and appreciate our Swedish Bolinder 4-cylinder hot bulb semi-diesel or crude-oil engine which, I later discovered, had been installed in 1914 and was the largest and oldest of its kind anywhere in the world.

John not only pointed me towards a government quango with funds, which subsequently paid for our first set of architectural drawings, but also kept an eye on the *Yavarí* in my absence. Of even greater and more long-lasting benefit, he identified a young naval rating who would visit the ship from time to time to bale out the rainwater from the bilges. When the young man came to complete his national service, John employed him on a part-time basis. His name was Máximo Flores Flores and from that day he could barely be separated from the *Yavarí*. Máximo's straight black hair, broad nose and full sculpted lips reminded me of the classic Indian features depicted on pre-Inca pottery. He was in his early twenties, married with two small boys, called William and Henry. He clearly had a flair for both marine and mechanical engineering, and proved himself to be a quick and adroit pupil of John's, and he loved the *Yavarí*. As soon as it was feasible he slipped seamlessly from John's employ to ours and has been the mainstay of the project ever since. Yet he came from such humble beginnings. He is one of a very large family with several peripatetic fathers which lived on the peninsula of Chucuito in a two-roomed adobe dwelling or *chosa* (croft) where his mother kept a handful of chickens, guinea pigs and six cows. In the dry season, she would row each cow across the water to the islands of *totora* reed to supplement their diet. She exchanged their milk for quinoa, barley and kiwicha, which in turn enabled her to supplement the family's diet of potatoes. In those days national service was compulsory, but even had it not been, Máximo, like his contemporaries, would have signed up just for the three square meals a day and the uniform. Today there is no technical challenge too great for him. He knows intimately every single nut and bolt on the *Yavarí* and understands every sigh and heartbeat of the Bolinder engine; he is both methodical and resourceful and his contribution to the remarkable appearance and condition of the *Yavarí* is unquantifiable.

John, the American, was a perfectionist. Everything he did and said was worth waiting for, but – *caramba* – was he ponderous and slow! His other failing was women with whom, on the contrary, he was far from slow. He said himself that he simply could not resist a pretty woman and that he found all Puneñas pretty. Despite being in his late fifties, with white hair and a sun-beaten, craggy and often unshaven face, and several missing teeth which he claimed to have lost while 'tilting for a lady fair', he cut quite a dash with the ladies of Puno. However, the Puneña who was the first to sweet-talk him into marriage was as devious as she was malevolent, and the next thing I knew was that while my back was turned she had more or less appropriated the *Yavarí*. She instructed John to paint the saloon, then moved her furniture in, hung her frilly curtains (*frilly curtains at the portholes!*) and invited her friends and her daughters' friends to join her. Within no time at all she was running a bordello which, by all accounts, became *the* place to go in Puno. When I next returned, sparks flew and John removed her and her effects, but by then she had her sights set on a far brighter horizon – the USA. She beguiled poor John until he had got her to the States whereupon, as she'd always intended, she divorced him. Sadly, or happily for John, other Puneñas were lying in wait for him so that after the fourth – or was it the fifth? – wife he eventually retired back to the States an exhausted and a much poorer man.

When naval architect Tim Parr arrived from the UK, I went to meet him at the airport in Lima. Conspicuously tall and immaculately turned out in his London pinstripe as before, there was no mistaking him. For a couple of days I hurried him around Lima to meet relevant people and then we returned to the airport to fly up to the *Yavarí*, or that was the intention. We got as far as Arequipa, an hour's flight to the south, then learned that the twenty-minute flight to Juliaca had been cancelled. Thankful for the precedent of the benighted trip with Andy from VSEL, I cast around for an alternative way up to the lake and, to my relief, this time we were lucky; there was a train leaving at early dawn the following morning. Somehow we managed to run the gauntlet of petty thieves and pickpockets with our many pieces of miscellaneous luggage but the challenge was finding a couple of seats. In the end we found two opposite the lavatory and although the inclining mechanisms had long ago jammed and I had more or less to bend Tim in two in order to shoehorn him in, we were grateful for them. It was a twelve-hour journey, very smelly, very slow and very cold, but the *altiplano* outside the window was as spectacular as ever.

Like Andy, Tim took no notice of the altitude but unlike Andy, who travelled and stayed at the 4-star hotel at VSEL's expense, Tim was travelling at my expense. He was booked into the Hotel Ferrocarril where both room and water were cold. I salute him forever that he didn't complain. The hotel, which is no longer a hotel, was the oldest in Puno, or maybe in Peru, or even in the world. Anyway, the owner, whose forebear had been one of the enterprising Italian merchants who settled on the lakeside in the mid-1800s, had been very good to me so I tried to be loyal. Undeterred, on the afternoon of our arrival, Tim was already on board and carrying out a full inspection of the *Yavarí*. The following day we were joined by the Peruvian naval engineer from Callao, who headed up the Naval Dockyard's Drawings Department. It was important for *Ingeniero* Pedro Vasquez and Tim to agree to the modifications proposed for the *Yavarí*.

Tim's principal input was to advise on how to modify a Victorian ship so that she complied with today's international guidelines issued by the International Maritime Organisation, known as the SOLAS (Safety of Life at Sea) Convention, while retaining as much authenticity as possible. At that time, Peru's Maritime Authority made no distinction between the standard of seaworthiness of a passenger ship that crossed the Atlantic and one on an inland waterway that was never further than thirty miles from shore. Peru boasts the largest fishing fleet in the world but has never had a passenger line and only a very modest merchant fleet. Through no fault of theirs, they had no experience of either passenger ships or ships of historic value. As far as the Maritime Authority was concerned, all passenger ships, regardless of size or where they sailed, had to be certifiable A1 at Lloyds for ocean voyaging. This meant that they expected the little old *Yavarí* high up on her entirely enclosed lake to meet the same standards as an ocean-going cruise liner like the old *Queen Mary*. Meanwhile, in all nations around the world with longer maritime traditions, the regulatory standards have been graded according to the size of the ship, the number of passengers, the ship's distance from shore and the severity of the local weather conditions.

Take the *Yavarí's* floodability as an example. A ship's hull is divided by partitions or bulkheads into watertight compartments so that if one or even two compartments are holed, the ship remains afloat (unlike the *Titanic* where they were not watertight because there was space above the partitions which allowed the water to overflow from one to another thereby ultimately sinking the ship). Tim calculated the number of compartments required by local regulations was excessive.

On every visit to Peru, I always made a courtesy call on the Admiral or senior officer of the Maritime Authority branch of the navy, and each time I would broach the subject as delicately as my position as a foreign woman would allow, but they would hear none of it. This put such constraints on the restoration of the *Yavarí* as to make it unachievable. I particularly wanted Tim to make this point with *Ingeniero* Vasquez because obviously it would come better from a man, who, though foreign, was a qualified Member of the Royal Institute of Naval Architects, than from me, a woman, both foreign and unqualified.

The knotty problem hovered like Banquo's ghost over all technical meetings and discussions and was an insurmountable handicap until comparatively recently. Mercifully, regulations have now become less rigid and more in sympathy with the integrity of the ship.

Whenever I run into cultural stand-offs like this, I remind myself to look at the situation in reverse and try to imagine how it would be for a Peruvian woman trying to change the rules of the Admiralty or Ministry of Transport in London – that is, if she was able to get an appointment in the first place.

Apart from the frustrations of that one issue, I enjoyed my visits to the various naval establishments and was always given a cordial welcome, probably because of my family associations with the Royal Navy. It was certainly because of this that I was invited to give a slide talk to the *Instituto de Estudios Histórico-Marítimos del Perú*. Ha! It had been bad enough giving a talk in English; the thought of giving one in Spanish sent my blood into a curdle. It's true that I had given a talk in Spanish for the

British Council before the short-sighted or parsimonious (or both) British government had closed it down, thereby forfeiting the loyalty and goodwill it generated. I was word-perfect but my talk had to be synchronised with the slides, otherwise I lost the flow.

When I accepted the navy's invitation it was during the very worst period of the *Sendero* menace, when blackouts were commonplace. Well, yes, you've guessed it. I was elevated to a dais and, having been very embarrassed by a most effusive introduction about my lineage of paternal and maternal admirals, I weighed into my talk. It was flowing along just fine when all of a sudden – disaster! The projector died; another power cut. Unfortunately, there was just enough natural light for me to be seen and so, to my horror, I was urged to continue regardless, and then to answer questions. It's braving such an experience as this that forges a person's character.

Living with terrorism had become a way of life. Although village communities in the *sierra* continued to be violated, tortured and gunned down by either the terrorists or the government forces, it made no impact in Lima, where life was tolerable, until one awful day in 1992. On 16 July two trucks, each carrying 1000 kilos of explosives, drove into Calle Tarrata in the fashionable Lima suburb of Miraflores and exploded, killing twenty-four people and wounding many more. The Limeños were shocked and outraged at the proximity, the audacity and the viciousness of the attack. People knew people who had been victimised 'in their back yard'. That was the day when life in Lima became *in*tolerable. From that day the *Sendero Luminoso* was doomed. General Antonio Vidal, leader of the elite anti-terrorist police unit, was immediately charged with bringing in the terrorist leader, Professor Abimael Guzman; failure to do so wasn't even an option. General Vidal did his job, and two months later the picture of Guzman in his striped prison fatigues was duly wired around the world.

But at the time of my talk in the late 1980s people were also deeply concerned about the state of the nation's economy. By the end of five years of Alan Garcia's presidency, during which he had appropriated the mines and tried to nationalise the banks, inflation was running at 7,649 per cent, which came to a cumulative rate over the five years of 2,200,200 per cent. Per capita income, within the formal economy, was just 720 US dollars per annum and, according to the official statistics, the 41.6 per cent of the population who lived below the poverty level had increased to 55 per cent by the close of his disastrous regime. Bread queues stretched around the block. The country was in crisis internally and, in the eyes of the world, had become a pariah state. The

'Kennedy of Latin America' had brought about the worst social and economic decline in recorded history, and he had to go. But he was wily, so before he could be charged with corruption or investigated for his questionable human rights violations, he got away. He fled in the dead of night, escaping through the back door as the police posse was forcing an entry through the front door.

He left the country on its knees and still in the grip of the terrorists. This didn't deter my mother, and I was thrilled when she expressed a wish to see why I had been seduced by the *Yavarí* and Peru. She was eighty, and like many of her generation who had withstood so much in wartime Britain, stiff necked about 'health and safety'. She dismissed the subject of altitude sickness and disparaged pills and potions for anything else. Nevertheless, without saying a word to her I managed to persuade my GP to prescribe various remedies she might need which, needless to say, she never did. On the contrary, she never faltered once throughout the most exhausting itinerary, and was nominated by our tour companions as the Group's Heartiest Gran. I don't think she was that smitten with the *Yavarí*, which still looked like a hulk, but she loved visiting Julian and his family and witnessing the ceremony of *El Rito del Corte de los Primeros Cabellos* of his daughter, to which, as Cinthia's godmother, I was invited. It is a traditional rite of passage that was practised by the Incas. When a child is about eighteen months old and ready for its first haircut, guests are invited and, following the senior uncle who makes the first cut, each one is required to cut off a lock in exchange for a gift which, today, is expected to be money. By the end of the ceremony, the rueful child looks rather like a punk rocker, but, on this occasion, a richer than normal punk rocker with a dowry.

After my mother had gone home I was lucky enough to be invited to visit one of the world's most remarkable bird sanctuaries. Located on the Pacific coast, *El Sanctuario Nacional Lagunas de Mejia* lies between Ilo and Mollendo. It was founded by the Arequipeño zoologist and conservationist, *Ingeniero* Mauricio de Romaña, whom *La Asociación Yavarí* was proud to have as a trustee, and a shy Englishman called Robin Hughes. It is five square kilometres (three square miles) of brackish lagoons around a river mouth, the only resting place in 900 miles of coastal desert for birds migrating on the long-haul flight north or south, and for the migrants on the short-haul journey between coast and *sierra* like the Chilean flamingo. Of the total community of 150 species, 80 are migrants, from the little sanderling on what might be its 6,000-plus mile flight north or south to the splendid osprey. Constantly under threat from the local farmers who want to drain it, this pocket handkerchief of a refuge is guarded by a dedicated team who ensure that it is always teeming with marine bird life.

I then ventured a little further inland and upland to visit again the Spanish colonial city of Arequipa. Known as the 'White City' for its convent and splendid seventeenth-century baroque churches built of the strikingly white *sillar* – the local volcanic rock – it lies at the foot of the dormant volcano El Misti, which I had hoped Andy would see from the plane. Whereas in my early years in Peru, Misti was always snow-capped, today that is no longer so.

Having got to know Mrs Michell (as she always referred to herself), her colonial house nestling next to the ornate Chapel of San Lazaro became a most welcome respite home and her gin and tonics, notorious for being long and strong, a welcome remedy for flagging spirits. Even when you couldn't get Schweppes Tonic Water (or Kellogg's Cornflakes, English Breakfast tea, Marmite, Maltesers or Cadbury's chocolate) in Peru, Mrs Michell's bar was always well stocked.

Arequipa was also home to the descendants of the first British families to settle in Peru. Like the Italians around Lake Titicaca, the British came out in the mid nineteenth century as bankers, merchants or railway engineers and administrators. They preferred Arequipa to Lima on account of the climate and formed a sizeable colony there. I met retired engineers who had worked for *La Peruvian* and knew the lake fleet and the *Yavarí* well. They more than rewarded my badgering them for their memories by producing photographs and architectural drawings squirreled out when *La Peruvian* was nationalised.

I was also able to spend time in the Municipal Library of Peru's second city, where I could look through the nineteenth-century

The Lake Titicaca fleet in 1900 (l. to r. *Yapurá, Coya, Yavarí*).

newspapers in the hope of finding reports of the *Yavari's* arrival and subsequent journey to the lake.

Important though the research was, my overriding concern was to raise money, so when I returned to London I was elated to find a letter from Sir John Smith inviting me to meet him. I took Tim along. Sir John was a director of a private bank as well as other financial institutions, and sometime MP for Westminster. Perhaps he is best known for having founded the Landmark Trust to rescue, restore and rent out architectural gems which fall outside the remit of the National Trust. He was also the founder of the Manifold Trust which had recently saved and restored HMS *Warrior*. As I knew from my visit, the *Warrior* was once the largest, fastest and most heavily armed ship in the world and Sir John was applauded for his benevolence in saving her for the nation.

Notwithstanding, I had been warned that he had no time for fools. Such a reputation made me nervous immediately because there was so much riding on this interview. We were shown into his office behind Westminster Abbey. Sir John was tall and austere and I inwardly quaked at his penetrating line of questioning, thankful that Tim was there for moral support and to handle the technical details intelligently. We were given twenty minutes to state our case. Exactly twenty minutes later, and without ceremony, Sir John produced his cheque book and wrote out a cheque there and then. I was ecstatic. That was the first of three donations he made over the years for which we shall always be inordinately grateful. He spoke of visiting the *Yavari*, but, sadly, the terrorism in Peru and his own poor health put paid to that. We should have greatly enjoyed giving him the welcome he so richly deserved.

But even with his support we needed more, and I hoped that with the change of presidency in Peru in 1990 people's attitude towards the country would change. President Alberto Fujimori, sometimes a Peruvian national and sometimes Japanese depending on expediency, was swept to victory on a ticket of total reform. By dint of shocking draconian measures he took Peru from a pauper state to being the fastest growing economy in Latin America. It became the country where everyone wanted to be to ride the wave. Banks of every hue, many British, had to be there and modernistic office blocks sprang up to house them while 5-star hotels and luxury apartment blocks quickly followed. As Shell UK negotiated a multi-million pound deal to extract gas from the Camisea field in the Amazon rainforest north of Machu Picchu, so British Airways, Rolls-

Royce, Landrover and all relevant British companies prepared to take up station in Peru.

Thanks to my trustee, Adrian Evans, who was well connected in the City, we approached all those blue chip British companies. The interviews which followed were palpably positive but no-one would commit until Shell's contract had been signed. On the day before the signing was due to take place, the deal collapsed.

The current of excitement had been so strong and the disappointment so great that it was hard to pick up from where I'd left off. I did get other interviews but the pattern was always the same. I received a warm reception and was always congratulated on the 'romantic and exciting' or 'extremely worthwhile', sometimes even 'astonishing', project. At this point in the interview, I found myself optimistically guessing the amount of the donation which would surely be forthcoming. I never learned, and the donation never came. I soon became disillusioned. The words were empty. The only person to write a cheque was dear Adrian because he felt so sorry for me.

Then, as everyone did in those days, I scoured the Directory of Grant Giving Trusts and Adrian offered to sign letters to the ones I handpicked as having potentially sympathetic objects, but only a few answered and then only with a rejection.

I had plenty of time and reason to reflect on why raising money for the *Yavarí* was proving to be so difficult but it wasn't a cheerful pastime because the problems were inherent and insurmountable. The ship was too far away from the United Kingdom for a start, and on a continent outside the British Commonwealth, little known by either the British public or British business. The aims of the project, although it would relieve poverty by generating jobs and income in the region, were not as obviously humanitarian as building an orphanage, and ships anywhere are notoriously expensive to restore and quick to deteriorate. I had been so confident of the little ship's appeal to what we like to call our 'maritime nation' that the bald reality was hard to accept. The North Americans, reputedly so generous, seemed similarly disinterested.

In the early years of the National Lottery there was occasionally one year when British projects operating abroad were allowed to apply. We applied. My volunteer at the time was an Oxford scholar of English called Clare who loved filling out application forms and particularly enjoyed adapting the actual needs of a project to the requirements of the

117

institution offering the grant and in their own jargon. The National Lottery was a case in point because much of the available funding was earmarked for projects which 'empowered women'. As ours was an essentially male-dominated project, this called for an advanced level of creative writing. We laughed a lot but did not win. I was later told that it was unlikely that the judges even read past page two of the form, which gave details of our management team. Far from being all-inclusive of sex, colour and class, our Board of Trustees was middle-class, white and all male.

Always at the ready to follow up on a lead, I raced over to Geneva in answer to a letter from a firm of naval architects. They felt sure we could 'work together' but it soon became apparent that their mission was to use me as a conduit to the Peruvian navy to whom they wished to sell their prototype high speed patrol boat for chasing drug runners. I was too naïve. With hindsight, I realise that the commission would probably have more than covered the restoration costs.

My hopes were so often raised and dashed in this way. I see from my diaries that throughout the twenty-plus years of the project, the pages are punctuated with entries like 'I wonder how I ever got myself into this?', 'How can I go on?', 'Was this what the Almighty had in mind for me?', or 'Is this really my destiny or am I on completely the wrong track wasting my few talents when, on another course, I might have been changing the world?' There have been intense black tunnels of hopelessness, but so often, just as I am at the point of stepping out of the shackles, something positive turns up which lifts my spirits to such a level of optimism that I feel sure that I am on the right track after all.

I was in just such a mood of darkness one day early in 1992. The project was already in the fifth year of its estimated three to four years' duration. A fat envelope flopped onto my doormat, addressed in a flamboyant hand and covered in the gaily-coloured stamps of Zimbabwe. I knew nobody who lived in Zimbabwe. I was mystified.

It turned out to be a letter written by a man called Carlos Saavedra del Carpio. His six-page letter left me dumbfounded. I read it again to make sure I had understood. My correspondent was a Peruvian, whose only dream in life was to live, work and die in Puno. Indeed, he had already bought the very plot in which he wished to be interred. Now, even Peruvians will forgive me for saying that in those days Puno was a ghastly place, dirty, cold and overpopulated, yet here was someone who longed to be there. Could I take this man seriously, I wondered.

He had been in the Peruvian navy, he wrote, but having witnessed atrocities on both sides of the terrorist divide, he had taken early retirement with the rank of Lieutenant lst Class, withdrawn all his savings and flown to Bristol to learn English. He had worked as a waiter, learnt English and then, with no more than a satchel for luggage (or so he claimed), had set out to walk round Africa which, at the time of his writing to me, he had been doing for two years. That was incredible enough, but more was to come. He had spent much of his service life at the naval base in Puno and kept loosely in touch with Julian González. Julian had written to tell him that 'an eccentric English woman' had bought the *Yavarí* with the mad idea of restoring her, and suggesting there might be job in it for Carlos.

I thought this was an extraordinary turn of events and Carlos an extraordinary man who should be reeled in. I wrote back immediately asking him whether we could meet.

Carlos had to return to England for a refresher course so one day he turned up at my house in London. I opened the door to a young man in his thirties, of medium height and sporting a generous *Laughing Cavalier*-style moustache. He wore a mackintosh, blue denims and a woollen skiing bonnet. His eyes were soft and brown and when he removed the bonnet he revealed a head of wavy chestnut brown hair. I would never have guessed that he was Peruvian or, as he preferred to be called, an Arequipeño. Arequipeños, from Arequipa, consider themselves to be superior to all other Peruvians and particularly to Limeños.

Carlos and I interviewed each other. It felt surreal to be in a London suburb discussing an antique British ship on a Peruvian lake on top of the Andes with a man who had most recently been sleeping in a mud hut in Zimbabwe. I asked him if he was a dreamer. He said 'Yes!' and I said, 'You qualify.' I offered him the job of captain. It was a landmark in the *Yavarí*'s story. From that day, Carlos dedicated himself to the *Yavarí*, where as the charismatic captain of a small crew he supervised the restoration work, maintained the ship to the highest of standards and entertained the tens of thousands of international visitors who came aboard. But more of him later.

You could say that what happened next was almost as astonishing. Remember, I still did not know which shipyard had actually built the *Yavarí*. I had a file full of photocopied documents from the James Watt &

Co. papers and every now and again I would dip into them to see if I had missed anything. One evening, I got out the file yet again and, as usual, got engrossed in deciphering the copperplate writing. I was marvelling at the detail contained in the inter-office memoranda when my eye was caught by a tail-end scribble squeezed into the corner of a page. A couple of capital letters was all I could read with the naked eye. I fetched a magnifying glass and tilted the page nearer the light. I could just make out what looked like the words 'Thames' and 'Iron'. What did this mean? It was 3 a.m. by this time, so a little late, or a little early, to 'phone a friend'. As 9 o'clock struck the next morning, I rang David Lloyd at the National Maritime Museum.

'About the yard which built the *Yavari*,' I said to remind him. 'Do the words Thames and Iron mean anything to you?'

'Of course they do,' came the reply. 'The Thames Ironworks and Shipbuilding Company, pioneers of the 48-hour working week, was one of the leading Thames shipyards of its day. In fact, they built the *Warrior*. "The Thames", as it was called, was a very consequential yard.'

I thanked him for the welcome news and set off to the Newham Public Library where he said I would find the relevant archives. The Thames, a yard much favoured by the Royal Navy, closed down in 1912 and unfortunately much of the company's archival material was destroyed in the Second World War. As I leafed through what there was I was amused to see that the yard, located in West Ham, London, E6, had been the birthplace of West Ham United Football Club. It is said that it all began when a casual team of shipwrights who kicked a ball around in their lunch break challenged the shipyard next door. Now they're in the First Division and call themselves 'the Hammers', but the crossed hammers in their coat of arms serves to remind us of their industrious beginnings hammering iron hulls together.

But so, so much more satisfying than that was to find in their yard list the entry: '*1861: Two Peruvian gunboats*'.

At long last, there they were in black and white. The James Watt Foundry had sub-contracted one of the country's most progressive shipyards to build the little *vaporcitos*. There in front of me was the evidence that the keel of my Victorian *Yavari* had first been laid in the Thames Ironworks and Shipbuilding Co., possibly on the very same slipway as the *Warrior* or even Charles Darwin's HMS *Beagle,* another illustrious ship on The Thames's list. This breakthrough was hugely exciting. I was sure that this proof of the *Yavari*'s origins and pedigree

(21)

LIST OF WAR VESSELS

BUILT BY

THE THAMES IRON WORKS, SHIPBUILDING & ENGINEERING CO., LTD.

Name	Type			Displacement. Tons.	Govt.	Date.
H.M.S. "Recruit"	12 Gun Sailing Brig	113ft. 0in. by 30ft. 6 in.		462	British	1846
H.M.S. "Vulcan"	Paddle Sloop	220ft. 0in. „ 41ft. 0 in.		2396	„	1848
"Vl__ir"	„	200ft. 0in. „ 35ft. 7 in.		1680	Russian	1848
"Francisco d'Asisi"	Wooden Paddle	230ft. 0in. „ 36ft. 9 in.		2818	Spanish	1850
"Isabel Secunda"	Sloops	230ft. 0in. „ 36ft. 9 in.		2818	„	1850
"Faid Gihaad"	Paddle Yacht	282ft. 0in. „ 40ft. 0 in.		2929	Viceroy of Egypt	1851
H.M.S. "Himalaya"	Troopship	339ft. 0in. „ 46ft. 0 in.		3947	British	1853
H.M.S. "Urgent"	Despatch Vessel	273ft. 0in. „ 38ft. 4 in.		2420	„	1854
H.M.S. "Perseverance"	„	273ft. 0in. „ 38ft. 4 in.		2420	„	1854
H.M.S. "Transit"	Transport	302ft. 9in. „ 41ft. 8¼in.		2775	„	1854
H.M.S. "Arrow"	Despatch Boat	160ft. 0in. „ 25ft. 0 in.			„	1854
H.M.S. "Beagle"	„	160ft. 0in. „ 25ft. 0 in.			„	1854
H.M.S. "Lynx"	„	160ft. 0in. „ 25ft. 0 in.			„	1854
H.M.S. "Snake"	„	160ft. 0in. „ 25ft. 0 in.			„	1854
H.M.S. "Meteor"	Wooden Floating	172ft. 6in. „ 43ft. 5 in.			„	1855
H.M.S. "Thunder"	Batteries	172ft. 6in. „ 43ft. 5 in.			„	1855
H.M.S. "Blazer"	Mortar Vessel	65ft. 0in. „ 20ft. 6 in.			„	1855
H.M.S. "Mastiff"	„	65ft. 0in. „ 20ft. 6 in.			„	1855
2 H.M. Mortar Vessels		70ft. 0in. „ 23ft. 0 in.			„	1855
H.M.S. "Alliance"	Despatch Boats	175ft. 0in. „ 23ft. 6 in.		578	„	1855
H.. "Alacrity"	„	180ft. 0in. „ 28ft. 0 in.		605	„	1855
H.M.S. "Vigilant"	„	180ft. 0in. „ 28ft. 0 in.			„	1855
H.M.S. "Nightingale"	„	106ft. 0in. „ 21ft. 8 in.			„	1855
H.M.S. "Violet"	„	106ft. 0in. „ 21ft. 8 in.			„	1855
H.M.S. "Bouncer"	„	106ft. 0in. „ 21ft. 8 in.			„	1855
H.M.S. "Hyæna"	„	106ft. 0in. „ 21ft. 8 in.			„	1855
H.M.S. "Savage"	„	106ft. 0in. „ 21ft. 8 in.			„	1855
H.M.S. "Wolf"	„	106ft. 0in. „ 21ft. 8 in.			„	1855
H.M.S. "Reynard"	„	180ft. 0in. „ 28ft. 0 in.		605	„	1856
H.M.S. "Fox Hound"	„	180ft. 0in. „ 28ft. 0 in.		605	„	1856
20 H.M. Mortar Floats		60ft. 0in. „ 20ft. 0 in.		85	„	1856
H.M.S. "Warrior"	Armour Clad	380ft. 0in. „ 58ft. 0 in.		8828	„	1859
H.M.S. "Minotaur"	„	400ft. 0in. „ 59ft. 3¼ in.		9870	„	1862
2 Peruvian Gunboats		100ft. 0in. „ 17ft. 0 in.		115	Peruvian	1863
"Absolon"	Armoured Gunboat	150ft. 0in. „ 26ft. 0 in.		527	Danish	1863
"Esbernsnare"	„	150ft. 0in. „ 26ft. 0 in.		527	„	1863
"Pervenetz"	Armour Clad	220ft. 0in. „ 53ft. 0 in.		3277	Russian	1863

List showing the output by the The Thames Iron Works
and especially '2 Peruvian Gunboats'.

credentials would be the X factor needed to crack the fundraising problem, and that now I almost had the ship's full and remarkable story to tell. I called up West Ham United F.C. and proposed that I give them a presentation. They appeared impressed and talked about including the *Yavarí* story in the museum they were about to build. I had the wind behind me and talked animatedly of the many ideas we could develop together, of their club sponsoring our project, of a retired West Ham player leading a group of their young club members up the Andes in the *Yavarí*'s footsteps and of challenging the local lads in Puno to a match. I left the stadium complex on a cloud, envisaging the future of this partnership, encompassing inner city boys from London's East End as well as the football crazy boys in Puno, and how it would flourish. Alas, like so many previous clouds, it wasn't long in evaporating; their expressed interest had been ephemeral and in due course died without trace. My visit to Avery's Weighing Machines, who now occupy the site of James Watt's Foundry in Birmingham, was a similar disillusionment.

Raising money through sponsors or charitable foundations was clearly going to be more difficult than I had ever imagined. I diverted my attentions to running the third *Fiesta* for the Anglo-Latin American Foundation (ALAF) which, together with Morven Hutchison of the Anglo-Peruvian Society, I had founded in 1986. We were lucky that the time was right and the countries' representatives enthusiastic about the idea.

The thought of staging a Latin American *Fiesta* in London came to me when my backpacking journey coincided in Ecuador with Quito's Foundation Day street carnival. It was such a jolly and colourful affair; bands played on every corner, people danced and made merry. People also drank, but not to get drunk; everyone was just happy to be enjoying themselves.

It seemed to me at the time that since the British last regularly danced round the maypole we have forgotten how to have fun as a community without becoming drunk and rowdy. On rare occasions like coronations and royal weddings we glow with the pleasure of wholesome street parties but this is not common practice due largely to the weather, a commitment to the daily routine and the work ethic. The Latin Americans, on the other hand, are blessed with the ideal weather and love to dance and enjoy life at every opportunity. Somewhere in between the two attitudes, I felt, there could be a happy compromise, and in the thirty years since that Quito carnival, I do believe the gap has narrowed.

The *Fiesta* was designed to raise awareness of Latin America in

London and the United Kingdom and to raise money for the street children of Latin America and the Salvation Army, at that time the only international humanitarian NGO operating in every Latin American country. The British image of Latin America was one of political coups and cocaine, earthquakes and military juntas. This display in London of all the eighteen Latin American countries and the warmth and fun-loving character of their people was intended to change all that.

We converted a corner of London's Battersea Park into a kaleidoscope of colour, each country boasting a pagoda in the colours of its flag and showcasing its music and dance, traditional costume, artefacts, food and cocktails. While llamas, alpacas, guanacos, Falabella horses, parrots, monkeys, snakes, Paddington Bear and Harry the giant tarantula looked on, everyone danced and everyone sampled each national cocktail. It was a lot of fun. The Parks Police were astonished by the good conduct. They told us the next day that had it been an entirely British event 'the River Thames would have flowed with blood'.

It took a lot of organising and distracted me absolutely from The Yavarí Project, but meanwhile Peru was growing in stature under President Alberto Fujimori and on the very day of the ALAF *Fiesta*, 12 September 1992, the long-awaited news broke – Abimael Guzman, leader of the Shining Path, had been arrested. The Peruvian contingent at the *Fiesta* erupted. It was, for them and all their friends, the most glorious news and when their celebrity singer, Julie Freundt, led the 2,000-plus Peruvians in their old favourite *Soy del Perú* (I am Peruvian) it was a moment of unbridled joy. The caged bird had been freed and could sing again!

The story of the capture later unfolded and was better than any Frederick Forsyth thriller. When the police chief, General Vidal, picked up Guzman's trail it led him from the *sierra* to a middle-class suburb of Lima. Vidal then closed in on a house which he put under the surveillance of his unit disguised variously as dustmen, road sweepers and telephone engineers. He needed firm evidence before he could pounce. It was eventually produced by the 'dustmen'. In the dustbin they found the spent tablet boxes of medication for psoriasis from which Guzman suffered. When pictures of him in prison uniform were beamed around the world, Peru celebrated. The reign of terror was over.

CHAPTER 11

Captain Carlos Settles in and the Inauguration of the Yavarí Museum

WITH ALAF ALSO OVER, IT WAS time for me to return to Peru and the *Yavarí*. It was customary in those days for me to arrive on board, say *Hola!* and then retire to my cabin for four days with a bucket and a death wish. It was *siroche* or altitude sickness for which I knew of no prophylactic or cure. Carlos considered this a complete waste of valuable time and eventually, driven by frustration, he called the naval doctor. The doctor duly came and took what looked like a vet's horse syringe out of his bag and without a by-your-leave, stuck it into my buttock. I never dared ask what was in the syringe but within the hour I was up and carrying out a full stem-to-stern inspection of the ship.

* * *

So far, we had concentrated all our attentions on Peru, but remembering that 40 per cent of Lake Titicaca belongs to Bolivia I thought it was high time we paid a visit to the relevant Bolivian authorities. Although Puno and La Paz look close on the map, it takes a day to pass through two passport control posts, change buses, take the quaint vehicle ferry across the Straits of Taquina and advance one time zone.

I took Carlos with me and we called on the Bolivian navy, the Peruvian Naval Attaché, the British Ambassador, the former Bolivian Ambassador to the Court of St. James, Sr Eduardo Arauco Paz, who was a good friend from ALAF days and well respected in La Paz, and all the principal operators within the tourist industry. We then hired a car to drive back along the lake's eastern shore investigating the little ports along the way where the *Yavarí* had once called. We imagined the *Yavarí's* future itinerary would include landfall at each one, lunch with the *campesinos* and a guided tour of the early village churches built of adobe and adorned with primitive murals. We also drove up to Sorata, the village from where the *Camino del Oro*, the Path of Gold, winds nearly16,000 feet over the pass of Abra Illampu, around the shoulder of Mount Illampu, and then plunges down into the cloud forest of the Yungas region of Bolivia where much coca is grown. The Path is well known for its seams of gold, which attract speculators and gold diggers in stetsons and tartan shirts seeking their fortunes. We envisaged groups chartering the *Yavarí*, and sailing around the lake to be dropped off within easy reach of this hinterland trail. Carlos and I were to return to it some months later.

In our hire car, we duly arrived at the Bolivian/Peruvian frontier town of Puerto Acosta which was in full *fiesta*. We were waved down by a policeman who, eyes glazed and breath reeking of alcohol, declared that the papers relating to the car were not in order. We could have slipped him a coin or two, but Carlos was something of a firebrand in those days and this was more than enough to set him alight. We ended up in the police station only to be told that all personnel were busy at the *fiesta* so we should prepare to spend a night in the cells.

'*Ridiculo!*' Carlos exploded first, then launched into a long and loud diatribe as to what the police force could do and whose influence he would bring to bear if we were not attended to immediately. Sure that he was making things worse, I was saying 'Hush!' and 'Sssh!' in the background when the inebriated policeman suddenly decided to head off into the *Plaza de Armas* where everyone else was dancing and making merry. He returned a few minutes later marching respectfully two paces behind his Chief Superintendent. The Chief, his hat somewhat askew, looked furious at having had his *fiesta* interrupted. He strode across the room and fell heavily into the chair behind his desk, opened the folder containing the documentation of our hire car and scowled at its contents. The problem was that our car was white but in the logbook it was described as blue. The Chief looked up and glared at us.

'Show me proof,' he said belligerently, 'that your car has not been stolen and re-sprayed.'

I couldn't imagine how we could possibly prove it and was thankful not to be the one having to answer. Carlos answered at length, but his explanation didn't sound very convincing to me. I was afraid that our car might be impounded and I didn't dare think what punishment might be meted out to us.

The Chief listened, scowling. Then, as if suddenly bored by the whole matter and longing to return to the *fiesta*, he thumped his desk and announced that he didn't want to hear any more because he was going to punish us anyway.

I waited with bated breath.

'I shall have to fine you...' He paused for maximum effect, while dollar signs danced before my eyes; I swapped a nervous glance with Carlos. 'Your fine,' continued the Chief aggressively, 'is the cost of...' another pause, '...six candles for Our Lady of Miracles. You are to buy them immediately and bring them back here to the station.'

We hurried out before he could change his mind. In view of the Chief's mood and our precarious position, we felt that Our Lady of Miracles well deserved her six candles.

* * *

Some weeks later, we returned to Sorata where thick snow made it almost impossible to get up to Abra Illampu. We jumped into the back of a decrepit truck heading up the western slope to the pass. A lot of snow had to be shovelled away to clear the road, but eventually we reached the top and were dropped off to walk down the eastern slopes of the Cordillera Real where the snow had barely fallen.

It was an Inca road which was good because it was laid but bad because the stones and boulders were round and smooth and it was easy for the foot to slip in between them. Moreover, because the Incas knew nothing of the wheel, the climbs and descents of the road were stepped and so deep that each tread required a giant stride. I found it extremely challenging. Carlos, on the other hand, did not, and in spite of carrying a heavy rucksack containing all our camping gear he bounded ahead from boulder to boulder with the ease of an ibex. By day three, I knew he was frustrated by always having to wait for me. It was a giveaway when he insisted on relieving me of my daypack *and* camera, thus leaving me with absolutely nothing to carry.

I was neither walking nor bounding. I was stumbling and slithering over the stones and crawling up the steps like a toddler climbing the stairs.

It was so tough that I rejoiced, but under my breath of course, when we walked into a two-day storm that compelled us to hole up in a wattle shack which turned out to be the 'village shop'. We had to stoop to enter. On the wall facing the entrance hung another saucy poster, this time of a half-naked white *belle* advertising vehicle lubricants. Three shelves in a dark corner held cigarettes, matches, half a dozen tins of tuna fish and some elderly potatoes. In the opposite corner was a bed of sorts. The *campesino* shopkeeper appeared in a short-sleeved shirt and shorts and a knitted woolly bonnet with ear flaps, his *chullo*, a legacy from the *sierra*.

When he said I was welcome to use his bed I loved him immediately. It was constructed of wooden slats on an iron frame but it could have been a super-sprung luxury bespoke Savoir mattress for the pleasure it gave me. Carlos slept on the floor and the shopkeeper moved next door and snored his way through the night.

We ate many tins of tuna while the torrents cascaded down outside until, as suddenly as it had begun, the rain stopped. By this time we had picked up a local guide. His name was Sylverio. Less than five feet tall, he was an elf-like, skinny will-o'-the-wisp, weathered, toothless and always in a pixie bonnet. His only other belongings appeared to be the ragged shirt and shorts he was wearing, a staff and a bottle of the local *aguardiente*. He said he could lead us over the swollen rivers and then pick up the path further down the valley. We were by now on our descent through the cloud forest but the path, with its stairways up and down, was unforgiving and the suspension bridges crudely slung over the rivers were in a hideous state of repair. Often the rotten wooden planks were tied with fraying rope and either loose or missing altogether. If I looked down I could see the foaming river beneath. I tried not to but once upon a time, according to Aimé Tschiffely[8] who rode from Buenos Aires to Washington DC in the 1930s, nervous travellers were blindfolded and carried across on a stretcher by Indians. Which would you prefer?

Each time we asked Sylverio how many more bridges there were to cross and how much further we had to go, he would take a swig from his bottle and, waving his hand in the air, proclaim, '*más arriba, más arriba*' – still much further. On the last day, we started out at dawn as usual and, still heading down from Abra Illampu, walked up and down, down and up, and on and on, till mid-afternoon. Still Sylverio wasn't giving anything away as to how much further we had to go to our destination so we – or I should say I, because Carlos was tripping along happily behind

Sylverio – kept doggedly going. We had probably done at least 16 miles when suddenly, like a mule when it decides that enough is enough, I could go no further and stopped dead. My feet were agony, my legs were agony, my heart was pounding and my head just said 'Can't!' I collapsed on a rock, miserable and on the verge of tears. Carlos came back to tell me there was only a little way to go. I said I didn't care how far or how near we had to go, I wasn't going anywhere.

Carlos simply leant forward, grabbed me around the waist, tossed me over his shoulder in a fireman's lift and together we reached Chusi village and the end of the trail.

The story of Carlos carrying me, often told and each time embellished, astounded all who heard it, but nothing was as astounding as the version which came back to us. In the best tradition of Chinese whispers, roles had become reversed and, according to the revised tale, I had carried Carlos. Thenceforth I was regarded with the awe appropriate to such a feat.

But not, I hasten to add, by Michael Palin, known the world over for arguably the BBC's most popular televised travelogues. A visit to the *Yavarí* was to feature in BBC TV's *Full Circle* in which Palin travels from Alaska via China, Japan, New Zealand, Southern Chile and the Andes, the Amazon rainforest, Colombia and back to Alaska. We were excited by his coming and intent on giving the *Yavarí* a serious makeover before he arrived. In my British way, I had tried to kickstart the programme of painting, polishing and preparing the photographic exhibition in good time, but 'when I saw the wind, I changed the rudder'. In other words, I shut up and let events prevail. It is a Peruvian custom going back generations to leave everything to the very last moment and, no matter what, I was never going to change that. Carlos knew no other way and over many years of anguish I learned to hold my tongue and my breath and let him do it his way. I was never disappointed. At the eleventh hour, orders were barked to left and right followed by a flurry of activity and, while I kept well out of the way, the job got done.

The day Michael Palin was due, we were still painting the ship when he rang from the Bolivian/Peruvian border explaining that they had had all their film kit confiscated and apologising that they would be late arriving. Hallelujah! But even when he and his crew did turn up an hour or so late it was a question of 'Mind the wet paint!' The filming was a triumph. He and his crew put us instantly at our ease and, with only one re-take, we had finished by the day's end.

Early the next morning we accompanied him to the station to continue his journey to Cuzco. He was on the train doing his piece to camera when, heralded by loud shouts, the station master appeared in a fury, waving his flag and expostulating about the station being a strategic and security-sensitive establishment and that it was absolutely forbidden on pain of a fine or imprisonment to take photographs.

Of course you can imagine that, for a travelling presenter as experienced as Michael Palin, all permissions had been sought and given, including entry permits for all his film equipment and filming in stations, but in Peru you should 'always expect the unexpected'.

The upshot of that visit was five minutes of the *Yavarí* in Episode 8 of *Full Circle* which has been shown all around the world and is even now being repeated somewhere at every moment of the day. People have come to see the ship in their thousands from far and near 'because we saw Michael Palin's visit'. It would be impossible for us to quantify either the value of this publicity or the extent of our appreciation.

* * *

At this stage, apart from the shortage of money, the principal areas needing clarification were how to modify the drawings submitted by the naval dockyard in order to make them achievable as well as acceptable, and whether the historic Bolinder engine could be restored and, if not, whether it should be replaced by a modern diesel. I took these two imponderables back to the UK.

No sooner had I got home than I received a letter from a young man who had read about the *Yavarí* and was particularly interested in making the Bolinder engine the subject of a project required of him by his company. Richard Lee spent a month examining and reporting on the mighty beast and felt certain it could, and should, be restored to working order.

As for moderating the Peruvian navy's inflexible stance on the drawings, I could only think that if I had another set prepared in the UK which met with the Department of Transport's interpretation of SOLAS, at least then there would be something in black and white to argue with. I put out an SOS to five firms of naval architects. One responded immediately and, knowing that he risked making no money out of it, Ian

Biles of Maritime Services (International) Co. generously undertook the charge.

* * *

By this time, we were ten years into the three-to-four-year project, and they had been tough years. Tough at the outset because of terrorism and the state of Peru's economy, and tough throughout for want of money and the time and energy needed to raise it. But we had struggled through and, as a result, were all the more determined to succeed. This was lucky because what was constantly debilitating was being mocked by the skeleton crews of the SS *Ollanta* and, until she was scrapped, the *Inca*. Both ships were berthed in the port with us and their crews had nothing to do but sit and watch us at work on our old hulk and, like the rest of Puno and the navy, deride our efforts. In fact they thought we were *locos* (mad), and referred to us as such. They were probably right, but neither Carlos nor Máximo thought so. They were both fiercely proud and protective of their *Yavarí* but Carlos could be quite volatile, and his fuse was shorter than Maxi's. I never knew exactly what went on when I wasn't there, though I did hear of confrontations and run-ins when Carlos felt he had to defend his beloved ship.

At any rate we survived, and by degrees the project began to earn grudging respect.

Carlos had no trouble recruiting extra crew members when we needed them, and they wore the uniform donated by Mrs Michell with pride. Teodocio Cahuana Pino was one of them. Teo turned up asking for a job and became Máximo's assistant. With hands like hams and commensurate strength, he was worth three ordinary men. Teo came from the *altiplano* where his father had been a herdsman on a *hacienda* which owned countless thousands of hectares. The *haciendado* should have educated Teo but didn't, and because his father was always on the move following the alpacas to new pastures Teo was seldom near a school so his education was scanty. What he knows today he picked up in the navy where he did his national service. After two years he went out to seek his fortune with the roughnecks panning for gold in the Amazon basin. No fortune was forthcoming, nor did he like the mosquitoes, so he returned to the *altiplano* to help his father manage his smallholding. The 1969 Agrarian Reform had radically changed the lives of all landowners and their *peones* (farm hands). All *haciendas* were divided up and redistributed to the farm hands. In Teo's case, the land was divided between ninety families but none was given title (which remains the status today) and the parcel was only just large enough to provide a subsistence existence. In other words, a good idea but a poorly executed one. Teo married Anastasia, who worked occasionally in the community shop, and borrowed money to buy a truck. By scraping a living they just managed to keep five children but Teo desperately wanted to give them the education he never had. Since joining the *Yavarí*, he has been able to do that.

Carlos now had a permanent crew of two and part-time members when required. He ran the ship with naval discipline and treated his crew as navy personnel. Every morning on the dot of 8 a.m., accompanied by a reveille on the bosun's whistle, the Peruvian flag (and the Red Ensign when I was on board) was raised and saluted and orders for the day given out. From those early days, this procedure, known as *honores*, has hardly missed a beat.

The clockwork routine and hard work had apparently not only been noticed but had also earned grudging recognition. One day, out of the blue, the port captain suggested that we retrieve the *Yavarí's* wheel, bridge telegraph, binnacle, compass and engine-room clock which were being jealously guarded in the museum in Arequipa. It took us many months of correspondence and many US dollars as security, but we were eventually able to reinstate these treasures on board. Polished up, the telegraph made by J. Stone & Co. Ltd. of Deptford, London, the binnacle and the engine-room clock made by Dobbie McInnes & Clyde Ltd. of Glasgow, Liverpool and South Shields, looked absolutely fantastic reinstated where they belonged. The compass, also made by Dobbie McInnes, still retains the fine silk threads which define the degrees, and orientated itself correctly without needing to be calibrated. One day I hope we can boast our distinguished Brown & Harefield 6-bar capstan crown currently 'on loan' to BAP *Puno*. There is plenty of brass on board the *Yavarí* but, happily, at high altitude it only needs a clean now and again.

The ship was now in a condition to be recognised by the Institute of Culture as Peru's first floating museum and, although we hadn't yet begun work on the engine, we were ready to open the vessel to the public. We were proud to be given the registration number INC Museo Flotante (RN No. 384/ING) and invited the British Ambassador to perform the inauguration ceremony.

The event attracted attention but nothing like the day the *Yavarí* was launched in this very same port on Christmas Day 1870. As reported in *El Comercio* on 5 January 1871, it all began in Puno cathedral with a solemn mass of thanksgiving 'with *Te Deum*' celebrated by the Bishop who then led the president of the court, the mayor, other dignitaries and the congregation down to the port which was already crowded with and surrounded by the Indians who had flocked from miles around. They had never seen a vessel of this size on their 'Sacred Lake' before, still less one made of iron and powered by steam. They understood about the wind, but steam – this was a phenomenon. They came in their *fiesta* finery in an unstoppable stream, *totora* reed boats garlanded with flowers turned up from all corners of the lake, and the doors of the machine shops were decorated like triumphal arches. The *Yavarí* lay in her cradle on the slipway flanked either side by *'el bello sexo'*, the fair sex, from Puno and surrounding villages, *'dressed with such harmony and good taste as to resemble a tree-lined avenue in April'*.

The band played the national anthem as the flag of Peru, with the *Yavarí's* name on the reverse, was raised and then the vessel was blessed. First the religious benediction, followed by the maritime, and then the signal was given for the *Yavarí* to be slipped. It was 3 p.m. Just as she began her descent, there was a hitch and a gasp of horror from the crew on board and an *'enfriamento del fuego de entusiasmo'* (a cooling of the fire of enthusiasm) within the crowd, but the fault was soon found. Such had been the anxiety caused by the hitch that when the *Yavarí* began her descent again there was an uproar of jubilation, the crew jumping up and down, the women waving their handkerchiefs and the men throwing their hats in the air. And when she hit the water, loud hurrahs were raised by one and all. The excitement was huge and at the lunch afterwards given for the prefect and all the authorities there was great celebration and congratulations all round.

But not a mention of the English engineers. Indeed, in *A History of the Building of Steamers "Yavarí" and "Yapurá"*, written in 1949, Humberto Espinar, Superintendent of Ships, Puno, writes:

> *'It is worth noting that all work at the Station, from the fitting of the first rivet, the assembly of the ships, the laborious building of the pier to the opening of the channel has been accomplished solely by Chiefs and Officers of the Peruvian Navy assisted by the lower ranks of the same service.'*

Letter dated 27 December 1870, from First Lieutenant M. Melgar, Puno Naval Base to the General Command of the Navy, Lima reporting the *Yavarí*'s launch on 25 December 1870.

* * *

On our big day in 1998, with the Ambassador, John Illman, and his wife, Liz, on their way up from Lima, we weren't going to let a little slight like that bother us. We too were going to celebrate. However, I was dismayed to hear that the Ambassador's suit had gone astray in transit. I knew that the mayor, regional president and all the local dignitaries and their wives would attend the inauguration ceremony dressed as if for royalty, and that the service chiefs and police would be in dress uniform, liberally adorned with medals. It would be a most humiliating diplomatic *faux pas* if the British Ambassador were to turn up in an open-necked shirt, jacket and grey flannels, but I could see no way of saving the situation. The Ambassador was tall and broad and the Puneño Indians short and stocky, so buying or borrowing was out of the question. I prepared to hang my head in shame. We drove to the 5-star hotel where he and his wife were to stay, and the manager was waiting for us. The manager! The manager was of European extraction, of exactly the same build as the Ambassador, and he was wearing an immaculate grey suit... Face would be saved after all.

We celebrated by dining that night in the 5-star hotel restaurant by invitation of the four-star general in command of the army's Frontier Regiment, a very senior appointment. He was tall, dignified and, when in mufti, impeccably dressed. He was refreshingly cultured and, as a self-confessed anglophile, delighted in quoting Milton and Shakespeare. Apparently he was the perfect gentleman and never more so than as our host that night. So much for appearances – three years later, in the purge to flush out all those aiding and abetting President Fujimori's infamous *éminence grise*, Vladimiro Lenin Montesinos, he was charged with corruption and sent to prison.

As it turned out, the inauguration ceremony went very well. The Ambassador, looking very much the part except for his Hush Puppies, underlined the significance of the *Yavarí* as a symbol of our two nations' historic relations. The dignitaries looked pleased, as if they had been responsible for those relations and for safeguarding the ship, the media swarmed over the *Yavarí*, and people laughed when, assailed by nervous tension, I thanked *la marinera*, Peru's national dance, instead of *la marina*, their navy.

Buoyed up by this success I went, cap in hand, to see the man said to be the richest in Peru. He ran an empire which included interests around the

Lake Titicaca area. Over the years, in my search for money, I had attended many tourism trade fairs and done the rounds of the British companies in Lima, although I knew from my Cusichaca days that I was wasting my time and theirs too. However, a few Peruvian companies gave us goods in kind and the British Embassy replaced our stolen steering chain.

Money was what we needed, so it was critical to make a good impression on Peru's richest man, if indeed he would see me. Someone with influence made the appointment. I was shown into the empire's boardroom where tabletops, flanking the sides of the room, glittered with Peruvian silver *objets* and the walls were hung with priceless textiles. I was admiring these textiles when the door opened. I spun round ready with my smile and servile greeting but it turned out to be a lackey who had come to dust. Soon after another lackey appeared, this time to offer coffee, and so it went on. After the mandatory delay, the door opened again and yet another man of modest height entered. This time I barely turned round, but when I did I saw he was holding his hand out to me. It was *him*!

I had rehearsed a business-like approach down to the last subjunctive, but he seemed in no hurry. Instead, with his nose in the air, he slowly inhaled and then exclaimed, 'Aaaah, how beautiful is your perfume, *Señorita* – what is it?'

Flattering? Charming? Latin? Or was it just gamesmanship? If it was the last, he won. I forgot every subjunctive forthwith and came away with the word 'No' resounding in my ears.

* * *

It was 1998, and other winds of good fortune were blowing in the *Yavarí's* favour. By this time I had much less patience than when I first launched the project, and I had come to the conclusion that employing a Peruvian administrator was essential. By a happy chance, the media coverage of the inauguration attracted the attention of a young girl who wrote to us c/o the British Embassy, applying to work for the project. Trustee Ellie, by this time Griffis de Zúñiga, and I interviewed Giselle Guldentops and, having given her the hard facts about the meagre pay we could offer, gave her twenty-four hours to think about it.

Giselle was a delightful freckle-faced wisp of a girl, the daughter of a Dutch father and a Peruvian mother of African ancestry. Petite and pencil-thin, she was the only Peruvian yachtswoman to hold a Master's ticket at all and hers was for boats of up to 100 tons. I couldn't imagine her handling such a craft in a force eight gale, but that didn't matter because she was doing a course in naval engineering and earning her course fees in PR and marketing. This was clearly our girl – a rare jewel, qualified in all the relevant areas. But could she live on our pittance?

When she rang the next day to say 'Yes', it marked another high point in the life of the *Yavarí*. I was soon to learn that, wisp she may be, but Giselle would prove deceptively strong and extremely competent as our part-time administrator, handling all the ghastly bureaucratic and fiscal obligations, our PR and press, our technical procurements and any other task that everyone else tended to shun. She does things the *criollo* way, the only way of getting anything done in Peru. When Peru was a Spanish colony, anyone of pure Spanish parentage born in Peru was known as a *criollo*. Today there are *criollo* food, music, art and style, which are native Peruvian with Spanish overtones. The *criollo* way in business and bureaucracy takes time for outsiders to understand. It is informal, sometimes irregular, and requires subtle intuition and patience. Unless you are prepared to pay or are in a position to grant a favour in exchange for prompt attention, patience is always a prerequisite in Peru, but, as I had seen with Dr Aramburú, much depends on your social status. Mine was temporarily elevated to the dazzling heights of the diplomatic corps when I was invited to stay at the British Embassy residence. My visit coincided with the Lord Mayor of London's official visit to Lima so I was swept along to many of his official functions. Travelling behind darkened glass in a cavalcade of Range Rovers and black limos sounding their sirens along streets cleared by police outriders was an unexpected thrill for me. Within a mile, I and my inflated ego felt very important and I thought how easy it would be to become infatuated with such a life style.

Alas, the ego didn't remain inflated for very long. A day later, I was walking back to the Residence, very much on the alert as becomes second nature in Peru, when a car screeched to a halt alongside me. Two youths leapt out. One blocked my path and the other snatched my bag. Within twenty seconds they were back in the car and the driver had accelerated away, bald tyres squealing on the tarmac...

Although robbed of a little money and my passport and notebook, which was a real nuisance, at least I was left unscathed, unlike the next time I was accosted. That happened in Puno during the *Candelaria* celebrations, when pickpockets from far and wide foregather to pick off both the locals and the foreign innocents. Being well aware of the hazards

I emptied my pockets, hid a couple of notes in my money belt, also well hidden, and set off to mingle confidently with the crowd.

It was a pleasure to be able to relax knowing that I had nothing of value on view. Once I had seen enough, I headed back, away from the town centre and towards the ship. Most people were watching the procession, so the streets on the edge of town were almost empty. I noticed a couple of lads idly kicking a football about and another couple of teenagers looking on. One of them came over and asked me the time. Nobody in Peru, let alone Puno, is remotely interested in the time. Sirens and alarm bells should have exploded in my head, but no, I was charmingly courteous and, because I had recently looked at my watch, I didn't need to pull up my sleeve to look at it again. I told him the time.

I walked on a few hundred yards, stopped to talk to someone, and was walking on when another youth appeared from a shop doorway. He too asked me the time. I was in such a relaxed frame of mind that it never occurred to me that this was in any way odd. Without a moment's pause, I pulled back my sleeve to look at my watch. The fact that it was plastic and cost £12 was of no matter; in Puno, Rolex or plastic, a watch is worth stealing and trading. Before I knew it, that one youth had been joined by a gang of seven more, including the four I had passed earlier. They surrounded me, some grabbing, some jumping on me, and minutes later they had overpowered me and dragged me into an alley. They were shouting at one another about what to do next, and while one grasped my neck in a half-nelson the others manhandled me roughly, tearing at my clothing as they fumbled for my watch and my money belt. I tried hard to punch and kick but made no impression at all. There were too many of them and the half-nelson was cutting off my air supply. Within minutes I was suffocated and fell to the ground unconscious. I don't know how long I lay there but they surely must have thought I was dead and that they would be in the dock for murder. I assume they ran away in a panic, because when I did eventually come round the alley was empty and, of course, no-one in the street had seen anything.

I had been lucky, but it taught me a lesson. By far the most upsetting result of the incident was that for a couple of years afterwards I couldn't sing. I love to sing, so when I heard of a physiotherapist who specialised in vocal cords, I hurried to see him. He was foreign, spoke with a strong accent and held his treatment sessions in a house in Rotherhithe, in East London. I was surprised that there was neither receptionist nor nurse on the premises; he and I were completely alone. There had been much in the press about the police hunting a serial killer who strangled women. The idea sprang into my mind, and I shivered as he ordered me to 'Come closer' in his guttural English. 'I need to put my 'ands arrrund your neck...' But I survived and, furthermore, he restored my singing capabilities.

* * *

Returning to life in Lima in 1998, I found that my feeling about Giselle, that I could rely on her and that when I had to fly back to London the tasks which I had to leave undone would get done, proved absolutely justified. Up until that moment, every time I left Peru, in spite of assurances to the contrary, the *Yavari's* administrative affairs would be dropped in a drawer and forgotten. I couldn't expect the *Socios* to be hands-on functionaries and, besides, communications by telex or fax were tedious. Even people I had paid to keep a light burning for the *Yavarí* in my absence had been hopelessly unreliable. Giselle changed all that and on her own initiative set about bringing order to the informal status, both legal and fiscal, of *La Asociación Yavarí*.

It was such a refreshing change that when I did get back to London that year I felt able to broach again the possibilities of involving young people. The idea attracted another volunteer, a young but retired army officer whom I shall call Andrew. Having served in all the contemporary theatres of war, including Bosnia, Rwanda and Iraq, Andrew had taken early retirement and joined The Yavari Project full of enthusiasm and military discipline. He offered to design and market the project as a young person's gap project.

The Lions and Rotarians in Puno had welcomed the idea of hosting our young, so he built a package around that fact to include working on the *Yavarí*, trekking in the Andes, lake conservation work, teaching English and/or assisting in a children's home. Both on the Cusichaca Project and when I represented Gap Activity Projects (now called Latitude) in Ecuador, I had seen how such a programme benefited the young people of both guest and host nations, and I wanted very much to replicate it. It sounded irresistible, and Andrew was energetic in promoting it to schools, but for some reason the scheme did not take off.

However, undeterred, Andrew was keen for another job. 'Now what would you like me to do?' he asked.

Maybe this was the moment to embark on a different part of The Yavari Project, and turn another long-held dream into reality.

CHAPTER 12

The Yavari's Epic Journey to Lake Titicaca

EVER SINCE THE EARLY DAYS OF the project I had longed to sit down and digest all the archival documents that I had photocopied about the *Yavari's* journey from London to Lake Titicaca. My ambition was to explore the route that the ship might have taken overland, to talk to the people on the way and see whether the story had been handed down or if their folklore bore any evidence of the *Yavari*. Rory Bowen, a Spanish-speaking volunteer, helped me to extrapolate a synopsis of the journey from the many letters and memoranda I had accumulated written in nineteenth-century curlicue copperplate of the most extravagant kind.

The Peruvian authorities wrote copiously to one another and I have since unearthed more contemporary documents but the essence of the story remains the same. In the nineteenth century when the two gunboats arrived, times were troubled in Peru and one of the troubles was Bolivia. The need for a naval base and a ship on Lake Titicaca suddenly became a matter of urgency and it was that which gave rise to the whole fascinating story of the *Yavari*. Bearing in mind how far the southern col of Peru was from Lima and that all personnel and correspondence between the two had to go by sea on a three-day voyage, what was attempted and what was achieved was, as described by Dr Romero in his *Historia Marítima*, '*en verdad, obra de romanos*', in truth, a feat worthy of the ancient Romans. This is how the saga unfolded.

To start at the beginning: in 1860 Peru was provoked into declaring war on Bolivia. Although the war never materialised it brought the southern *sierra* and particularly the Lake Titicaca region and its potential wealth of natural resources to the attention of President Ramon Castilla.

During his first term, Ramon Castilla, probably Peru's most visionary president, had brought stability out of the chaos which followed Peru's final break from Spain forty years previously in 1824. At home, he had introduced many radical fiscal and social reforms, including the abolition of slavery and forced Indian tributes, while abroad he made a serious attempt to repay the country's considerable foreign debt (principally to Great Britain). It was his dream that profits from the guano trade would enable him to do this.

Come his second term (1858-62), and still bolstered by the successful guano business, he determined to exploit the natural wealth of the southern highlands. Copper, silver, precious metals, minerals and wool, and the riches of the rainforest beyond the Cordillera Real, such as timber, coffee, chocolate, coco and Peruvian bark (quinine), were there to be garnered. If these resources could be brought to the lakeside, collected by ship, delivered to the mule-trail heads and transported to the coast, they could be exchanged for the manufactured goods coming in from Europe (and America) of which silk hair nets, velvet carpeting, pink silk hose, muslin handkerchiefs, threads, ribbons, grand pianos, brass bed-heads, champagne and woollen clothing from Yorkshire were among the most popular.

It was hearing of a small 55-foot iron paddle-wheeler being built in pieces in New York for delivery to and use on Lake Titicaca (though in fact there is no historical evidence of it ever having arrived) that inspired President Castilla. The practicality and benefit of such a boat or, better, a larger ship, were immeasurable. Orders were given for one of 300 tons to be built for the lake and, being the world leader in pin-built ships and boats, Great Britain was the obvious place to do it.

Aware also of the need to protect Peru from its three other neighbours, Ecuador, Colombia and Brazil, the President established another naval base in the Amazon for which two warships, plus two smaller craft for river exploration, were ordered from the Samudra Brothers' shipyard on the Thames. In the early days of my research, correspondence in Peru's archives concerning this particular order confused me utterly because it appeared so similar, and because Yavarí is the name of the river forming Peru's frontier with Brazil, and the Yapurá is a tributary of it. Indeed, I was often told that the *Yavarí* had been intended for the Amazon and had been delivered from the Atlantic via the Amazon.

Specification.

of a pair of Marine Engines of 60 horse power
for two Gun Boats for the Peruvian Government

Engines to be Non Condensing and to have two
cylinders each 16 inches diameter and a stroke
of 16 inches, with covers bolts and glands complete,
pistons with metallic packings and double piston
grease cups, and springs complete.

Slide Valves. of the usual kind with back spring
and rods, with bolts and nuts and doors as usual.

Shaft of wrought iron with a double crank,
plummer blocks of iron, fitted with brasses
lined with patent metal, bolts and nuts,
grease cups and water pipes, and foundation
frame for support of the cylinders, of cast iron
with guides for the connecting rods; bolts and nuts
complete.

Working Gear and Eccentrics of wrought iron,
with double eccentric gear for starting and
reversing the engines, with levers, quadrants, &
links complete.

Connecting Rods of wrought iron, fitted
with brasses lined with patent metal, cross
bars and guides, with gibs and cutters
complete.

(1)

James Watt & Cos three-page Specification for a pair of 60 horse power marine
engines for two Gun Boats for the Peruvian Government.

Propeller Shafting of wrought iron, with bolts and nuts, plummer blocks lined with soft metal, grease cups &c. and bolts and nuts for securing them to the ship.

Stern Tube of brass lined with wood, with glands, pins and nuts complete.

A Screw of brass about 6 feet diameter and about 7 ft 6 ins. pitch fitted with bearings of wood, with bolts and nuts, screw frame, cross bar, hook for blocks, guides for lifting it on deck when under sail alone.

Boilers of the Tubular kind and to be two in number with brass tubes, the fire plates to be of Low Moor iron, the rest of the plates of Best Staffordshire iron, fitted complete with fire doors, damper doors, grate bars and bearer bars, gauge cocks and glasses, blow-off cocks and surface cocks, feed valve boxes and pipes, safety valve gear, manholes and apparatus complete.

A Superheater at the bottom of the chimney with stop valve and pipes, steam pipes, and exhaust pipes.

A water heater complete for waste steam, a feed and a bilge pump to be fitted to the engines with pipes, valves and cocks complete.

Chimney with hood, and waste steam pipe, stays, pins and nuts complete.

(2)

Racks for wood fitted on each side the engine in the engine room in the usual manner, with flooring plates for the engine room.

A Donkey Engine to feed boilers, pump out ship, and wash decks.

The whole of the foregoing materials to be of the best description and workmanship and fitted complete and packed in boxes ready for shipment and delivered alongside a ship in the Thames or in the Docks.

No portion of the foregoing materials to weigh more than four hundred weights.

In 1861, responding to the President's wishes, the Peruvian Ministry of War and the Navy contracted Antony Gibbs & Sons to assist them in commissioning a 300-ton paddle-wheeler to operate as a gunboat and as a commercial tramp steamer on Lake Titicaca. The ship was to be built in kit form in order to be carried up to the lake piecemeal so no individual part was to weigh more than 14 *arrobas* (3½ hundredweight) being the maximum carrying capacity of a mule. Furthermore, *'en ningun caso'* – on no account – was it to be propeller driven.

Admiral Ignacio Mariátegui sailed for England to order this vessel, and others for the Amazon. He and Antony Gibbs, London, explored the possible shipyards but it soon became clear that no yard was yet capable of building such a large vessel in such small 'mule-sized' parts. In July, Antony Gibbs advised the Peruvian Ministry that instead of one ship of such tonnage, they should consider ordering two smaller gunboats of 140 tons each, which would be propeller driven. This was a popular model at the time, but Antony Gibbs recommended the James Watt Foundry in Birmingham as being the specialists. At this early stage, recognising that Lake Titicaca was above the tree line, Antony Gibbs raised the question of what to do about fuel.

Mariátegui, the Peruvian emissary Juan I. de Osma, and a representative from James Watt & Co. met at Antony Gibbs' London office to discuss requirements and place their order. An order for such a craft was not unusual, but the altitude of its destination was. After some discussion with the foundry in Birmingham, James Watt & Co. wrote the letter of agreement which I had found in the Birmingham City Archives.

There were also details regarding the Specification for the 60 hp steam engines; they were designed to consume 12 tons of coal in 24 hours, with a speed of 10 knots, to be of the best description and workmanship and fitted complete and packed in boxes ready for shipment and delivered alongside a ship on the Thames or in the Docks. No portion was to weigh more than four hundredweight maximum. The component parts of the vessels were also assembled in Birmingham for dispatch to London.

On 28 June 1862 the two gunboats and their steam engines, in 2,766 individual parts packed in boxes, left London in the *Mayola*. They were accompanied by Engine Erector William Partridge, who was leaving his wife, Ann, and their five children in Harborne just outside Birmingham, and seven skilled tradesmen. In March 1862 Gilbert Hamilton of the James Watt Soho Foundry in Birmingham wrote to the London office

Details of monthly wages and hotel expenses for William Partridge and his team.

expressing some concern as to the make-up of the team to accompany the ships' parts to Peru.

> 'Mr Langdon on the 14th inst. simply says "six men"; say 3 for Engines and 3 for Boats must go. We assume it is meant that the 3 men for the ships are to be supplied by the shipbuilders and the other 3 by us. How should these 3 be divided. We do not think the boilers can be properly put together without two riveters independent of the ships men. Probably one man suffice for erecting the Engines with [illegible] help and this leaves the other two from here to fit the boilers.'

The final team, some from Birmingham and some from the Medway not far from The Thames shipyard, amounted to seven, who were Joseph B Astbury, Andrew Dyer, Charles William Scott, John Buckham, George Blaxland, William Kemp and Joseph Thomas. Partridge was chosen because 'William Turner declines to go to Peru,' wrote W.S. Garland from Birmingham to London, 'so we therefore made the offer to Partridge (who is the better man of the two), and he agrees to accept the appointment if the conditions besides the amount of pay suit him.'

They were contracted for four years and paid between £24.00 (£2,228) and £40.00 (£3,713) per month, of which a percentage was remitted directly to their families back home and a further percentage held by the Peruvian Government until completion of the contract.

These Englishmen would probably have known little of the terrain or the living and working conditions which lay ahead, but in the spirit of the Victorian age, and like so many of their kind who delivered pin-built ships to remote corners of the globe, they were undaunted.

The *Mayola* arrived at Arica on 15 October 1862 and the cases were unloaded. The authorities in Tacna, the regional capital, 37 miles inland, were alerted and the word put around the mule-train contractors that the challenging job of delivering 2,766 parts of two *vaporcitos* to Lake Titicaca was in the offing.

But it wasn't until May the following year, 1863, that the Naval Ministry sent Lieutenant Amaro Tizon from Lima to assess the exact weight of the consignment and decide how best to transport it to Tacna, and onwards and upwards to Puno at 12,500 feet above sea level. At the same time, he was appointed to be the first captain of the *Yavarí*. Indeed,

1865 View of the port of Arica, Peru.

at this stage William Partridge was confident that if the navy could provide two extra *mecánicos,* a carpenter and the drawings and inventories compiled at The Thames, they could get one ship reassembled in six months. However, following a lengthy correspondence between the Ministry of War and the Navy and the *Comandante General de la Marina*, it was established that none of the relevant documents which were sent to Lima could be found. Reassembly would depend on Partridge's memory and experience. His response to this news is not recorded.

Tizon estimated the total weight to be 4,200 quintales, or 463 tons (the equivalent of two diesel locomotives), and that it would fill nine wagons of the train travelling to Tacna across the Atacama desert. He also recommended that the gunpowder provided with the four 24-pounder Armstrong guns be stored on the coast until the *vaporcitos* had been reassembled.

In August, *Comandante* Ignacio Dueñas sailed from Lima to Arica to take charge and get things moving. He spent a fortnight in Arica during which time he arranged for the train to collect the boxes and transport them to Tacna and gave instructions for them to be unpacked there, and the parts laid out on the platform in the order in which they would be required for the reassembly in Puno. Imagine arranging 2,766 parts of

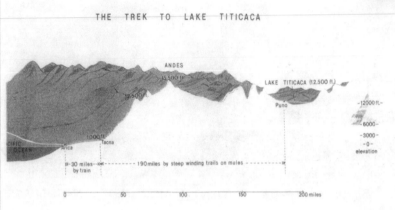

THE TREK TO LAKE TITICACA

Top: Cross section of the route from Arica on the coast to Lake Titicaca 12,500 feet above sea level.

Middle: The perils of Andean transport!

Bottom: Porters and mules sheltering from the polar winds of the Andes.

two iron steamships, various iron plates, pistons, rivet tongs, sections of boiler, funnels and flogging hammers, as well as the engineers' living accoutrements such as wash stands, pillow slips, a coffee mill and a sugar box, in the right order, and without the instruction manual which would have been in English anyway. Leaving First Lieutenant Eduardo Robinson and Astbury in Arica to supervise and see that the warehouses were emptied, Dueñas, Partridge, the other six Englishmen and the posse of naval personnel Dueñas had brought from Lima rode up to Tacna, 1,800 feet up in the foothills of the Andes, on the first stage of their journey up to the lake. The train left Arica in September.

In the meantime, a meeting had been called in Tacna of the transport contractors and, based on the weight assessment estimated by Tizon, the task of delivery to Puno put out to tender. Colonel González Mugaburú won the commission, beating a competitor offering one thousand mules on the basis of the claim made by his *arriero,* Don Lucas Quelopana, who said that he could do the job in six months with only one hundred mules. The price was right and he was confident that he could complete on time. The contract was signed.

In October, Quelopana and his one hundred mules began to move the first loads out of Tacna. Happy to see the job underway, Dueñas put Second Lieutenant José Manuel Silva and, again, Astbury, in charge of dispatch, with, I assume, extra manpower from among the naval team who had come from Lima, and prepared to leave for the lake.

On 7 October, Dueñas, Partridge, the same six Englishmen and the naval personnel set off on horseback to ride the 190 miles up to Lake Titicaca. The naval posse under Dueñas's command consisted in total of eight naval officers, one surgeon, eight engineers and eleven sailors whose job it would be to set up the naval base in Puno, survey the lake for navigation and work with the Englishmen to prepare for the gunboats' arrival. Accompanying the posse were two naval guards, a bosun, and six First Class gunners. In October the desert was at its coolest and the rainy season in the *sierra* had not yet started, but the ride was no trot in the park. It was a gruelling and perilous climb, and although the locals could make the journey in nine days it was a valiant effort for the Englishmen and for the Limeños who had come from the coast to attempt the same. The distance was not the worry, but the altitude and the pitiless climate offered no mercy.

The first community which the expedition passed through was

Tarata, probably half a day's ride from Tacna, then on 12 October Dueñas was seen in Pizacoma. Pizacoma lies at nearly 13,000 feet, which means they climbed 11,000 feet in four days over some of the world's most rugged terrain, jumping across crevasses, climbing huge rocks and following crumbling tracks such as Flora Tristan described, all at altitude. On the way a young Peruvian midshipman had a tumble nasty enough to be recorded, and one's heart bleeds for George Blaxland, the youngest of the English team. He had had a serious fall on the *Mayola* coming out to Peru from which he had not fully recovered and, at the time of the hike up the mountains, he was also suffering from a liver disorder. We can only admire that Victorian phlegm.

After such an ordeal all members, Peruvian and English alike, expected and deserved a warm welcome when they reached Puno, but there was no one there to meet them which annoyed Dueñas and, worse than that, apparently no arrangements had been made to accommodate the Englishmen.

Within a month there was already an argument in the making as to the exact total weight of the consignment. Quelopana maintained that he agreed to transport 3,000 quintales but, as there were 4,200 quintales, he complained of having been misled. Pieces of the ships were found abandoned by the River Maure. Quelopana may have been a crook, or he may have had a problem incentivising his handlers, and indeed his mules, to carry such heavy and awkward cargo. From the very start, pieces got left behind. The porters, the mules and their handlers came principally from around Tacna and the coast, and were obviously not comfortable with the altitude or with the unwieldy loads.

Two months into 1864, tragedy struck. The wretched George Blaxland succumbed to his ailments. The doctor thought he would not recover, and he was right. The cause of his death on 15 February 1864 was officially reported as TB. Such a sad turn of events, and so far from home.

Because he was a Protestant, and probably the first Protestant to die in Puno, he was not allowed to be buried in the Catholic cemetery. Instead he was laid to rest in the tranquillity and solitude of Esteves Island, close by within Puno Bay. In his will he left his best Sunday suit to his father and £10.00 (£948) to his family. His parents were informed and, by the same mail, the navy sent a desperate appeal for a replacement engineer from England, letters which took three and half months to reach Britain. Blaxland's loss was more significant than at first appeared, as he had been

The muleteer Don Lucas Quelopana's Contract to deliver the *vaporcitos* to
Lake Titicaca in six months.

responsible for numbering the pieces of the gunboats in The Thames'
shipyard. Although Partridge had the experience and had supervised the
construction of the ships in The Thames, this must have added to the
challenge of rebuilding the ships without their drawings. Blaxland was
replaced by John Thomas, iron shipbuilder, duly contracted on 14 May
1864 on a monthly wage of £26.00 (£2,466) and *'to be provided by the
Government free of charge with all customary and necessary rations for
his proper and comfortable maintenance.'*

By May 1864, Dueñas was becoming increasingly frustrated and
vocal that the pieces were not arriving and that those that did arrive were
the lighter items, not necessarily those needed first in order of the rebuild.
Quelopana was already a month behind schedule and had only delivered
one third of the consignment. Dueñas calculated that at that rate it would
take two years, nine months and thirteen days to complete the job. Little
did he know that circumstances would intervene and that it would take
twice that time and more for the pieces to be delivered, and even then not
all of them. Quelopana was brought to account but remonstrated again
that he had been misled and that some of the pieces were too heavy for
any of his mules or porters to carry. Please could he have thirty more days

The Spanish fleet threatening to re-invade Peru at the Battle of Callao, 2 May 1866.

to put things right? Letters flew between the prefects of the various regions and villages between Tacna and Puno. Yet, though Quelopana was still being paid, the parts were not arriving. A senior security official, José Maria Sanchipa, was provided with a horse and a guide to take him from Tarata as far as the River Maure, from where he was to make his own way; his job was to look into the problem. June, and Quelopana was appealing again for a further sixty days and to be exonerated from carrying the heaviest pieces of equipment. By July 1864, transport had come to a halt. A letter dated 15 July from Tacna to Commander Dueñas at the naval base in Puno said, '*se encuentra paralizado el traslado de las piezas de los vapores*' – 'transport of the pieces of the steamers is paralysed'.

While it was frustrating for the team in Puno, there was much to do to prepare the port. The naval team, Partridge and the Englishmen set about building a 1000-foot jetty, a shed for general stores, a machine shop and a carpenter's workshop, and the slipway. A civil engineer called Davis was sent from Lima to oversee the work. By this time Dueñas was completely exhausted, in fact too exhausted to carry on. The strain and the altitude had done him in. He retired to Lima to restore his health and Second Lieutenant Manuel Mariano Melgar took over as Base Commander. There were further arguments with Quelopana about money, and also about his incompetence because many pieces were being found along the trail from Tacna to Tarata. Finally, and not before much valuable time had been lost, he was sacked.

Meanwhile, the reason the transportation of the gunboats had ground to a halt was because, down on the coast, a Spanish squadron supposedly on a scientific voyage sponsored by the Spanish Crown had landed on the Chincha Islands, Peru's principal source of guano, and raised the Spanish flag. They then entered Callao harbour and looked menacing. Shamelessly duplicitous, the incumbent President Juan Antonio Pezet struck a deal with them while simultaneously procuring armaments and four warships, of which the *Huascar* from Lairds of Birkenhead was one. Some thought this was underhand, even dishonourable. One such was General Mariano Ignacio Prado from Moquegua in southern Peru. Backed by the people of the south, including the Puneños, he led a revolution against the President. The navy was entirely distracted by the outlandish Spanish invasion and abandoned the *vaporcitos*, though confiscating their four 24-pounder Armstrong guns for use in defence of

Copy to Lopof
13 Sept /65.

Puno Peru South America
August 3rd 1865

To Messrs James Watt & Co
       Engineers 18 London
              Street London
                     Gentlemen
                            The Gun Boats for the
Lake of Titicaca are in much the same state as
they were three years ago, we have not yet commenced
to do any thing at them; neither do I see any prospect
of doing so for some time to come. There are about two
thirds of the materials for one boat in Puno, but there is
nothing come in for the last six months. We have done
nothing at the Mole since the middle of December
last; and I begin to think that it will never be wanted,
and my opinion is that we shall leave Puno without
having done one days work at the boats, in about ten
months our contracts will be completed and the men
say that they will not remain here after their time is up.

This country is still in a very unsettled state, the
Revolution is not yet at an end; neither do I see any
prospect of its speedy termination. the general opinion
is that the Government will fall, the rebels are now within
a short distance of the Capital, Lima. Part of the Fleet
including the two new Frigates which have just arrived
out here as fallen into the hands of the rebels. The ports

William Partridge writing from Puno in August 1865 to say that they had been unable
to do any work on the project for six months!

the country. These guns were never seen again. From that moment, the *Yavarí* and *Yapurá* would never become gunboats.

In 1865 civil war brought southern Peru to a standstill. For Partridge and his men, who had already been twiddling their thumbs waiting for the parts to arrive, this was clearly a disappointing development but accepted with the sangfroid typical of the age. I found firsthand evidence of this when, on one of my many visits to the Birmingham Library, the archivist surprised me with a file that had recently come to light containing three letters written by Partridge in Puno and addressed to James Watt & Co., Engineers, 18 London Street, London. I imagined the journey the letters would have taken – transported first by mule to the coast then dispatched on a sailing ship, or maybe even a steamship, round the Horn and back to London docks for delivery, maybe by pennyfarthing, to London Street and then by train to Birmingham.

In February 1865 William Partridge wrote:

'*The Spanish question still remains unsettled and the Peruvian Government are very short of funds so much so that several public works have been stopped and ours amongst the rest. They are owing us 3 months wages, and we are much better off than others in the Service. Our job is now all quiet and likely to remain so at present. I think our contracts will be completed before anything is done to the gunboats.*

Messrs. Scott, Astbury and myself have just returned from Cuzco, the ancient capital of Peru where we have spent the last few weeks very pleasantly. The journey is a rough and tedious one having to travel upon mules for about 600 miles on bad roads and to cross rivers which are rather dangerous, but we have been amply repaid for our trouble and expense for the remains of the old palaces and fortresses of the Incas are well worth the trouble and some of these old buildings are most beautifully executed...' (This was written over forty years before Machu Picchu was 'discovered' by Hiram Bingham in 1911.)

By April 1865, things had changed little. Partridge wrote again:

'*I am still leading a very quiet and comfortable life in Puno. For the last four months our job has been at a stand and there is every prospect of its remaining so for some time to come. Up to the present time there has not arrived in Puno moor (sic) than two thirds of the materials for the first Boat. Nothing has come in for the last five months and I begin to think that the Steam Boats will never be put together. The President of Peru, and a few of his ministers have taken upon themselves to settle the question with Spain contrary to the wish of the Country. The consequence is that the people have risen against the Government and the whole of the Southern provinces are in a state of Revolution. Many lives have already been lost. A division of the revolutionary army left Puno on the 15th inst. to meet the Government troops who are marching in this direction. In a few days we expect to hear of a General Battle but I think the revolutionary party will have to give up, the President still holds the capital Lima and has a much stronger force than the other party. Things are in a very unsettled state all through the country. In reference to the Arsenal and Mr. Costas' boat, I fear that nothing will be done for a long time to come. Mr. Costas has been a prisoner for more than two months.*

Three days ago, Mr. Joseph Thomas was out shooting, the barrel of his gun burst and blew off part of his thumb and part of the second finger on the left hand, the Doctor has taken the whole of his thumb off and his hand is in a very bad state, but there is no fear of his losing his hand. With this exception I am happy to say we are all in good health and comfortable.

We are a few months behind with our money but this is quite safe. I remain, Gentlemen, yours etc.

The reference to 'Mr. Costas' boat' and the fact that he had been a prisoner was particularly interesting to me. Until recently, I have always half expected my claim that the *Yavarí* was the first iron vessel on the lake to be challenged. Often the locals refer to a vessel of unknown type and size called the *Aurora* which they claim was already on the lake before the *Yavarí* was launched. They may have been referring to the American 55-foot iron paddle-wheeler which had inspired President Ramon Castilla, but there is no evidence of that craft having been delivered. I hoped therefore that their claim was myth and legend, but I remained a tad uneasy until one day, to my delight, in the National Maritime Museum I came across the general arrangement by Alexander Stephens' shipyard for an iron schooner called *Aurora*. It was dated 1870, the same date as a letter I found in the Puno archives from Don Geronimo Costas, by then Vice President of Peru, asking permission to use the slipway in Puno to reassemble his vessel, the *Aurora*. The slipway would have been occupied at the time by the *Yavarí*, whose keel was laid in 1869 for her launch in 1870. I believe that is evidence enough to reinforce my claim that the *Yavarí* was the first iron steamship on the lake. At the time that Partridge was writing, Costas, as a Prado supporter, had apparently been locked away by the rebels.

In August, Partridge wrote again; the theme is the same:

'The gunboats for the Lake of Titicaca are in much the same state as they were three years ago. We have not yet commenced to do any thing at (sic) them neither do I see any prospect of doing so for some time to come. There are about two thirds of the materials for one boat in Puno but there as (sic) nothing come in for the last six months. We have done nothing at the mole since the middle of December last; and I begin to think that it will never be wanted and it is my opinion that we shall leave Puno without having done one days work at the boats. In about ten months our contracts will be completed and the men say that they will not remain here after their time is up.

This country is still in a very unsettled state, the Revolution is not yet at an end, neither do I see any prospect of its speedy termination. The general opinion is that the Government will fall, the rebels are now within a short distance of the capital, Lima. Part of the Fleet including the two new frigates which have just arrived out here as (sic) fallen into the hands of the rebels. The ports have been blockaded but the blockade ships have fallen into the hands of the rebels and the ports are open again. Puno is in the center of the Revolutionary Provinces consequently we know but little what steps the Government is taking to suppress the rebellion.

For the last few months we have received but little money, and are now several months in arrears but I think our money is quite safe. Puno is a very dull place and being so long without employment we are getting tired of it. We are all still in the *enjoyment of good health. Hoping this will find you well. I remain, Gentlemen Yours very truly Wm. Partridge.'*

Partridge was prescient in his opinion because, come the completion of their four-year contracts, all went home except William Kemp, and another team took their place.

Partridge stayed on till 1868. Had he returned in fifty years he would have been surprised to find that Puno, far from being a dull place, had become the cultural and commercial centre of the south. Puneños travelled frequently to Buenos Aires, Argentina's capital, in preference to Lima, for its education, sophistication and culture. In 1865, however, Puno was probably very dull indeed.

James Orton, an American naturalist who spent much time in the *sierra* and who died crossing Lake Titicaca to be then buried on Esteves Island beside George Blaxland, wrote about Puno in 1867 that, apart from the university, cathedral and three newspapers, the population of 5,000 were mostly Aymaras, *'in sombre garb, silent and sullen as nature in this latitude and altitude,* [they] *move to and fro as if in mourning. They are poor and indolent but why should they work in this sleety region, which yields nothing but small potatoes...'*[9]

On 15 March 1866, in an attempt to resurrect the project of transporting the ships' pieces up to the lake, the Prefect of the province of Chucuito, that rides with Puno region, wrote to the Lieutenant Colonel Prefect of the Department of Puno, '...*se sabe que se tiene la orden de alistar 1000 Indios para trasladar de Tacna las piezas de los vaporcitos de Titicaca'* – your order has been received to recruit 1000 Indians to transport the pieces of the *'vaporcitos'* from Tacna to Titicaca – and says he has passed the word around to the governors of his province. In April there was a change of heart and the order was rescinded because two new *arrieros*, Don Marino Muñoz and Don Natanial Chocano, had been contracted to complete the job. However, as a result of the unrest in southern Peru, every kind of trouble was brewing among the Indian community. Puno was in uproar. The people had backed General Prado, but as soon as he took office as President he re-imposed the indigenous tax which President Ramon Castilla had lifted. There was a revolt among the Indians against this tax and other abuses inflicted on them by the *criollo* authorities. Described by the British Embassy in Lima as a class war, it was not exclusive to the Lake Titicaca region; it spread from Puno

The Anglo-Peruvian team which reassembled the two steamers seen here standing proudly in front of the *Yapurá*.

to the surrounding communities of Huancane, Azangaro and Capachica. A popular hero called Juan Bustamante emerged to defend the Indians against the ruling elite, and asked aloud, '*Hasta cuando serán los indios considerados como cosas y tratados como esclavos?*' - 'How long will Indians be thought of as things and treated as slaves?'

Colonel Andrés Recharte was deputed to quell the rebellion and, damning his reputation forever, appealed first to Bolivia to lend him troops. Being unsuccessful, he led a division of the Peruvian army instead to quash the uprising and then to assassinate its hero Bustamante. Presumably for this reason, charges of treachery against him were dropped and, for his own safety, he was sent to Tacna to resume the transportation of the two steamers.

The year 1868 was marked by a momentous earthquake and tsunami, which shook 900 miles of the seaboard from Lima south to Mejillones. It caused a tidal wave so great that whole ships were flung up onto the beach and Arica and its port were destroyed completely.

Inland and up in the *sierra* the correspondence between regional prefects and the naval base in Puno continued to tell of pieces of the steamers strewn on the trails up to the lake. Between Tarata and Quilla, two pieces of iron were found and between Tarata and Chero, five more. One letter even included a sketch and measurements to help identify the wooden items that had been seen. Renewed calls went out to supply 400 Indians to get the job done.

By the end of that year, although parts were still missing, enough had been assembled in Puno to build one ship, no matter to which of the two ships the parts really belonged. The *Yavari*'s keel was laid on the first day of January 1869, despite her sternpost – the critical part which joins the keel with the deck and supports the rudder – still being somewhere on the mountainside. The team called for one to be sent from Lima, and improvised a temporary one so as to get on with the job. Come February, another tragedy befell the Englishmen, even more calamitous than losing Blaxland:

> '...*que el 9 del que cursa, se volcó en aquel lago un bote del vapor 'Yavarí' donde fueron de paseo al islote llamado Esteves, algunas personas visibles de Puno de las cuales perecieron seis ahogadas, entre ellas el Sr. Coronel Prefecto de aquel Departamento Dr. Narciso Arestegui, el ingeniero del Apostadero D. Francisco Martin, el Constructor Naval D. Santiago Sutherland, el Calderero, D. Jorge Hill, el Comerciante D. Cujenio de la Sota Romaña, y un joven D. Federico Cortantarte, cuyos cadáveres aun no se han encontrado; salvandose siete personas de las trece que iban embarcadas, a virtud de haberse hacido de proa del bote.*'

In other words, on 9 February, engineer Francis Martin, shipwright James Sutherland and boilerman George Hill were taking the prefect of the Department and nine other passengers across the bay to Esteves Island in the *Yavari*'s lifeboat when it capsized and they, the prefect and two others were drowned. The remaining seven passengers survived by virtue of sitting in the bow.

Another account of the incident maintained that the three Englishmen were rocking the iron lifeboat, which was, of course, a novelty on the lake, to demonstrate how stable and seaworthy it was. The water was calm, so such an accident is hard to imagine, although one can't rule out the fact that it was Mardi Gras and *fiesta* time in town. As when Blaxland died, there was an immediate and urgent call for these three men to be replaced as soon as possible.

At first, I had assumed that the bodies of the drowned were never recovered, but just as I was writing this book, new evidence came to light. A faded, almost illegible photocopy of a letter dated 18 February 1869 from Manuel Melgar, commander of the naval base in Puno to the *Comandante General de la Marina* in Lima, reveals that they did find the corpses and the Englishmen were subsequently buried in a cemetery for Protestants, as indicated by the town hall. Their effects were inventoried and, presumably, sent to their families in Britain. Next time I am in Puno, I shall try to locate the graves of the three Englishmen and suggest that they be recognised.

By 25 December 1870, the team had managed to rivet together one hull from the iron plates that had been delivered. Some belonged to the *Yavarí* and some to the *Yapurá*, which meant that the rivet holes were not necessarily aligned, but it was good enough. The delivery had taken so long, and although it still wasn't complete, it was now time to get on and do the best they could. A long list of parts, dated 1870, was sent to Lima. It included 60 planks of Oregon pine of different thicknesses and lengths for the superstructure, yellow pine planks for the decking, plus 50 pounds

The earliest known photograph of the *Yavarí* taken in 1887 by Mr. Borgdoff of the U.S.S. *Iroquois*.

of three-, four- and five-inch nails, many iron angle bars, *llaves inglesas* ('English keys', or spanners) and sandpaper. In the case of the wood, it is likely to be an original order to equip both ships, but one has to assume that the nails, iron bars and spanners were to replace those left on the trail. Clearly there were still many parts missing when they came to lay the keel of the *Yapurá* on 30 April 1871.

The replacement team of Englishmen had now lost three of their members. Those remaining who joined William Kemp, the only man left of the first team, were Richard Hopkin, John Harris, Charles John Sanders, William Morse and William Pemberton. It was Hopkin who took over from William Partridge as Engine Erector. He supervised the team of twelve skilled tradesmen and their assistants who finally launched the *Yavarí* on Christmas Day 1870.

It was they who were subsequently also responsible for fitting her out for her maiden voyage on 14 June 1871. Although Antony Gibbs raised the question of fuel right at the start, at the time of the maiden voyage no answer had yet been found. Many excursions had been made in search of sources of coal near enough to make transporting it to Puno feasible, but there was none. Consideration was even given to shipping it out from England, which clearly wasn't practical. Wood was out of the question, so there was only one other alternative and that was *taquia* – or llama dung.

When I first read that the *Yavarí*'s original steam engine ran on dried llama droppings, I found it hard to envisage the sourcing process, but one of the llama's most attractive characteristics is that the herd defecates in one communal and tidy spot. Ephraim George Squier, a North American journalist, diplomat and archaeologist, wrote of seeing mounds of llama excreta, similar to rabbits', as much as five feet high. If that were the case, collecting the *Yavarí*'s requirements would not have been difficult.

That was one problem solved. The other which is often mentioned is the need for a dredger. The way out of Puno bay into the lake was too shallow for the *Yavarí* once she was loaded, so her berth to begin with was five miles from Puno town. While the team waited for the dredger, called *Zúñiga I*, to come from England, they tried to dredge by hand but it was a thankless task.

Jumping forward twenty years, an American passenger, Frank Vincent, described the same situation.

'At the end of a long pier on which the cars run, lay one of the

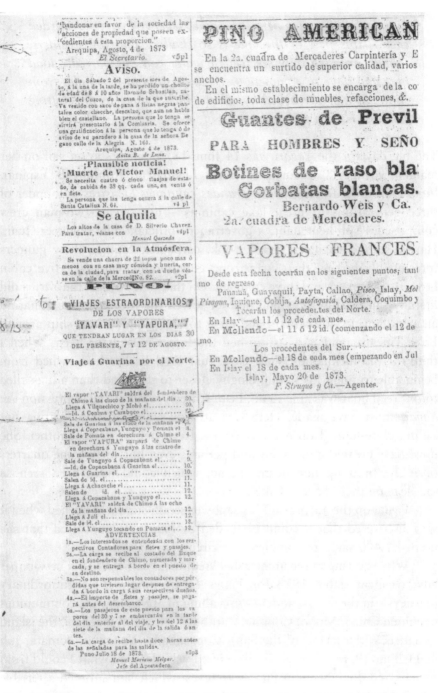

Dated 1873, the first advertisement for *Viajes Estraordinarios*! around the lake in the *Yavarí* and *Yapurá*.

two little iron steamers, of some seventy-five tons burden each... this part of the lake is so shallow that the steamers, though drawing only six feet of water can but partially load here and have to complete their cargoes about two miles from shore, at a spot reached by canal which, owing to the shifting sands, it is hard to keep open...'[10]

The big day for the *Yavarí* was 14 June 1871, when she set sail on her maiden voyage. Captained by First Lieutenant Romulo B Espinar, *'fundador de la dinastia de los grandes capitanes lacustres'* – founder of three generations of great lake captains – her twenty-two-man crew comprised a sub-lieutenant, a government official, chief engineer 'Juan' Harris, second engineer, guard, cook, carpenter, caulker, three gunners (presumably hoping their Armstrong guns would reappear), five cabin boys, three stokers and three coalmen. On that first voyage, the *Yavarí* did literally sail because they had not yet solved the fuel problem. What an amazing novelty for captain and crew to be sailing an iron ship around Lake Titicaca, and how astonished the locals must have been. When I think of the nickname 'Wind God' that Fred Parker had earned from being able to point his sailing dinghy closer to the wind than a lug-sailed *totora* reed boat was able to do, I can scarcely imagine the impression the *Yavarí* must have made. Here was an iron ship not only floating but sailing close-hauled on a direct course from one point to another. She must have created quite a stir and perhaps even horror in some quarters once she fired up her steam engine, which could have been seen as sacrilege on their 'Sacred Lake'.

Firing up the *Yavarí*'s 60-horsepower steam engine happened when it was discovered that it could be fuelled by *taquia*. It transpired that she needed 1,400 sacks to complete one circumnavigation.

While delving in the archives in Arequipa, I came across a newspaper advertisement dated 1873 for *Viajes Estraordinarios!* – extraordinary journeys – in the *Yavarí* and *Yapurá* calling in at the lakeside communities of Vilque Chico, Moho, Conima, Carabuco, Huata, Achacachi, the island of Titicaca (the Island of the Sun), Copacabana, Yunguyo, Pomata, Juli and Chimo (Puno). Subsequently, when I was gleaning what I could from the charred documents in Puno's archives, which had suffered a terrible fire, I found a file containing one or two of the passenger lists. The accommodation had the capacity for 20 first-class passengers, each one listed by name. Second Class also showed several names, but the 40 passengers accommodated on deck were merely listed as 'Indians' with no names, not unlike the 'woolie' cargo mentioned in the manifest as occupying the space below decks. It must have been a crowded ship.

The newspaper advertisement was dated 1873 when, soon after the *Yapurá* had completed her maiden voyage on 7 August, the two ships launched into their commercial careers, sailing round the lake in opposite directions. Fifteen years on, Frank Vincent gives us a further insight:

> *'The captain of my steamer, the Yavarí, though a native, spoke English. The engineer was an Englishman, who had been in these countries nearly thirty years. The steamer had four state-rooms, two for the ladies, with four berths in each, and two for the gentlemen with one berth in each. The majority of the male passengers were obliged, therefore, to sleep on the benches of the saloon... Our freight was chiefly lumber though I saw two piano-boxes labelled La Paz.'*

CHAPTER 13

Searching for the Footsteps of the Yavari

THE *YAPURÁ*'S MAIDEN VOYAGE MARKED TWELVE years since October
1861, when James Watt & Co. first agreed to build the two gunboats.
They had been twelve years of adventure and misadventure for the two
little steamers of which by far the greatest part had been spent on, or
scattered in bits and pieces beside, the Andean trails leading to the lake.

It is not clear from the correspondence which trail or trails were
used. Few place names are mentioned in the correspondence, but it is
likely that over the six years that the delivery took, each of the *arrieros*
would have chosen his favourite route. I assumed therefore that probably
parts of the *Yavarí* travelled up all three of the trails most commonly used
in the nineteenth century but, since the outset of my research, I had been
longing to find out the truth.

To me this feature of the project was like the favourite morsel you
leave on your plate till last to savour and enjoy. When Andrew asked,
'Now what would you like me to do?' it took me unawares. Here was a
conflict between sentiment and practicality. I absolutely did not want to
give my 'morsel' away, yet I realised that since he was keen, certainly fit,
and had the training and the time, it would make good sense. Although I
had strong reservations, I heard myself offering my 'morsel' to him.
Andrew was trying to overcome the chilling memories of his front line
experiences as well as face a breakdown in his family life, and I hoped that
keeping him challenged and busy would be good therapy.

I suggested that he work out a budget for an expedition the following
year, of three teams of four persons, to explore the three trails I had
identified. Then he should apply to the Winston Churchill Memorial Fund

for the principal grant and seek sponsorship for the remainder. Meanwhile, the project would pay for a fortnight's familiarisation visit to Peru. Andrew was exhilarated by the task and, equipped with maps of the area, went to it with a will. He called the expedition 'In the Footsteps of the *Yavarí*', and scheduled it for September 1999.

'Why the name *Yavarí*?' he asked, like so many before him. I couldn't tell him; it was a puzzle to me too. The Yavarí river forms part of the frontier with Brazil and the Yapurá is a tributary. Why call a ship earmarked for Lake Titicaca high in the *altiplano* after an Amazonian river? Carlos's explanation is so far the best. After several frontier disputes, Peru and Brazil finally ratified a Fluvial Convention in 1858. This convention was of such significance that the Peruvian government wished it to be marked by naming the *vaporcitos* after these two rivers. Yes, but what does the word mean? I have put the question to linguists, anthropologists and missionaries who work with the Ticuna tribe along the Yavarí river, but none could tell me the answer. Then one day, as I was writing this book, I received an e-mail from biologist Dr Richard Bodmer, who researches the Yavarí river in his rubber boom period boat of which he is justifiably proud, with the following extract. According to the French explorer and botanist Paul Marcoy writing in 1873, '*The name Yavarí which was written Yahuarí in the seventeenth century is derived from the number of Yahuarí palms (Metroxylon) which sheltered its bank at that time – these palm-trees do not exist now, or at least they are very rare.*'[11]

Yavarí remains a place name in the Amazon region of Peru. Who knows if this is the explanation, but it is satisfactory for now.

* * *

The team for our fact-finding expedition to trace the route of the *Yavarí* consisted of Andrew and two other trek leaders, Chris Hooker and Matthew (Matt) Powell; Captain Carlos and two of our crew, Máximo and Teodocio; Percy Calisaya, an anthropologist from Puno; my young cousin Sophie Orr; Ian Biles, MD of Maritime Services (International) Ltd.; me, and two *arrieros*, Victoriano Chata and Fraulan Fuentes, with their fifteen llamas. We planned to meet up in Tacna, but I began my journey in Arica which, having once been Peruvian (and raided by Drake), was the *Yavarí*'s port of arrival. I wanted to begin at the beginning...

* * *

In the *Yavarí*'s day, before the tsunami of 1868, Arica was a busy commercial port. Today it is a lively fishing port in Chile and a popular shopping centre for Peruvians. The seafood is worth a trip too, but having admired the little iron church designed by Gustave Eiffel and delivered in kit form like the *Yavarí*, and seen the photographs in the railway station of old Arica, I caught the train back to Peru. The railway track is one of the oldest in Latin America and the very one which bore Partridge, his men and the nine wagons loaded with ships' parts across the desert to Tacna. I travelled in company with a group of Indian women trafficking second-hand clothes which, amidst shrieks and giggles, they put on to bamboozle the Customs officials at the border. Each attired herself in five or six sweaters and as many thick woollen skirts and then pretended to look innocent when the inspectors walked through the train. It was a charade in which obviously everyone except me was a player but they included me in their merriment.

The train took me inland through the Atacama, the world's driest desert, then slightly uphill to Tacna, an oasis town today popular for its pleasant climate quite as much as for being close to the border with Chile and the gateway from there into Peru for fleets of second-hand Japanese cars and plenty of contraband.

The demarcation line between the desert and the outlying agricultural areas of Tacna is as stark as the one that lies along the Nile valley. Up to the line of irrigation the desert is featureless and lifeless. Then, within a stride, sterility becomes fertility and all is lush and verdant, alive with fauna and flora.

As arranged, we all met up in Tacna and, whereas Dueñas, Partridge and the team had unpacked the boxes of parts here at the railway station, we packed our bags in preparation for the adventure ahead, and Andrew delivered his first briefing to us as a complete team. I had no misconceptions as to how hard I would find the trekking, and had asked months in advance if a sure-footed mountain pony could be lined up for me. No pony materialised; instead, Carlos suggested I should ask the army if I could borrow a horse. I took Sophie with me to the barracks where we were met by a young good-looking jack-booted cavalry officer and escorted to their arena. The Colonel joined us and said he needed to see how competent we were as horsewomen before agreeing to lend us any of his horses. He ordered Agamemnon and Perseus to be led out. They were handsome creatures but immense, at least 17 hands high, with hooves the size of dinner plates, perfect for galloping across the desert but not ideal for tiptoeing along narrow and treacherous mountain trails. With some difficulty we were given a leg-up and told to walk around the arena. We walked and walked around and around, and around again, for far longer than necessary for a competence assessment. I assumed it was Sophie in her tight trousers which they were enjoying. Eventually we were instructed to trot for a couple of circuits before being called in and told to dismount.

'You,' said the Colonel, looking at me, 'could improve your seat.' (Well, how do you like that? The cheeky devil!) 'But I am prepared to lend you a horse.' (Sophie didn't want one; she had only come to keep me company.) 'Bring out Achilles for the *señorita*,' he snapped to the young lieutenant.

Well, Achilles was quite a different thing. Poor Achilles wasn't magnificent at all, clearly second string, and it wasn't just his heel that worried me. To my alarm, I noticed that he was blind in one eye. What would happen when the precipitous edge to the path was on his blind side? And how would he see where to put his dinner-plate hooves? I shuddered at the possible consequences. Besides, he was so tall I couldn't get on without a leg-up. Achilles was not suitable, but I found it awkward to say so to the Colonel.

So early next morning, as Victoriano and Fraulan were loading our equipment onto the llamas, who were looking their most supercilious, there was a terrific clattering of hooves on the nearby road, and a platoon of cavalry, jingling and jangling in full harness, came cantering into the yard and slid to a halt. The young lieutenant, straight off the front cover of a Barbara Cartland romance, jumped down.

I spotted Achilles with his huge hooves, breathing heavily, head hanging low and looking dreadfully forlorn.

'I ought to tell you, *Señorita*,' said the handsome cavalier, 'that you must only ride Achilles for three hours before stopping to allow him to drink and eat, and don't forget to loosen his girth six centimetres. When he's drinking you need to count the times he swallows, because he must swallow thirty-two times before eating, and twenty-two times after. He likes to graze, but he must have four kilos of ground barley every day as a supplement, and when he's finished you should walk him on the leading rein for at least one hour to allow him to digest. At night he must wear a rug and be hobbled.'

No, no, no! This was supposed to be a journey of reconnaissance, not an Achilles benefit ride, and anyway the army wouldn't provide the rug or the hobbles, still less the barley.

Carlos came to the rescue. In response to a frantic wink from me, he handled the matter the *criollo* way so no feelings were hurt, and the platoon and Achilles clattered away, *amour propre* still intact.

A Peruvian television company was keen to film our departure and our arrival at Lake Titicaca and apologised for not having time to film the in-between. As we prepared to depart, we welcomed the film crew who arrived in time for the *Pago a la Tierra* ceremony dedicated to *Pachamama*. According to Inca mythology, *Pachamama* – Mother Earth – is a benevolent fertility goddess who, if worshipped, makes harvests fruitful and offers protection for new departures such as meetings and journeys.

Victoriano and Fraulan laid out a miscellany of votive offerings, including coca leaves, flowers and libations of *chicha* (maize beer) and *pisco* (grape brandy), and we joined them in asking *Pachamama* and the *Apu* mountain gods to smooth our path and keep us safe.

The twelve-person expedition was divided into three teams of four. Each team would search for evidence of the *Yavarí* on one of the three trails used in the 1860s for transporting goods to the lake from the Pacific coast.

At the edge of the town we split into the three groups, two of which had satellite telephones and call times. All three had a schedule of rendezvous days and places. In my group were Andrew, Máximo, Fraulan and, for this first leg, all fifteen llamas.

For the trek I had insisted that Máximo and I were in the same team. Maxi, a trusted friend of many years and a perfect companion, comes from the Lake Titicaca region and is an Aymara Indian, a tribe which preceded the Incas by many hundreds of years and the only tribe known to have resisted Inca dominance. They are a strong willed, resilient and feisty people and, like all highland Indians, stocky in stature and immensely strong. Recognising my frailty at such high altitude, Maxi was very willing and more than able to add my daypack and water ration to all the other equipment he was already carrying. I don't believe he even noticed the extra load. That was the plus side of my team.

Unfortunately, for several reasons, I had had a serious confrontation with Andrew and wished we were not in the same team, but for the sake of the enterprise I tried to be magnanimous about it. It didn't make things any better that on the first leg of the journey he led us miles out of our way up a winding and treacherously narrow trail which led to a mine

The 1863 map of the trails up the Andes which I tried to follow on our trek in 1999.

shaft. The mine had long been abandoned and was very much a dead end, so in military terms it was right about turn! As we turned around on the narrow ledge which was our track, I was thankful I was not aboard Achilles.

The foothills of the Andes, in which such mine shafts are plentiful, resemble a moonscape. Overlooked by towering, jagged peaks of what was once molten volcanic rock, the dry riverbeds and narrow trails snake their way up the folds and strata of the cold russet-coloured mountains. Sometimes we passed a scattering of cacti or a bromeliad, sometimes a dusty acacia or stunted bush, but this is a barren land. Because it had rained early that year, in places there was the faintest idea of a green hue to the rock face where brave desert plants were just reappearing, but in general it was dry, bare and empty of plant life. Occasionally a gecko or lizard would slither off the path in front of us, or a valiant passerine flit by, while overhead a raptor might glide into view. Whenever we came to any human habitation, vultures would be keeping watch from a good vantage point. The sky was a fierce cobalt blue and the heat intense. Turning back, we could look down over the desert to the haze in the west which disguised the Pacific shoreline.

* * *

Our first rendezvous was Tarata, for Dueñas and the Englishmen a half-day's ride, for us three uphill days away and the last community of any size between Tacna and the *altiplano*. It would have been no more than a settlement in Partridge's day. Today it is a small town typical of all small towns in the southern Andes. It definitely needed a coat of paint, but was enhanced by eucalyptus trees, flowering shrubs, roses and dahlias and a lively bird life that included my favourite, the humming bird. Colonial church, police station and modern municipal town hall overlooked the central plaza. The fountain in the middle, topped by a bronze statue of a soldier bearing arms, was dedicated to the fallen heroes of the Pacific War against Chile (1879-83). We saluted, figuratively, to other ghosts of the past like General William Miller from Kent who fought alongside General José de San Martín and Admiral Lord Cochrane in Peru's War of Independence before achieving his own notable victory at the Battle of Tarata (1822), which helped turn the tide in favour of the revolutionaries. Later, during the War of the Pacific, the Peruvian Admiral Lizardo

Moreno also passed this way in 1882 as he fled from Arequipa, having – as his critics say – 'surrendered' the town to the Chileans. He, on the other hand, in a letter he wrote on the *Yavarí*'s ward room table (still in use to this day), maintained that the alternative would have meant a bloody massacre, mainly of Arequipeños.

Tarata is situated on one of the routes over the Western Cordillera. On a map in the Royal Geographical Society dated 1863 it is easy to see the contemporary mule trails leading to Puno. Squier was also heading for Lake Titicaca at exactly the same time as the *Yavarí*'s parts but on a route a few degrees to the south. He writes most engagingly of his experiences. On one occasion he met a train of one thousand llamas coming down the trail and, on another, a mule train carrying powdered copper or iron ore led by an *'educated horse with a sonorous bell attached to his neck, to warn approaching travellers to stop at some spot where the road is wide enough to prevent their being run down outright or toppled over the precipices by the heavily laden train that plunges behind the equine leader.'*[12]

The little town is the gateway to the *altiplano* from the coastal desert and must have seen much traffic. It is not a 'must-see' town but within the surrounding area are stone-age cave paintings providing evidence of a culture dating back to 8,000 BC. They also imply that these same trails were used by early man for travel and trade up and down the Andes, from desert seaboard to over 22,000 feet. With the llama as his beast of burden he exchanged salt, seashells and guano fertiliser from the coast for potatoes, wool and grains from the *sierra* and exotic feathers from the rainforest. When the Spanish arrived in the sixteenth century they brought with them their mules which, in spite of the altitude and harsh conditions, were more practical as pack animals. A mule will carry or drag up to 400 pounds, whereas a llama will spit contemptuously and refuse to move if a load exceeds 100 pounds. So by the nineteenth century mule-trains were commonplace and could do the journey in approximately nine days. However, we could not afford to be distracted from our mission, so with a bow in the direction of prehistoric man and a vow to return we turned our attentions to the immediate and to nightfall.

There was not a great choice of places in Tarata to pitch our camp, but we were given permission to occupy the town's football pitch where the television crew caught up with us to do their interviews. Andrew insisted that, in the best traditions of the British army on a route march, we had to be 100 per cent self-sufficient. This meant doing a big shop for the next leg of the journey thereby exceeding the hundred-pound weight limit imposed by each of our fifteen llamas so we were asked to carry our own rucksacks. Well, I knew one person who wasn't happy with that plan although the others appeared to relish the added challenge and physical exertion. It reminded me of the ten British soldiers who looked after our logistics at Cusichaca, who would run up mountains with 50-gallon drums strapped to their backs – for fun!

It was clear from our briefing in Tarata that, now knowing our pace – and I was by a long way the slowest – we would not reach the lake within our allotted time frame. This was a bitter blow, but at least in Tarata we could hire a truck for a few hours whereas it would be out of the question once we were on the *altiplano*. Moreover it would help us cover a particularly severe, and slow, uphill section. None of us enjoyed cheating but there was no other choice.

Before dawn the next day we broke camp and, together with the llamas, climbed into the back of the truck. Although disdainful of humans, llamas make delightful and easy travelling companions. On the trail, they eat and drink sparingly, are very clean and neat, and as they trot daintily along on their little cloven feet they hum to one another, until they get spooked and then they bolt. When they are working they wear tassels in their ears. Our leader wore red, white and blue tassels and a bell around his neck while his followers were only entitled to wear red and white. At dusk they huddled together in readiness for the night during which they slept within a rope corral, some standing and some lying down with elbows jutting out at the back like camels. All we heard were spasmodic muffled grunts which we liked to think meant contentment. They are proud beasts and showed their low regard for us by laying back their ears if we got too close and, if we didn't heed the warning, by spitting with deadly accuracy. I thought of Hilaire Belloc's silly and rather unkind ditty and wondered whether he had been a victim.

The Llama is a woolly fleecy hairy sort of goat
With an indolent expression and an undulating throat.[13]

The truck coughed and spluttered as we zigzagged our way slowly up the mountainside towards the snowline. The cold was hypothermic but the sunrise, red and pink sliding into orange and yellow over the highest of the mountain peaks, now covered in snow, was glorious.

In the Andes, the climate is extreme and in one day can vary as much as 63°F, or 17°C. Even moving out of the sun into the shade it can drop 20°F, or 6.6°C. It is always very cold at night but in the day it can be viciously hot one moment, driving rain or hail the next, or blowing a pitiless icy wind which bites into one's very vitals. Trekking in such conditions is not for the faint hearted. I felt for those lowland Indian porters charged with carrying the *Yavarí*'s cold, angular iron parts too awkward for a mule to carry, who, however hardy, couldn't endure the severity of the *sierra*. To make matters worse, because of the inherent difficulties of transferring money from Lima, and the uprisings and invasions which distracted the navy, the porters' and muleteers' wages were always irregular and frequently overlooked altogether. We know that many of them deserted, simply abandoning their cargo on the trail (which is why we harboured the unlikely dream of finding a piece of old iron still lying where it had fallen).

The purpose of our mission, of course, was to find out more about the *Yavarí*'s own journey, to ask people along the way whether their grandfathers or great-grandfathers had ever spoken about mule trains passing by carrying parts of an iron ship. You would think it would have made an indelible impression and worked its way into their folklore. With such informal research in mind, we had appointed Maxi, Teo and Percy to each of the three groups as they could speak the ethnic Aymara language.

As it was, where the truck left us on the *altiplano* was around 14,000 feet above sea level, in the middle of absolutely nowhere and with not a soul in sight. In the very distant far-away we could just discern the mountains, but we were now in what they call the *Despoblado* – the uninhabited high plains. Specks between us and the horizon turned out to be alpaca. Even llamas don't really enjoy being so high. I was glad there was a track, because tramping through the tussocks of needle-sharp *ichu* grass and unfriendly *paja brava* (angry straw, which speaks for itself) would have been sheer torture. At this altitude we occasionally saw individual specimens of the tree *polyepsis tarracapana* or *queñoa*, as it is known locally. Maxi knew his local flora and pointed them out to us. It grows at the highest altitude of any tree in the world and, withstanding as it does the harshest of climates, its trunk is stunted and gnarled and its short branches swept sideways by the prevailing wind. Each specimen now is a landmark, as its numbers have been so depleted.

As the truck disappeared back to Tarata, I wondered whether

Andrew knew exactly where we were. We gathered round his satellite map of the region prepared by the super-modern US Defense Mapping Agency in Bethesda, which I was trying to reconcile with my copy of the RGS's hand-drawn map dated 1863. Both were difficult to read as the wind tried to snatch them out of our hands, but Máximo and Teo had a native hunch and that was good enough for me.

Once again we split up into our groups, one heading off in a southerly direction towards the Bolivian border to explore the route through Pizacoma where we knew Dueñas and the Englishmen had been seen, another on the northern route, and my group on the north-eastern route. The hardiest of the three groups carried their own backpacks while the rest of us took advantage of the llamas. Having identified the next rendezvous point, we wished each other well, waved goodbye and trudged off.

It was silent and strangely eerie being left alone in such an expansive panorama. I was glad to be with Maxi and Fraulan. Andrew and Maxi both carried their rucksacks and Fraulan his bag of coca. I carried a day pack for my two litres of water, sun hat, sweater, my red expedition anorak kindly donated by a sponsor, a rainproof cagoule, lipsalve and two conventional pre-digital cameras, batteries and spare rolls of slide and positive film. The llamas carried the tents and camping equipment, main rations, satellite telephone and my rucksack.

* * *

It was still early as we trudged off along a crude track that would take us near to the River Maure. As I knew for certain that the *Yavarí*, or parts of her, had crossed the river I was excited. For what seemed like most of my life, I had imagined the moment when I would be treading the very path that the mules carrying pieces of the ship had trodden before me. We were now on the *puna* – the barren wastes of the bleak Andean tundra. The cold was polar intense and our route meant walking into a biting head wind, and I mean biting. I tried to cover my face with a scarf but it was torn off like a leaf from a tree. There is no mercy on the Peruvian *altiplano*. My eyes watered and my nose ran and after four hours' walking my face, fingers and toes were so numb from the cold I could hardly remember what they felt like. When I could face the icy blast, I looked up and what I saw around me was awe-inspiring. *Puna* scrub or dry pale green *ichu* grass stretched away to the far horizon where it fused into the faint grey outline of the mountain peaks beyond. All around me was a vast, empty and fearsome space but its grandeur and savage beauty were overpowering. I have never, before or since, become blasé about the *altiplano*. The emotions of wonderment and spirituality well up inside me and I think of the *Te Deum* – 'Heaven and earth are full of the Majesty of thy Glory'. It is the majesty of the God who 'laid out the earth above the waters' (Psalm 136) or the majesty of the *Apus*, the Indians' sacred gods of the mountains, or Viracocha the creator god. However, it all began, Big Bang or no, we have inherited natural wonders the majesty of which are humbling.

And they offer a physical challenge. We paused periodically for a swig of water and a piece of chocolate, but by the time Andrew began talking about looking for a campsite, my heart was thumping and my lungs were raw from the air, so rarefied and so exhausting to inhale at over 14,000 feet above sea level. Every muscle agonised as I struggled to put one foot in front of the other, the soles of both smarting from the stones underfoot.

For logistical reasons we sited our camp a few kilometres away from the River Maure which lay to our right, although from the map I envisaged the mules approaching it from the other side. As the river winds, we had deviated very slightly in favour of a more direct route.

A night camping on the *altiplano* is an experience never to be forgotten. Andrew was not feeling well that first night, so it was left to Maxi and me to look for space to pitch three tents. With difficulty we found an unforgiving patch of hard, stony ground between the tussocks of *ichu* grass. These tussocks, which look innocent enough in the grand vista, are in fact as sharp and as unfriendly as an angry porcupine.

Maxi found a stone to knock in the tent pegs and with frozen hands we fought the wind that was trying to tear the tent out of our hands. Neither Fraulan nor Victoriano participated in any activity other than loading and unloading their llamas and looking after them at night. They preferred to eat and sleep apart from us and, on this occasion, Fraulan had already taken his llamas away to another patch to corral them. We had brought a little primus stove with us which Maxi now lit and heated up a dish of potato, rice and tuna. It was hot and sustaining.

The sub-zero intensity of the cold that night froze my tent rigid, every zip fastener, my water bottle, my brain and my body. Fantasising about electric blankets, I folded my shivering self into the foetal position, slithered down deep within my sleeping bag and waited sleeplessly for the dawn. Only when my mind had thawed enough to think could I empathise with the mules, burdened with heavy loads, the *arrieros*, and, most of all, the lowland Indian porters, who had to be dragooned into undertaking the assignment over a century before. I could now understand only too well why so many of them deserted, even here in the middle of nowhere. In a country where earthquakes, wars both civil and frontier, and other misadventures were frequent occurrences, the journey had been an astounding Herculean feat.

In the morning, it was no ordeal to dress because I hadn't undressed. Seasoned campers like the army team at Cusichaca had told me that it was imperative to undress before getting into the sleeping bag. They had four-season army issue sleeping bags which were like eider ducks' nests and so, so toasty warm. I did not have such a bag and I could not, I simply could not, bring myself to undress to get into mine. Did I suffer unnecessarily? I don't know, but I couldn't wait till morning came.

On this particular morning I was impatient to find the River Maure, so after a breakfast of stale bread dunked in hot coffee, we started out. Naturally I took Maxi with me. Frankly, in the inhospitable terrain of the Andes, I wouldn't go anywhere without him. I was thankful that Andrew chose to stay behind.

It was a long trudge over sharp stones, dodging the tussocks as we went. I wished I had spent more time in the gym before leaving London and I also wished that I had indulged myself with a new and more extravagant brand of hiking boot. As it was, my feet were very sore and my ankles were not well supported. If I sound feeble, let me say, even at the risk of over-emphasising the point, that walking across the *altiplano* is not like walking across Salisbury Plain. It is hard work, and all the time you have to breathe in enough thin cold air deep into the lungs to oxygenate the blood and power the muscles. It was a trial of endurance, and had I not had a goal I would gladly have sat down and said 'To hell with it!' but there was no turning back now. I had to reach the River Maure.

The view ahead and one hundred and eighty degrees around us was of a grey-green swathe of tussocks stretching as far as the eye could see towards the horizon and the distant snowy peaks of the Western Cordillera of the Andes. Away from the mountains, the curvature of the

Dinner with Anastasia on the last night of the trek.

The *Yavarí* is a popular outing for local schoolchildren.

Giselle.

The Bolinder engine stripped down – grinding the crankshaft (l to r: Antonia, Julian, Tatu and Máximo).

The Bolinder rebuilt.

A very happy crew – engine repairs successfully completed!

Engine trials 1999.

Captain Carlos at the
wheel.

Tatu and Carlos firing up the boiler to operate the winch.

The *Yavari* still out of reach of the cradle.

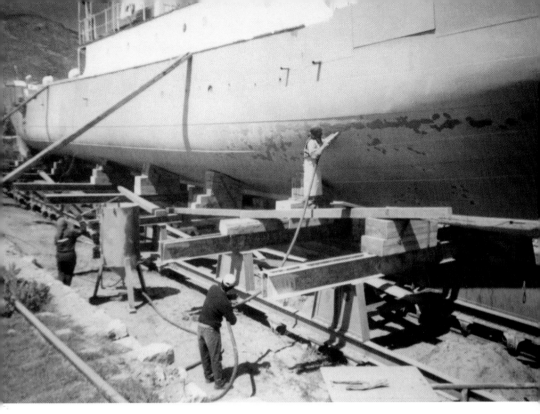

Sandblasting the hull.

The propeller removed for cleaning.

Bridge telegraph.

The restored binnacle.

The Dobbie McInnes
& Clyde compass.

Restored cabin ready for B&B visitors.

The author with the crews of the *Yavarí* and the *Yapurá* (BAP *Puno*).

BAP *Puno* (*Yapurá*).

The author relaxing
at the *Candelaria*
fiesta.

So much achieved by
Back row l to r: Author,
Adrian, Antonia, Per.
Front row: Carlos,
Maximo, Teo.

The *Yavarí* 'dressed overall' at her pontoon.

The *Yavari* off Suasi Island.

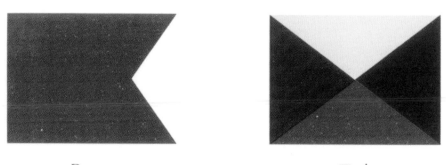

Bravo — Zulu

Bravo Zulu – the Naval signal for "Well done".

earth was marked by a faint line where the scrub blended with the sky. Between it and us the emptiness was absolute. We appeared to be the only living creatures, just two tiny specks, in an infinite and awesome sweep of desolation. We continued to walk, Maxi a little ahead but keeping my pace.

When we next scanned our surroundings, we did spot other signs of life. Far away to our left a herd of alpaca was quietly grazing, while to our right, and to our astonishment, we picked out a Peruvian army barracks so cleverly camouflaged we almost missed it. The vision of a jeep, and being driven back to camp, flashed into my mind. But the barracks were beyond the river and I first wanted to relish our arrival at the riverside.

At this point in its course the River Maure is broad and shallow and flows slowly over the plain. I collapsed on the bank with a groan, surprising a pair of teal just paddling past. They swivelled their heads in my direction, but realising that I meant them no harm, they glided on their way. 'How dare they look so relaxed?' I thought crossly, before putting my mind to conjuring up the scene of a hundred mules head to tail bearing the *Yavarí*'s and the *Yapurá*'s iron plates, bags of rivets, tons of chandlery, tools, steam boilers and steam engines over the *puna,* and porters stooped under the weight of sections of propeller shafts.

Having rested a moment and enjoyed the river's gentleness and sparkle, Maxi and I made our way over to the barracks. It turned out to be an outpost of the cavalry but, alas, there was not a horse to be seen and, worse than that, no sign of a jeep either. The corporal in charge of a skeleton team of soldiers confirmed this very bad news so, with dusk falling fast, Maxi and I turned to head back to our camp site.

As we tramped back, me weary but happy and Maxi probably wondering whether I would make it, I had time to think about why it felt so good to have achieved my goal. I never intended that unearthing the facts behind the incredible story of the *Yavarí* would become such a personal odyssey. When my curiosity was first aroused I imagined it would be a short-term research project over, perhaps, a couple of years. In fact, it has taken more than twenty-five. Moments like these, I mused, made it all seem worthwhile and I left it at that. I wanted to enjoy the sensation of achieving an ambition of (nearly) a lifetime, because I knew that if I delved further for justification of the years spent on the project I would find it hard. I preferred to dwell on the *Yavarí*'s odyssey rather than my own. Extraordinary that anyone should think, in the first place, of carrying a ship up to one of the world's highest waterways which only became recognised as the world's highest 'navigable' waterway because of the two steamers. I thought too of the expedition's ill fate. Had *arriero* Quelopana completed the delivery in the six months that he estimated, the parts would have been in place and their reassembly well under way before the Spanish invasion of the Chincha Islands which brought everything to a standstill. It was, however, miraculous really that in light of the delays and mishaps they were able to gather up the individual parts scattered randomly over the hillside and piece them together to make a ship. Miraculous too, that the ship is still afloat today...

But, then as today, the *Yavarí* is nothing if not a survivor.

And it was the question of survival that was uppermost in my mind as we neared our camp. I did not look forward to another and many subsequent nights camping on the *altiplano*. Anyone who has been camping – and nearly everyone has at some time – will know that the romance which surrounds living under canvas is a fantasy. It is simply unmitigated discomfort. I'm not talking about a walk-in family tent with a porch and windows and a Calor gas stove. No, I'm talking about life in a basic tent, about fumbling with glaciated fingers to unzip the flysheet and the main flap, crawling on hands and knees over stones and other extraneous knobbles hiding under the groundsheet, trying to dry clothes putrefying in a rucksack, and sleeping in a bag which is never warm enough. After a long tiring walk, one feels like an armchair, a log fire and a gin and tonic, not a grope in the dark for the torch, the thermos and a tin of bully beef.

The discomforts of camping as well as the cold at these altitudes which I have tried to describe prevented any proper sleep. I determined that I would never go camping again and, more immediately, I also determined to revisit the idea of finding a pony as soon as we came to any likely looking habitation.

CHAPTER 14
On the Altiplano

IN THE MEANWHILE, THERE WERE COMPENSATIONS aplenty. The scenery was never less than breathtaking; it was wild and it was windswept; it was both chillingly inhospitable and magnificent at once. Sometimes we came across a dry-stone corral and sometimes an adobe or stone *chosa* or a community of two or three *chosas*, and we would stop in case someone was at home. These *chosas* were primitive. The roof was of grass, the floor earthen and the one windowless room contained the barest of necessities – a table, a couple of plastic chairs, two or three cooking pots and tin mugs, and some empty tins and bottles. The 'bedroom' was defined by a bed behind a clothesline of miscellaneous garments strung across one corner of the shack. A ledge of adobe at knee level around the wall served as a bench and as a dormitory to the ubiquitous free-range guinea pigs. The only light came from the open door in the day, candles at night and the glow of *ichu* grass burning in the adobe oven. We sometimes saw kids with ruddy cheeks and runny noses playing with a marble outside in the dust. The older ones might ask for sweets or a pencil, the younger ones just stared with big round black eyes. Most probably we were the first foreigners they had ever seen. Next door to where the family lived, an outhouse, smaller but of the same materials, was where the alpaca fleeces or llama skins, sacks of potatoes and farming tools were kept.

I was impressed by how hardy these peasant folk are and how far, far removed our lives are from one another. Obviously they thought the same about us, feeling and asking us the price of our boots and anoraks and looking uncomprehendingly at our satellite telephone.

These tough, inexhaustible people live off their beasts and the edible tubers that grow at high altitude of which the potato is king. *Solanum tuberosum*, called *patata* by the Spanish who first brought it to Europe, originated exactly where we were, in the *altiplano* of southern Peru. Thought to have been cultivated eight thousand years ago, it has now become the world's fourth staple food. Of the five thousand varieties grown around the world, the International Potato Centre in Peru has identified four thousand three hundred that grow in the Andes. One *campesino* household, such as the ones we came across, might grow as many as twelve varieties, each cultivated specifically to withstand the diverse and harsh climate; rains, drought, frost, El Niño, La Niña – any or all can kill a crop in the *sierra*.

The additional value of the potato is that it can be freeze-dried and stored indefinitely without losing any of its nutritional properties. I had heard much about 'the world's first freeze-dried vegetable' and had seen quantities of dehydrated potatoes on sale in Puno, but had never seen how it was done. On the trek we came across several *campesinos* in the throes of the procedure, so Máximo was able to explain what they were doing.

Having selected the variety they wish to store, they lay them out on the ground for three days in order for the potatoes to freeze in the low temperatures at night and thaw in the heat of the day. Then they trample them to squeeze out the water, remove the skins and leave them for another two days. The end result is a shrunken, rock-hard, knobbly potato the size of a horse chestnut, called *chuño* if it's brown and *tunta* if it's white. The taste is subtle but the big plus is that both can be stored for years, to be rehydrated for making soups or stews when required. On market day in Puno, the stalls overflow with sacks of different varieties of tubers, and along the pavements designated for the sale of potatoes Indian women sit cross-legged behind small handfuls or huge mounds of *chuño* or *tunta* and all kinds of different shapes and colours of potato.

One day, we came across an old woman sitting on a wooden stool outside her adobe *chosa* not far from the track. Typically she was wearing a bowler hat, plaid blanket held in place around her shoulders with a nappy pin, several skirts, thick socks and, not typically, trainers. Maxi introduced us and she was surprisingly forthcoming. She told us her name was Clementina and that she was eighty-five years old. She was the daughter of an *arriero* and she did remember her grandfather talking of parts of a ship which had been carried through his village. We egged her on, and although she had no more to tell of the *Yavarí,* she held us transfixed with her memories of accompanying her father and his mules up and down to the coast. She could remember by name exactly where they had watered and grazed the mules on their nine-day journey.

It was frustrating to think that, had we had more time, we would surely have found others of Clementina's age with memories as lucid and we might have learned much more. Indeed, that was one of the principal reasons why being self-sufficient and sleeping in tents proved to be so unsatisfactory. It isolated us from the locals. We saw few people in the day because they were out with their livestock. Night-time or 6 p.m. when it got dark was the time to make friends, and even then it took a good while to break the ice and win confidence. *Campesinos* are reserved and tight-lipped even with urban Peruvians, let alone foreigners. Their daily life is tough, the climate harsh, and their history of having been invaded and oppressed by the Incas, then the Spanish and, most recently in this part of southern Peru, the Chileans, has taught them to be guarded. On the surface they are not unfriendly but I learned at Cusichaca that it takes a long time and plenty of hooch totties to get beneath the surface. Even then we foreigners can never be sure whether we're being told the truth or what they think we want to hear.

From talking to the people we did meet, it became clear that they were happy to offer us their hospitality in exchange for sharing our rations. They billeted us in their adobe outhouses reserved for storing alpaca fleeces and warm and cosy llama hides. This soft option won unanimous approval so the tents became 'surplus to requirements' in double-quick time. No-one was happier than I was. Now only the search for a pony remained outstanding.

Sometimes our trail would take us over *bofedales* – swampy valley bottoms of emerald green and deep pools of water alive with ducks and waders of which I was surprised to recognise several species, such as rails, coots and pintails, which I associate with sea level habitats. However, definitely more exotic, I thought, were the *puna* black ibis, and the black and white mountain *caracara* with orange cheeks and yellow feet that stood ramrod straight and still as a heron, watching as we trekked past. I should love to have stopped and watched him, but alas, there was 'no time to stand and stare'. We had to keep going. I did miss a kindred spirit with whom to chat along the way, but we walked such distances apart that no-one was within earshot.

Sometimes we passed through wide valleys between sage-green slopes terraced through natural erosion, or went scrambling over rocky outcrops and slithering down shale escarpments dominated by battlements of serrated rock or red sandstone fantastically carved by the wind into faces and figures. It was hard going, and the extreme climate constantly changeable. One moment we were in shirtsleeves and then, heralded by ear-shattering claps of cracking thunder and blinding streaks of lightning illuminating the whole sky, murderous dark black clouds would roll into view. I would wriggle out of my daypack, dig inside it for the storm gear, fight my way into anorak, hat, hood and gloves, and wriggle back into the daypack before getting drowned in a terrible storm and lashed by the wind. Half an hour later, the sun would be beating down again so that all of the above had to be reversed.

Every other evening Andrew would put a call through on the satellite telephone to Chris who was leading the group furthest away to the south. If he failed to make contact, he checked in with our liaison operator in Lima.

Days later, we rendezvoused with one of the other groups in a village of fifteen shacks, one of which was a shop with a back room spacious enough for eight of us to lay out our sleeping bags. Apart from Clementina's recollections, there had been no other memories of the *Yavarí* to report. We had allowed ourselves to get excited about a piece of old iron we found lying in the *puna* scrub. One of the llamas was persuaded to carry it so that we could have it analysed in Lima. We enjoyed speculating about it but no-one was too surprised when it was later identified as a piece off a twentieth-century truck.

However, what we were discovering from our conversations with local people was that the Chilean invasion of 1879 and their subsequent fifty-year occupation had made such a powerful impact that most preceding history, including the arrival of the gunboats, had been obliterated. The War of the Pacific was fought both at sea and on land and nowhere more fiercely than in the south of Peru as the Chileans battled their way north to Lima, which they then occupied for two years. Contemporary accounts speak of the havoc they wreaked and what they stole as spoils of war, including the majority of the books from Peru's National Library; in 2007, with due ceremony, 3,778 books out of an estimated 2,500 kilos were returned. The humiliation of defeat, most keenly felt in the south, has left a deep-seated sense of resentment, and whereas for many Peruvians their most vivid history begins with the Incas, for the people of southern Peru it begins with the Chileans.

* * *

Having planned the next leg of the journey with the other group in the back room, Máximo and I left the others relaxing and washing clothes, to go looking for a pony to hire.

We quizzed everyone we met along the road but no-one could help; we walked up long tracks to *haciendas* where horses grazed, but nobody was interested. Eventually we reached a village where we were told of a farmer who might be able to help us.

The farmer wasn't at home but his son said he thought he had gone to the village and would be back in a *'ratito'*. We circumnavigated the village asking for him, but he was nowhere to be found. Twenty-four hours later he returned unshaven, crumpled trilby pushed well back and breath smelling strongly of cheap alcohol giving us a clue as to where he might have been.

'Yes,' he said. 'I do have a pony, but it's for sale not for hire, and I'll throw in the saddle and bridle as well.'

This was the obvious option – to buy a pony and sell it in Puno. We showed interest, though not too much.

The farmer told me to jump on the back of his motorbike and took off towards the foothills. I clung on for dear life, not knowing where on earth we might end up or whether I was ever likely to see Máximo again. The bike slipped and bucked over hillocks and ruts until we reached a paddock in which there stood a shaggy, dirty white pony the size of a Dartmoor. The farmer slung a rope round its neck and jumped on; kicking it aggressively, he cantered in small circles around me shouting about how docile it was and how it would be ideal for the *señorita*. As animals are for work and not kept as pets, I was immediately impressed that once Moro, for that was his name, had been brought to a standstill he allowed me to give him a timid pat. He did, indeed, seem docile and I was hopeful that we might be able to bond in due course, but I needed Máximo to talk numbers. I had about as much clue of this pony's monetary worth and how to negotiate a fair price as I would about buying a second-hand carpet off a Turk. When Máximo turned up, I asked him to strike an Aymara bargain.

We agreed on 170 US dollars to include saddle, bridle and head collar. I was pleased but the farmer looked *very* pleased so we'd obviously paid over the odds, but we had paid for added value. Moro changed my whole perspective of trekking in the *sierra*. He was kind, quiet and sure-footed, as good and steady going downhill as he was going up. He stood still while I wrestled with my daypack and the dry and wet weather gear routine, and he never seemed to tire. Best of all, I could mount him unaided. He became a very dear friend.

The only snag was his saddle. Its high narrow pommel cut deep into my inner thighs. I took it in turns to walk and ride which dear Moro allowed me to do, standing quietly while I got on and off.

Maxi, Moro and I caught up with Andrew and Fraulan and carried on to our next group rendezvous, but from this point on, my life changed. I had a pony to ride in the day and a roof over my head at night. Trekking took on quite a new and improved hue...

A few days later we met up with both the other groups in Mazo Cruz where we slept in the police station. I wasn't surprised that the southerly group had picked up more positive references to the *vaporcitos* because Pizacoma, where they had been, is mentioned a couple of times in the archival correspondence. Percy reported having met a *Señora* Dora Garnica who said she had known the story of the *Yavarí* since childhood and that she had seen bits of old iron on the road to Tarata. It was unclear whether she had seen them sixty years ago or yesterday, but in either case it was probably as fanciful as our dreams had been back in London to think they were parts of the *Yavarí*.

Although the precise information we sought was scarce on the trek, we did learn a lot about customs and modes of transport in the *sierra* both today and in the nineteenth century, and that we had chosen the right trails to follow. We also learned that the demography had changed in the last 150 years. In the 1800s it was common for *campesinos* to own their own herds and pass them down from generation to generation, or to work on a *hacienda* from cradle to grave, but the Agrarian Reform changed all that. Today, many *campesinos* prefer to look for work in the towns, so the companies that now own the herds employ anyone prepared to live the harsh life of the *altiplano*. This is likely to be one reason why the gunboat story didn't resonate with more people.

* * *

For the third leg of the journey our gentle giant Teodocio took over from Máximo as my chaperon and as pathfinder for our team, because the next rendezvous for all three teams was to be at his home.

He led us over a rocky escarpment which dropped away to make the Titicaca basin. We picked our way, or rather Moro picked our way, through gateways of stone monoliths the size of Stonehenge, over slippery boulders and past cacti and stunted shrubs. Still there was bird life and still the scenery was dramatic. I realised how incredibly lucky I was. The weather was more settled for this leg of the journey and by this time Moro and I had grown to know one another, so with Teo leading us and Moro treading carefully through the 'wild west' terrain I was able to gaze about me and enjoy the extraordinary privilege. More than that, I could chat and point things out to Moro. He was a pair of ears and, although I got little response, it was somehow more gratifying than talking to myself.

One night we stayed at a *hacienda* which had once owned thousands of hectares but, as the *haciendado* explained, at the time of the Agrarian Reform the government had parcelled up the majority of his property to make over to the *campesinos* and he had been left with 150 hectares.

'The Ministry of Agriculture had very little idea of the true value of the land,' said *Señor* Romero. 'They supposedly took the location and the fertility of the soil into account and came up with a number.' There was no argument, no come-back, he said. 'So we just had to get on with it. In fact, 150 hectares is not enough to run large herds of alpaca as we did before, so I now run a stud for breeding them.'

To judge from his appearance and his dilapidated *hacienda*, this market was clearly not as lucrative a business, and although he didn't complain *Señor* Romero looked wistful and weary.

'So *that* didn't stand me in very good stead.' he remarked ruefully, pointing at the foetus of a llama in a glass case. 'According to folklore, the foetus is considered to be an amulet of good luck. There's one buried in the corner of every Andean *chosa*.'

We had to agree that in this case it did not appear to have lived up to its reputation.

Señor Romero later explained that because of the Agrarian Reform the breeding stocks of both alpaca and the unique Peruvian trotting horse, *el caballo de paso,* had suffered drastically. In this falling market, the pure breeds had been snapped up by American stud owners who now controlled the best bloodlines. By degrees, he told us, Peruvian breeders have been buying back in an effort to restock and restore the tradition.

Peru may never fully recover from the Reform. It seems to an outsider like me that both landowners and *campesinos* lost out. Most landowners seem to agree that land reform was due but the way it was done bred deep bitterness and many took what money they had left out of the country. Like landowners anywhere in the world, some treated their labourers well, some abused them. Where the Reform fell down so badly was not in the concept but in the execution. No-one, least of all the government, appears to have taught the *campesinos* how to farm their own land; until then they had never been responsible for their own livelihood. Under the Incas they farmed for the state and under the Spanish they were either tied or dependent on the *hacienda* for employment, its school and its chapel and were probably in hock to its shop. Since Independence, except for those *serranos* who owned their own herds of camelids, the peasant worked for a landowner.

Following the Reform some co-operatives were started up, but Teo's experience is more common. *Campesinos* throughout the highlands farm small plots, some on the *altiplano* like Teo's, some in the valleys, and some up and down the steep terraced sides. According to the law of inheritance, property is divided between the heirs, so plots become smaller and more widely scattered over generations. For many, conditions are not conducive to making a living, even at subsistence level. It is small wonder that migration into the towns has become so constant.

When we reached Teo's home at Sacuyo, it was obvious why he was anxious to move his family to Puno. His home was an adobe shack like all the others we had seen, primitive, crude and bare. I was shocked. Because Teo had not been with us very long, I had only ever seen him on board in his *Yavarí* uniform. Now that I saw him in his own surroundings I realized that he, his wife and five children were living at the lowest of poverty levels.

His wife Anastasia cooked us *chuspé*, a typical Andean mutton stew, in a dented, blackened cauldron on the flickering flame of a single gas ring. Plastic plates were washed off under a tap outside. Some of us ate inside by the light of candles and a hurricane lamp, huddled up on the adobe ledge, aware of the guinea pigs scampering and squeaking underneath. The others sat on the wall outside under a night sky bright with stars sparkling like diamonds on black velvet in a jeweller's window. It was a tired but happy gathering.

We slept in what had once been the *hacienda*'s school which, like the chapel and the shop, was crumbling away. It was a sad sight. I tried to imagine it, like a remote tumbledown farmhouse in Europe, being snapped up as a 'weekend retreat' or by a foreigner wanting a retirement project. There have, indeed, been rumours of foreign companies buying up Peruvian land. I enjoyed that idea more than the one suggested to me by a Peruvian sage who envisaged Peru following the world trend and becoming an urban society, leaving the *sierra* forever.

As we approached our last overnight stopover at a solitary *chosa* on the trail, we were alarmed by ghastly bloodcurdling screams. Out of curiosity I involuntarily looked over in the direction of the hideously chilling sounds and immediately wished I hadn't. Two llamas were having their throats cut in preparation for the market on the morrow. I had witnessed a similar scene on a sheep station in Australia and knew that decapitation and skinning would quickly follow. I hurried off to unsaddle Moro.

The television crew met up with us and accompanied us on our last leg which took us to the edge of the *puna* looking down on Lake Titicaca. The water was dark and sparkling. It was the moment to imagine how this first sighting of the lake must have seemed to Partridge and his men. It was also a moment of triumph.

The expedition, which had taken us three weeks, was over. It had not thrown up as much evidence of the *Yavari*'s journey as I had hoped, but I put that down to the effects of the Chilean occupation, the demographic changes and the natural reserve of the Indians. Had we spent more nights intoxicating ourselves with them, we would probably have learned more. However, we learned a lot about the *modus vivendi* on the *altiplano*, we had seen a way of life that not many have seen and the uniquely robust people who live there, and most significantly of all we had experienced at first hand the gruelling conditions that made the *Yavari*'s delivery such an unparalleled achievement.

We know that we were on the trails commonly used in the nineteenth century. If we assume then that each *arriero* followed his preferred trail, which I think is reasonable, then it would be safe to conclude that a percentage of the *Yavari* and *Yapurá*'s 2,766 individual parts were carried over each of the three trails we had followed.

We might never have done it had Andrew not organised it and raised the sponsorship, but I wish that in the report he submitted to the Winston

Churchill Memorial Trust he had qualified the achievement with details of the distances that Partridge and we covered, and the altitudes we reached. He mentioned neither. It has always been my intention that the last leg of the journey, from Teo's '*hacienda*', where we had all rendezvoused for the last time, to the lake should become known as the 'Yavarí Trail' and recognized as such like the Inca Trail or the Pennine Way. Someone needs to walk it again in order to record its co-ordinates. Any volunteers? Please get in touch!

CHAPTER 15

Sailing, Slipping and
Going Aground Drill!

PERHAPS IT WAS LUCKY THAT HER guns never reached the *Yavarí* because in 1876 she was hijacked by Enrique Bustamante, a revolutionary on the run to Bolivia. He had joined Nicolas de Piérola in an attempt to overthrow President Mariano Ignacio Prado, who had himself caused such an uproar leading his own revolt in 1865. In time Piérola was to become president for two terms, but not before having to flee the country for his own safety. Bustamente, in his flight, found the *Yavarí* moored at the island of Soto in the north-eastern corner of the lake and, frightening the crew into submission, set sail for Bolivia where he grounded the ship and ran. She was later rescued and then sold by the navy to Don Guillermo Speedie on a ten-year contract which also obliged him, among other conditions, to dry-dock the *Yavarí* on a regular basis and to dredge the canal. He did neither, so the contract was cancelled. The ship was then made over to Don J.L. Thorndike, who was already heavily involved in developing the railways in southern Peru.

The railway from the coast, built by the 'Yankee Pirate' or 'Railway Messiah' Henry Meiggs, reached the lake in 1874 and one of the passengers on the first train to use the line was the American naturalist James Orton, who was so unimpressed with Puno. With the arrival of the train came the availability of coal. Although it is not noted, it must be assumed that the *Yavarí* switched over, but what *is* recorded is that as soon as the Peruvian Corporation took over running the fleet, they 'jumboised' her hull, cutting her in half and inserting another 50 feet. It is common practice today, but this was 1895 and represented truly cutting

Bolinder 4-cylinder hot bulb semi-diesel engine.

edge technology which the locals must have watched spellbound, as I'm sure they also did when the *Yapurá* was widened by three feet. At the same time, *La Peruvian* also built a new slipway and machine shops and commissioned the SS *Coya*.

The extra weight and length did not help the *Yavarí*'s old steam engine, which was already in a poor state of repair, so in 1914 it was decided to replace it with the latest marine engine – the Swedish-built Bolinder four-cylinder hot bulb crude oil engine.

Cleaning this 'collector's piece' was the next challenge that awaited us on return from the trek. In anticipation Máximo had charged me with bringing from England fourteen specific spanners including a set in sequence from 1⁵⁄₁₆ th inch to 1¹³⁄₁₆ th inch. I didn't know then that there is a lot more to spanners than the one I use to fix the saddle on my bike. Pre-war, post-war, Whitworth, British Standard fine thread and so on, to say nothing of American English or metric. Oh, yes – the subject has a language of its own! I settled for a series of second-hand pre-war Whitworths only to be found in a Government surplus depot. They were so heavy I had to squeeze out a tear of anguish when pleading my case with Gatwick's baggage handlers. At least I didn't have that problem with the three-inch glass cylinders also for the Bolinder. The difficulty in that case was finding a glassblower dedicated to making laboratory phials and pipettes and there are, or were then, only six left in the country.

Volvo had given us the money to strip the engine down, clean and restore it to full working order. We imagined we were but a heartbeat away from sailing out of the port for the first time in nearly fifty years, but there was a shock in store for us.

The crew now consisted of Máximo, Teodocio, Antonia Quispe, Tatu Zapana, Freddy Cahuana, Basilio Pacori, Julian González, Manuel Quispe the *watchiman*, occasional part-timers and Moro. Moro lived with us in the port on a diet of lake algae supplemented with carrots and apples until Teo took him back to the *altiplano* to live with his father. Tatu reminded me of Ronnie Corbett and was every bit as funny. Antonia was Teo's niece and also came from the rugged *altiplano*. Carlos recruited her and only learned later that she and Teo were related. Antonia was orphaned at the age of twelve when her parents were allegedly poisoned in a vendetta killing. It was too costly to hold an autopsy but circumstantial evidence left little doubt. Antonia, living at the same level of abject subsistence as her Uncle Teodocio, was left to fend for two brothers and two sisters, feeding them from a smallholding, clothing them and bringing them up. She had trouble fighting back the tears as she told me the story attesting to the hardship and pain which she had endured. She has never asked for sympathy, but her appreciation of the security and harmonious life on board the *Yavarí* has been obvious.

John Kusner, the eccentric American engineer, was by now in declining health, but he would visit to see what we were doing to 'his' engine. We stripped it down, every part being meticulously labelled and marked by Máximo before being stowed away somewhere on the ship. Once we had it stripped down, John came to see the condition of the crankshaft. Having already tested the engine successfully, neither he nor any of us expected to find any problem when he suggested turning the shaft manually for his inspection. He took his time to pronounce but when he did he stunned us. He said it was damaged.

Apparently the engine had been run without lubrication and the surface of the crankshaft had become rough to the touch, with hairline scratches. It needed to be smooth. We checked out all the workshops in Puno but none had the equipment necessary to sand or polish out the blemishes. Three marine engineers travelled up to Puno one after the other, at our request and expense, to examine the problem. Each one pronounced the same. The crankshaft would have to be removed and shipped to Lima, the only place in Peru with equipment capable of grinding a crankshaft of that size. According to all three of them, there was no other way. We baulked at the cost and we baulked at the risk to the crankshaft, bumping along on a low loader to Lima, and the possible effect its removal would have on the integrity of the *Yavarí*. There had to be another way.

A gloom settled on the ship but it didn't last long because nothing is impossible for the *Yavarí*. John and Máximo put their heads together and, using a Singer sewing machine motor, devised the cleverest of grinders for us to do our own grinding. We took it in shifts on our home-made sanding machine to pare down the almost imperceptible millimetres required to smooth the surface. Whoever was not masked and grinding was cleaning some other piece of the engine elsewhere or providing cold drinks and chocolate sponge biscuits to the workers. The process took three weeks and was declared an outstanding success. The next problem we faced was that the main bearings had been similarly damaged. They are lined with a soft white metal which, in the *Yavarí's* case, had been scarred. According to John, speaking in his slow mellifluous American voice, 'We need to find some Babbitt metal to reline these bearings.' I had no idea what he was talking about and until I came to write this book I assumed the word was Babette. The American Isaac Babbitt invented a soft-metal antifriction alloy in 1839 to prevent wear on load-bearing surfaces. (Yes, I've learned a lot over the years about naval engineering! I wish I thought it would be useful to me from now on.) Pure Babbitt metal, which would be ideal for our Bolinder, was going to be difficult to find because the custom in Peru is to adulterate it to make it go further. We imagined it would be the same story in Bolivia but we looked there anyway, and Giselle searched in all the shipyards and workshops in Callao.

We were on the point of ordering it from Britain when a local mechanic appeared at the gangplank carrying two bricks of pure Babbitt metal inscribed 'Made in England'. He had found them in a corner of his workshop. We presumed they had come out from England with one of the ships; they were exactly what we needed.

We employed the retired shipwrights who had worked for ENAFER (the state-owned railway company) who took ownership of the lake fleet when it was nationalised in 1972, but we had to quicken their pace. They were used to working at a state railway pace, whereas we had a deadline. We had to be ready for the arrival of Per Fonser from Sweden, the birthplace of the Bolinder. Per was a self-taught Bolinder expert, and after a ten-year correspondence we had at last arranged for him to visit. He had earmarked three weeks' leave from his regular job and timed it to coincide with our having completed the rebuilding of the engine. He was expecting to tweak a few levers, fine tune a few valves and set sail. I collected him from Juliaca airport, but didn't dare tell him exactly what state the engine was in. When he looked into the engine room his face turned to the colour of chalk, and it was not because of the altitude. It was shock. All there was to show for the precious Bolinder, which he had travelled half the world to see, was a naked crankshaft.

Once he had absorbed the impact and realised that before he tweaked anything, he would have to help us rebuild the engine from scratch, he turned his heart and soul to the task. Without a word of Spanish, but with his flair for leadership, engineering knowledge and plain enthusiasm, he masterminded the cleaning of every part and the subsequent rebuild in just three weeks.

On the eve of his departure he told us that we could sail on the morrow, but that we should know the risks of breaking down. He gave us a choice: either we could continue tinkering after he had gone to iron out likely glitches, or we could take the risk and sail. I looked around at the expectant faces of our crew and said, 'We will sail'.

We borrowed from the navy their helmsman, five sailors to make up the crew numbers, life jackets and various other pieces of essential equipment. Early the following morning our strongest members turned the flywheel and lined up the pistons before we fired up the Bolinder's cylinder heads with kerosene blowtorches. The roar of the naked flames sounded like an angry dragon breathing fire. After a forty-minute warm up, Per gave the signal for the injection of compressed air and, with a mighty *phumph*, we had lift-off.

In passing, I should point out that this engine is the largest and oldest of its kind in the world and we have known grown men cry when they see, smell and hear it in action.

We did our own crying when one day the telephone rang and an anonymous caller offered us two of the Bolinder's three missing blow torches for a price. We ground our teeth, negotiated and paid. Maxi spotted the other one in the flea market but, unfortunately, he didn't spot the two candle lanterns for reading the compass at night missing from the binnacle. One subsequently reappeared, if we were prepared to pay for it, and in contrast, a kind visitor, Trevor Chambers, volunteered to make us the other one.

For the first time in nearly fifty years, the *Yavarí* sailed out of the port under her own steam, belching vapour at first black then grey, then white then back to black, and then white again. The locals looked on amazed, and the mocking from the skeleton crew on the SS *Ollanta* finally fell silent.

We had to bear in mind the conditions attached to the permission to sail as made clear to us by the captain of the naval base. We only had permission to go as far as 'the first buoy'. The first buoy was within 300 yards of the jetty. Even if we had tried, we could not have stopped in such a short distance. The next buoy marked the entrance to the channel out of Puno Bay and into the lake. At this point it was much too narrow for us to turn. Carlos, Per and I exchanged glances with each other and then with the navy helmsman, who nodded. Without a word, we motored on. We could worry later about explaining to the port captain why we had disobeyed his orders.

We spent two glorious hours 'at sea' testing our speeds, going astern, going full ahead and basking in the admiration of the tourists in their motor launches heading for the islands. Although there was still work to do to perfect the engine's performance we were jubilant, and as we sailed back into port we raised the signal flags 'Bravo Zulu', meaning 'Well Done', and rejoiced. Still in overalls, with no time to change, Carlos, the crew and I squeezed into a taxi with Per and, with dangerous haste, reached the airport just in time to pipe him through the departure gate bound for Sweden and home.

* * *

Our next guest was Christopher Hobson, an architect of note for his experience in designing for luxury yachts and trains. It was our ambition that the *Yavarí* should be able to cruise on the lake for two or three days, which meant converting the empty hold into luxury cabins for twenty passengers, with a shower and loo in each. Christopher came up with minutely detailed designs with reading lights over each bunk, a shower pod that doubled up as the loo and a hook to hang a dressing gown on, but try as we might to fit them into the very limited space, besides taxing Christopher's patience to its utmost, we simply could not and had eventually to abandon the idea. Of course, it would still be nice to do but we mustn't be distracted by such thoughts when we haven't yet achieved day cruising.

Two events marked 2000 as a momentous year. The first was the resignation of President Alberto Fujimori. His *éminence grise*, Vladimiro Montesinos, had been rumbled for grievous crimes of corruption and money-laundering and was on the run. Fujimori declared that he knew nothing of any of it and left to attend an international meeting in Japan. He faxed his resignation from there. Peru was thunderstruck. Puno, in particular, was thrown into a state of bewilderment. Puneños loved *El Chino*, as they called him although he was Japanese, as much as they had once loved Alan Garcia. Each president in turn makes a point of endearing himself to Puno. It is a critical constituency because it is a frontier district, because it is poor and because both the Aymaras and the Quechuas are important people to please, since they can be very troublesome when they are displeased. During a presidential campaign, a lot of time and energy is spent making friends with Puno and it seems to pay off. It was therefore a double disillusionment, when 'their' Alan Garcia let them and the country down so badly, followed by 'their' *El Chino* resigning so suddenly and ignominiously.

The other momentous event was taking the *Yavarí* out of the water for the first time in more than forty years. The condition on which Orient Express, by this time deeply invested in Peru's southern railways, would allow us to use the slipway in Puno was that we restore the 100-year-old boiler, steam winch and flat bed.

We tackled the boiler first. It was a locomotive boiler standing at least 12 feet high and 15 feet long. The hole through which to shovel the coal was only just big enough for our diminutive comedian, Tatu, to crawl through. The butt of many good-natured jokes about his size, Tatu now came into his own and was able to clean the inside of the boiler thoroughly. It was a disagreeable job, which he did with his usual good cheer. The boiler hadn't been used for at least ten years so we were wary of just how much we should dismantle and clean, and how much we should leave well alone. The safety valve was a case in point. From England we were being advised to dismantle and clean it; otherwise, if the valve didn't open we would be blown to Bolivia in the explosion. The locals, on the other hand, were advising us that since it had worked perfectly well last time it had been used ten years before, it was much better to leave it alone.

We did leave it alone, but were cautious when it came to building up the pressure. As we watched, the hand on the pressure gauge crept up from 20 pounds to 30, then 40, then 70. A nail-biting moment. But 70 was not enough to haul the *Yavarí* out of the water – it had to be at least 90 pounds. We stoked with coal and flung the water in as the tension and pressure mounted until – hooray! – we had reached 90 pounds and hadn't yet been blown away. The words 'Bravo Zulu' came easily to mind.

We had then to repair the flat bed and its short railway down the slipway to the water and build the *Yavarí's* own cradle to her hull's exact measurements. This is a skilled job because if you get it wrong, the ship falls off the flat bed. We were taking no chances and soon ran to ground the cradle specialist who had worked for ENAFER, when they owned the lake fleet. He was easily coaxed out of retirement to demonstrate his expertise in measuring, cutting and fitting the wooden blocks which would hold the *Yavarí* firmly in position. The Scottish winch (1893) was such a quality piece of machinery that it only needed a wipe over with an oily rag and it worked beautifully.

However, the water level of the lake was so low that year that, having got the *Yavarí* into position to be hauled out, we couldn't push the cradle out far enough to get it beneath her hull. A friend with a jeep tried to push it out but couldn't, so Carlos went off to the 'labour exchange', a traffic roundabout where casual labourers congregate, and gathered up twenty of the strongest to push it out to its optimum distance. There was only one snag – they refused to take off their trousers to wade into the lake. Born to lead, Carlos was down to his underpants in moments, and without so much as a gasp trotted into the glacial waters of the lake to set an example. The men cheered but were left with no choice but to follow. They looked sheepishly in my direction and then, accompanied by much embarrassed laughter, slowly downed their trousers and tiptoed in behind Carlos.

The *Yavarí* was in position; the flat bed and cradle were in position. It only remained for us to bring the pressure of the boiler up to strength, but because this took several hours we decided to sleep on site and start stoking it at 3 a.m. It was cold lying *al fresco* under the stars, so around midnight I retired to the warmth of the machine shop and found a piece of greasy cardboard to slip between Teo and the winch as my 'mattress'. At 3 a.m. we began stoking up the boiler. The needle on the pressure gauge moved slowly but steadily from 60 pounds to 70, and by 7 a.m. had reached 90 pounds which, from the dummy run, we knew was enough. Maxi set the levers for the winch to start hauling. I was afraid the cable might snap because the *Yavarí*, lying about 40 yards from the water's edge, did not want to move. Then, almost imperceptibly, we could see her bow inch forward. As she rose out of the water there was a gasp of horror. She was in her cradle, but lying at an angle. With some trepidation we carried on hauling, but I must say I was relieved when the winch was switched off and she was safely wedged either side on her blocks.

We sandblasted the hull and tested it for weak spots with the ultrasonic meter. It was at this point that we were bamboozled by the 'slag' in the iron. The meter gave us feverish readings which oscillated so many millimetres between frames and strakes as to completely undermine our confidence in our assessments. According to our reading of the meter, only small patches appeared to be less than regulation thickness. Cyberspace filled with figures and instructions as we sought advice from our knowledgeable contacts in the port of Callao and the UK, but to our surprise the expert diagnosis turned out to confirm our findings. Even after so many years in the water, only three small patches had to be cut out and replaced. We cluttered cyberspace once more to establish how to insert patches into an iron hull. As luck would have it, around the slipway lay a surfeit of old iron which was handy, but the nub of the problem was how to weld iron to iron. We learned soon enough that no purist would ever do such a thing. But we had no option. To resolve the issue, we found ourselves conducting another cyber-debate about the rights and wrongs of welding iron. I can hear Tim Parr's voice to this day: 'Steel is welded; iron is riveted or bolted'. He was adamant, but the Puñenos were only offering to weld.

Eventually a specific welding material was chosen, and we went ahead to break with all known practice and weld iron to iron. Well, it satisfied the Peruvian Maritime Authority who inspected the hull and presented us with their certificate of approval. Indeed, so far the patches have remained watertight and the *Yavarí* has remained afloat. When it becomes dangerous is welding near rivets, and it's often impossible to avoid them. They heat up then cool, and become loose and no longer watertight.

Carlos supervised the works. My job was principally to anticipate our needs, buoy up morale, serve refreshments, chat up our contractors, inspect the work, keep a photographic and written record, and pay the bills.

We were doing just that when there was a heart-chilling cry. Tatu had fallen off a ladder. He was unconscious. Carlos and I managed to get him into a taxi and rushed him to the hospital five miles away while Máximo ran off to fetch his wife, Agrapina. It was a Saturday and the doctor who was supposed to be on duty was nowhere to be seen. After a shameful delay we contacted him on his mobile. Tatu, by this time, was dying. He had had a stroke, and whether or not a quicker response might have saved him, we shall never know. Agrapina got to his bedside just in time, and Tatu died later that day. Carlos and I were already enraged by the poor attention he received, so when they simply slung a sheet round Tatu's body and stuck it in a shed to free up the bed, Carlos was almost at the doctor's throat.

We were desperately saddened by this loss. Tatu was the yeast in the bread, always cheerful, funny, kind and hardworking, and his passing left a gaping chasm in our team.

Immediately, though, we had to pay the bills at the hospital, look after Agrapina who appeared confused with shock, record Tatu's death with the coroner, and make arrangements for his funeral.

So nothing could have surprised me more than, as I was waiting for Carlos outside the morgue, suddenly to find myself surrounded by a dozen or more belligerent Indian *señoras* led by Agrapina. They were blaming me for Tatu's death and demanding that I cover all the expenses of his funeral, declaring that in Peru the employer was responsible for everything. I didn't know whether this was true or not and felt a natural inclination to agree, but Peruvian law can get foreigners into deep water. Instead, I did my best to placate the volatile women until Carlos reappeared. He told them to stop harassing me and that we would speak to them later.

It turned out that it was not my responsibility but we made a generous contribution anyway, and the crew acted as pallbearers. We processed slowly through the town to the cemetery collecting many mourners on the way. It was no surprise that Tatu had been much loved.

We restored our friendship with Agrapina, and on the anniversary of Tatu's death we were invited to a feast to mark the day and make many votive offerings to the gods for the safekeeping of his soul.

Much subdued, we finished our work on the *Yavarí* and returned her to her berth in time for a veteran car rally to use her as their staging and check-in post. They had driven from Brazil, through the rainforest, Argentina and Bolivia, and were aspiring like mad by the time they reached our altitude. The contestants included a 1946 Chevrolet, a

Packard, an Austin Westminster, a 1950s low-slung Jaguar and an Alvis. They were accompanied by a team of 4x4s who were also rallying, but spent a lot of their time towing the old veterans out of trouble.

* * *

Whenever I returned to London I reported to the Trustees. On this occasion, they wished to 'report' to me. I had already lost one and our trusty treasurer; now two of the remaining three Trustees felt it was time to stand down. They reasoned, gently, that when they had agreed to become Trustees they had thought it was for four or five years, not thirteen, as indeed had I. In fact, recently I came across a note from one to another which said, 'This project has the smell of decay about it'. That was written in 1995, and their resignation was in 2000! I thanked them warmly, and Tony Morrison, for sticking with it, and ran home to find my address book.

While visiting the *Yavari* with his wife Christine, Peter Lea made the fatal mistake of letting slip that he was an accountant *and* owned an oldish narrow boat equipped with a Kelvin engine – i.e. he was a veteran boat enthusiast. He was the natural person for me to ring. Then Hallam Murray, who cycled from California to Tierra del Fuego passing along 'the wrong' side of Lake Titicaca, made a similar mistake, saying, 'If I can ever do anything to help, please do let me know,' surely imagining I never would. John Illman, the British Ambassador who had inaugurated the *Yavari* as a museum in 1998, was by this time retired, but he most kindly agreed to sign on, as did David Harris, retired Commander in the Royal Navy where he trained as a shipwright, and had since become curator of HMS *Victory,* and then HMS *Belfast.* He and his wife Ishbel had also fallen under the *Yavari's* spell and, when asked, he said 'Yes'. Lesley Alexander took over from Simon as treasurer.

I was thrilled with this new team. They all had relevant experience and were enthusiastic and, most of all, encouraging. Over the years, the role of a trustee has become more accountable and now brings with it a heavier burden of fiscal and moral responsibilities. They need to keep a close eye on the workings of the charity and its director and I have been so lucky to have their support.

* * *

In 2001 we signed a deal with the Sonesta Posada Hotel situated alongside the slipway to build a pontoon at the rear of their hotel for visitors to access the *Yavarí*. This marked a graduation from the shelter of the port to securing the ship to buoys (oil drums attached to sunken cement blocks made by the crew) and being moored as opposed to berthed. A moment, thought Carlos, to drill the crew in 'man overboard' procedure and life saving. I had brought life jackets from England (heavily discounted) but was not planning to put one on. Instead, I watched as Carlos lined the crew up on the upper deck and, holding his nose, leapt off shouting "JUMP!" to his devoted crew. As a people, the Aymaras do not like swimming and Antonia, for one, had never been in water before, least of all polluted water, but they jumped. I was so, so thankful that my age and seniority were enough for me to be excused.

It then became clear that we had reached the stage when we needed detailed advice as to how to modify the vessel but at the same time retain her authenticity. Rightly or wrongly, we felt that what was required was outside the ken of the local engineers. We needed the on-site participation of a more experienced naval engineer or architect, who could advise us and the Peruvian engineers on how to comply with SOLAS without losing the ship's historic character, approve the technical drawings and, finally, supervise the work.

I put out a *cri de cœur* through a marine engineering journal. Some months had gone by, and I had given up hope, when I received an e-mail from a retired Lloyds surveyor called Adrian Chapman. He was curious about the project. From that moment he didn't stand a chance; within months we had flown him out from his quiet retirement in the Philippines and he was ensnared.

Adrian had surveyed fleets of ships, new and old, cargo and passenger in his time and he had worked a lot in the developing world. He was patient over language differences and sensitive to problems arising from lack of experience or the limited choice of materials and equipment. His experience stood us in good stead and with his help we prepared a set of fifty drawings and specifications in Spanish, which, following his visit, flew through cyberspace from the engineer's office in Lima to his home in the Philippines and to Tim Parr in Cornwall. This may sound simple and efficient, but the truth was nowhere near either. Neither of them lived within a country mile of a computer sophisticated enough to download the architectural drawings; neither of them found the Spanish engineering jargon easy to read; and neither of them agreed with the other on the proposed modifications anyway. They were both word-perfect on the SOLAS regulations but their approaches were diametrically opposed. Tim begrudged any change which compromised the *Yavari*'s authenticity while Adrian welcomed any compromise which was practical and meant we could get the job done. The challenge for me was to keep the peace between them, so whether I was in Peru or Putney it was vital to intercept and edit their e-mails to one another. It was diplomacy with a capital D.

Besides his extensive professional capabilities, Adrian was a lifelong bird watcher and his contribution to our knowledge of the birds on the lake and on the *salinas* lakes in the Western Cordillera was as much of a benefit as his prowess as a surveyor. One day, just as we were going ashore, right beside the pontoon he heard a twitter and stopped dead.

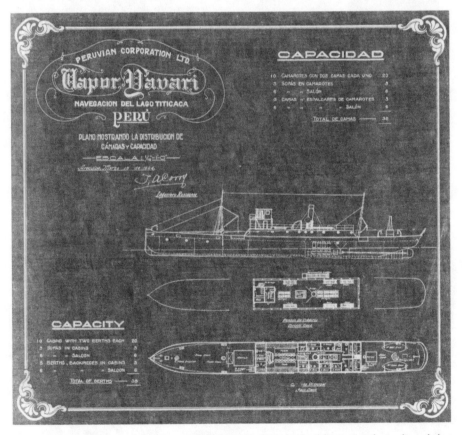

General arrangement of the *Yavari* dated 1927 after she had been 'jumboised' and the steam engine replaced by the Bolinder in 1914.

'There it is, there it is!' he whispered urgently, and there indeed was the multicoloured or seven-coloured tanager, as small as a robin but brilliantly coloured. What a joy, and to think how many times we had passed this spot and would never have known had it not been for Adrian's expert ear and eye.

Our intention has always been to modify the *Yavarí* to comply with international safety regulations and to meet the standards of comfort expected by today's discerning traveller. The original *Yavarí* was 100 feet long, a steam sailer with a bowsprit. It would be impossible to recapture that first 'incarnation'. Our ambition is to restore her to her 1920s incarnation, after she was 'jumboised' but before she was vandalised in the 1950s to serve as a tanker. We agree with our tourism consultant, Yasmine Martin, that the vessel deserves to become an up-market

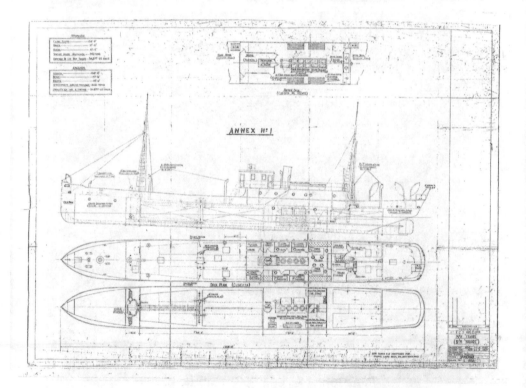

General arrangement of the *Yavarí* dated 1957 after being converted to a tanker.

boutique passenger ship for day cruises but such modifications need money.

When a potential investor, VIP, film maker or journalist expresses a wish to sail in the *Yavarí* we are happy to use the occasion to carry out engine trials and deck drill. Such an opportunity arose, organised by Yasmine, when it seemed appropriate to invite Per Fonser and Adrian to join us. We took advice from Adrian to ballast the *Yavarí* to make her sit better in the water.

In his customary way, Carlos left it to the very last moment to move the ship across to the port to embark the ballast. No amount of nagging made the slightest difference. With only days to spare before a group of important tour operators, and Peru's top television travel documentary presenter Rafo Leon, were due to arrive, he ordered a mountain of sand to be delivered to the quay. We motored over and tied up alongside, and Carlos disappeared to the labour exchange.

The next day, twenty strapping labourers reported for work. By day's end, they, Carlos and Antonia had shovelled sand into 1,334 canvas bags so that each one weighed exactly 66 pounds, tied them up with string, and humped them from the quayside into the hold of the ship, making a grand total of forty-four tons of ballast. When I saw little Antonia shouldering bags weighing 66 pounds I felt so ashamed I had to offer to help. I hoped they would say 'No, thank you', but no – I was told I could do the string-tying bit. A sop to the boss and easy, you would think, but not with nylon string and fingers like sausages. The bags stacked up so quickly behind me that I was soon mocked into early retirement, but I overcame my shame and returned to taking photographs of the workers. The result of loading the ballast was a remarkable improvement in the line, look and performance of the *Yavarí*.

Adrian and Per duly arrived and we sailed out of the harbour on engine trials. We notched up nine knots, the same as is recorded in the 1921 logbook. The hours of dedicated tinkering, cleaning and fine-tuning of the Bolinder engine had paid off. The vapour issuing out of the funnel was translucent, the beat of the engine even, the sky was blue and all was extremely well with the world. We patted each other on the back, hoisted the signal 'Bravo Zulu', and cracked open a bottle to celebrate.

When it was time to turn for home we motored back through the channel and turned to starboard towards the pontoon where we tie up. We rounded the marker buoy and, as usual, lined the ship up with the edge of the pontoon's floating platform prior to cutting the engine and gliding in alongside.

I was standing on the upper deck and heard Captain Carlos ring the telegraph to the engine room to reduce speed. Nothing happened. We sailed on towards the pontoon. I became concerned but had every confidence that captain and crew knew what they were doing. Then I heard Carlos ringing the telegraph urgently, three times, ordering 'Full Astern!' but still nothing happened; on we sailed.

By this time, we were almost alongside the pontoon. The shore was only 100 yards beyond it. As the pontoon came up on the port side and we sailed past it, I knew that nothing could save us – we were going to run aground. Carlos had now run back to the engine room skylight and, directing his loud hailer at the luckless crew below, was shouting 'Full Astern!' as if our lives depended on it, which it felt as though they did. The rest of us stood on deck in a state of unbelief at what was happening, either paralysed or, in my case, shouting my lungs out. From where I stood I could see that we were just going to miss the stern of the *Coya*, the 1895 ship-restaurant beached in the mud, but behind her was a man exactly in line with our bow. He was bent over in front of a brick wall with his back to the water, and was obviously unaware of the impending danger. I shouted and shouted, but he didn't hear and he didn't move. I could see it all vividly playing out in my mind – first scraping past the *Coya*'s stern, then killing the man, and finally crashing into the brick wall. From that moment of alarm, everything happened quickly. The engine was still 'full steam ahead', as we drove into the mud and came to an abrupt halt. It was a heart-stopping moment. We were aground. But we had missed the *Coya* and we had missed the man and the brick wall; in fact, we had slipped in so quietly, the man didn't even look up.

One moment we had been celebrating our success and patting ourselves on the back, the next we were looking just about as foolish as it is possible for a ship to look.

We took stock. We had to get off as quickly as possible before our keel sank irretrievably into the mud and, more importantly, before anyone saw us as, for sure, it would have been a scoop for the local press. We put out an SOS to the navy. Ideally they would have sent over the *Yavarí*'s sister ship, the BAP *Puno*, but alas, she was out on one of her bi-monthly exercises, so they sent a patrol boat. By the time it reached us, the *Yavarí* had well and truly settled in the mud and, pull as they might, there was no way of budging her. We didn't panic, but we were becoming quietly alarmed. Apart from the obvious reasons for needing to get off was the thought of the television presenter with his camera crew finding us there.

We held a wardroom conference to formulate a plan of campaign. Some relief came when night fell and darkness hid us and our red faces from view. Come first light, Carlos set off for the labour exchange once more. He returned with more men and with launches, and gave out the orders.

His plan was straightforward. 'By midday', he addressed the men, 'I want every bag of sand taken out of the hold and put into a launch.' He paused for that to sink in. 'Then we expect to pull the *Yavarí* off so that once she's free and floating again, you can re-load the bags.'

The men went to work while we sent ashore for refreshments, and by 10.30 a.m. the *Yavarí* was empty of ballast. Ropes were tied to strategic points on board and on shore and all the men pulled, but the *Yavarí* did not want to move. Her keel was well and truly embedded in the mud.

Adrian had the answer. All the men were to run at once from side to side, heeling the hull over as they did so, to let water in and release the suction of the mud. It worked! The *Yavarí* slid back into the water, the 1,334 bags of sand were re-loaded, and we were back at our pontoon by midday and the arrival of the VIPs.

It could all have been planned as a 'going aground' exercise. When people ask 'What happened?' I tell them that if the blame lay with the Bolinder it would cast aspersions on the engine, and if I said it was human error it would not be fair on the engine room crew. So there is no answer, but the practice was good for all of us.

Among the passengers for the VIP voyage were Robert Munro and his wife Rosemary, the first fare-paying passengers in the *Yavarí's* new life. They had come over from Paraguay out of curiosity to see the *Yavarí* which had been just a twinkle in my eye when we worked together at ALAF, the Anglo-Latin American Fiesta, in the early 1990s. We sailed out to and around Taquile Island, some 20 miles away. Robert loved it and saw the *Yavarí* being the principal attraction in Puno once she was able to take passengers sailing. He was so enthusiastic, as well as being bi-lingual in Spanish and a former banker, that I couldn't resist asking him if he would help us to get her sailing. He joined us as a Trustee and has been invaluable to me and the project ever since.

CHAPTER 16

Changes All Round

FOR SO MANY YEARS WE HAD focused our attentions solely on the *Yavarí,* and now I felt it was high time to look at matters outstanding which had been put to one side. One such matter was bringing closure to the life and death of George Blaxland, the young shipwright who accompanied the *Yavarí* from England in 1862 and who died in February 1864 just a few months after arriving in Puno. I knew from the archives that his body was buried on Esteves Island but had never discovered exactly where. I took Carlos and the crew with me to clear away the undergrowth and after some searching we found his simple unmarked grave of roughly cut stone slabs. We weeded and cleaned it and ordered a brass plaque to be inscribed with his details and association with the *Yavarí.* Then we invited the British Ambassador, Richard Ralph, to come up and unveil it. We performed a short ceremony to mark the passing of this young man so far from home and then, to the emotive strains of the bosun's whistle playing the Last Post, the Ambassador removed the Union flag from the plaque and laid a floral tribute. It was a strangely moving affair.

* * *

After 9/11 a friend offered me a 'friends and family' fare on a cruise to Antarctica. Such was the give-away that I could afford to invite Carlos to come with me so that he could see how a real cruise ship was run. We travelled overland from Puno to Ushaia in Argentina, stopping on the way at the Bay of Angamos to see where Comandante Miguel Grau, in command of the *Huascar,* had so gallantly fought and died in the War of the Pacific. The bay is now in Chile, a little way north of Antofagasta, and not conspicuous in any way, yet it was an enlightening experience to envisage where the Commander's final battle took place. For months Miguel Grau harried the Chilean navy, thereby distracting Chile from launching their land campaign into Peru, but on that fateful day, 8 October 1877, he found himself cornered. He fought to his death, and seeing where he actually died reinforced my appreciation of his bravery and his status as a national hero.

Since our visit, a plaque in his name has been unveiled at Cammel Laird's shipyard at Birkenhead, where the *Huascar* was built.

When we arrived on board the *Marco Polo* we discovered that the Captain had been informed that I was a ship owner (wrong) and Carlos was my captain. Thenceforth we were treated as royalty, with champagne, tours of the ship, crew's areas and engine room included, and whenever whales were spotted we were called over the PA system to hurry to the bridge.

The voyage was memorable for Antarctica, of course, but also for the honour and fun of sitting at the Captain's table for the only Captain's Dinner of the voyage. Carlos was pestered the next day by passengers wanting to know who the woman was on the Captain's right. He told them it was 'hush hush', but that I was President Fujimori's Head of the Secret Service and responsible for Peru's security. My reason for being in Antarctica was to carry out a reconnaissance of the Chilean and Argentine bases on the continent. It was such a silly story but made us laugh ridiculously because some people actually believed it!

The *Yavarí* and I enjoyed sixteen years with Captain Carlos. I owe him a tribute for being willing and capable of taking full responsibility for the ship and her crew and for entertaining the many thousands of international tourists who have visited the ship over the years. His professional competence made the project possible and his charm and wit made me laugh so hard and so much as to make the darker moments of the struggle actually seem worthwhile. When he came to leave to go exploring the Ancient World, we gathered his friends for one last sail. I was especially happy that Trustee Ellie, on crutches but dismissive of shipboard hazards, came all the way from Lima. As my oldest friend in Peru I have long enjoyed and learnt from her sideways look at life and its foibles. On return to port we lowered Carlos's commissioning pennant from the masthead. The deck was awash with tears when, after all the speeches were done, he bequeathed his naval sword to the *Yavarí*, took the salute and, for the last time, was piped ashore in the traditional naval way which he would expect.

This presented a natural watershed. It was time to look again at why we had been unable to fulfil Carlos's dream of captaining his own ship and entertaining his passengers at the Captain's table. We had presented several proposals to companies principally within the tourist industry and had been encouraged to get excited but then, for various reasons, been let down with a thud of disappointment. There were still a couple of proposals to which we were awaiting responses, but I no longer allowed myself to anticipate good news. Then one day we had a call from Ecuador, a follow-up call from two female directors of a high profile tour company who had visited the *Yavari* earlier in the year; Carlos had taken them out for a sail. Apparently they had been charmed by the *Yavari* and probably by Carlos as well. They were calling to invite further discussions. In spite of my resolve not to get excited, I couldn't help myself. I saw as many signs of Divine intervention as I did omens and auguries, lucky black cats, silver linings and the rainbow's end. It felt good, it felt right. The company had an excellent reputation, was financially sound, understood ships, was looking to expand its interests beyond Ecuador and, most compelling of all, they had experienced Lake Titicaca and the *Yavari* performing.

Our tourism consultant Yasmine Martin and financial advisor Robert Munro and I flew to Quito. We were quizzed in fine detail at the meeting but we answered well and came away with a positive feeling. We felt we had acquitted ourselves more than adequately and that, if we made one or two adjustments and compromises, we could expect a proposal of marriage. We celebrated in Quito's Plaza Mayor which, having recently emerged from years under scaffolding and dustsheets, looked spectacular. It is a jewel of colonial architecture and one of the first sites ever to be recognized as a UNESCO Cultural Heritage Site. Its beauty and the emphasis it gives to the value of history and conservation suited our mood perfectly. We saluted one and drank to the other.

We returned to our respective desks to amend our proposal. I was sure that this was the joint venture that had always been intended for us. All that had gone before had been in preparation for this moment. The *Yavari*'s five-star quality and potential, her location in Peru, and Lake Titicaca's popularity as a destination all pointed towards us signing a contract any day soon.

'Any day soon' never came, like so many hopes that had been dashed before by the *Sendero,* El Niño, political unrest, landslips, bad publicity, road blocks and demonstrations. This time it was a global recession crashing around our ears. Banks foreclosed, holidays were cancelled and, at a stroke, our dreams were over. The company pulled in its horns and we stowed away the *Yavarí*'s 'Bravo Zulu' signal flags that we had ready to hoist in celebration.

I put the collapse of our negotiations down to the recession but perhaps that was the excuse. Perhaps there was something more fundamentally wrong? Maybe I'd been at it too long and could no longer see things objectively. Yet I was still so convinced of the *Yavarí*'s potential. She has earned media coverage and publicity around the world and the Visitors' Book is rich in signatures and plaudits from national and foreign dignitaries, ambassadors, film makers, journalists, television presenters and even a Russian Naval Attaché who loved the *Yavarí* so much he bequeathed his naval cap to her as a memento. In 1910 Hiram Bingham sailed in her and I had no doubt that many more important passengers would visit the old ship and, one day, sail in her. I was also confident that the *Yavarí* would make a serious social contribution, as was always intended. As a Victorian maritime museum she has much to tell the children of Lake Titicaca, about Peruvian and English history and the close links between the two. As the 'grandmother' of the lake fleet she also has a responsibility for the lake's protection and conservation. The shoreline of this valuable source of fresh water has already been and continues to be polluted by human effluent and, more threateningly, by the mercury tailings washed in from the informal mines. It is now urgent to alert the lakeside communities to the far reaching and damning affects of contamination. The *Yavarí* is an ideal vehicle to broadcast the word.

All this seemed so obvious to me. I examined again the ways in which, over the years, we had sought but been unable to raise the funding. Was it, I wondered, because a First World trust was seeking funding for a Developing World project? Would an appeal come better from the Developing World project direct? Was I personally at fault? Had I got so lost in the trees that I could no longer see the wood? Was the Anglo side a deterrent? Maybe the *Yavarí* was just too old. As a museum she is interesting, romantic and nostalgic, but perhaps too risky as a long-term venture for a sponsor or investor.

The project had attracted the support of generous individuals and some organisations but none that would commit to undertaking the modifications. It was now twenty-three years since Tim Parr and I lunched together in London's Soho pizzeria, when he had told me that the project to restore the *Yavari* to full working order was likely to take, at the outside, four years. Where did we, or I, go wrong? Why did I envy Carlos, hanging his captain's cap on the hook and walking away? It was a bad sign. I had become weary and stale. I no longer enjoyed the responsibility, I no longer wanted to be introduced at parties as 'Meriel owns a boat on Lake Titicaca! Imagine that!' I didn't own the *Yavarí* and I was tired of denying it and then having to tell the *Yavarí* story, again. I was also sickened by my auto-response to meeting new people. My first thought was always, 'Is this person likely to be able to help us in any way?' The obsession was automatic. I longed not to have to worry any more.

When I confessed these thoughts to my UK Trustees they were sympathetic and we discussed what seemed like the most appropriate option. After all, Peru's economy was strong: mining, fishmeal and fruit & veg were producing an average annual growth of 7% in their GNP, while Great (?) Britain was, in company with most of the rest of the world, heading downhill fast into a global recession. Was it not time for us to suggest to the Peruvian *Socios* that they take on more of the responsibility for the short-term day-to-day running of the ship and also for raising the necessary finance to carry out the modifications?

I felt strongly that Peru was better off than Britain and that, for everyone's sake, it was time for me to hand over the baton. I recalled Saint Paul admonishing the Corinthians for arguing over whether it was better to listen to him or to his colleague Apollos. He explains that each of us has been assigned *a* task. He says, 'I planted the seed, Apollos watered it, but God made it grow.' I interpreted this as meaning that, figuratively speaking, I had planted the seed of the *Yavarí*'s revival and that it was now time for others to take it on, to 'water it'.

With Carlos's departure it was time to consider how best to move forward. We didn't announce that he was leaving until it was necessary but, on the quiet, we interviewed one or two possible replacements. They did not come anywhere near the mark, but then the mark he had made was high and indelible. It was going to be extremely difficult to find anyone to replace him. Platitudes like 'no-one is irreplaceable' rang hollow until, quite out of the blue, the most unlikely person in the world put their name forward.

Giselle, our Administrator, offered herself as an interregnum captain.

She would go up to Puno and take charge for six months. After all, she had her Master's Ticket, experience in naval engineering and, having accompanied each of our several visiting firemen to the ship, had a very thorough knowledge of the *Yavarí*. But Giselle was a Limeña. Her clothes, her accent, her jargon and her activities were emphatically those of the capital city. First of all, how would she adapt to the unglamorous life in Puno and, equally questionable, how would the people of Puno adapt to her? The people of the *sierra* don't much like the people from anywhere else, least of all from Lima, and how would our crew take to working for a woman and a Limeña at that? Doubts surrounded Giselle's exceptionally kind offer, but we accepted it with gratitude.

We met in Lima. Giselle was appointed temporary captain and, on hearing my arguments outlined above, the *Socios* of *La Asociación Yavarí* agreed to take on the management of the ship and search for the long-term financing. I was delighted to hear how enthusiastic they were and how positive they were about the *Yavarí*'s commercial potential. Their approach to the long term, however, was different. Before propositioning their friends and contacts to invest, they wished to show proof of the ship's earning capacity. They wanted first to upgrade the ship's interior and offer Bed & Breakfast on board. This would both produce an income quickly and impress potential investors.

I saw the idea as a distraction from the main objective, but said nothing. If they were now in charge it was better to agree with their initiatives. Giselle took up her post and ran into exactly the cultural problems we had foreseen, but more immediately she and the crew had urgent matters to attend to which required their united efforts. The water level of the lake was dropping and the local weather men could offer no assurances as to the volume of glacial melt and rain that could be expected come the next rainy season three months away. The *Yavarí* was in danger of grounding. Although her draught is 10 feet, she draws six feet. Each week, Giselle was out with the plumb line measuring how close the keel was to the lake bottom. As the days passed she became increasingly concerned and needy of advice and of decisions to be taken by me and the UK Trustees. The *Socios* had no practical experience of ships.

All options were examined before deciding that we should extend our pontoon from 44 yards to 76 yards so that the *Yavarí* could lie in deeper water and, at the same time, restore the existing one which was long past its life span. The rusting oil drums, cracking planks and fraying ropes would have given the UK's Health & Safety high strikes! It cost money to repair and extend the pontoon so money was sent from our UK Yavari Project account.

It was then time to refurbish the *Yavari*'s below-decks accommodation to a standard acceptable to the discerning visitor looking for Bed & Breakfast in the unique surroundings of a converted Victorian tramp steamer afloat in Puno bay. Giselle is a perfectionist. She modernised the galley, the bathroom and the lighting, and bought ethnic blankets from the islanders of Anapia. Sheets embroidered with the *Yavari*'s logo and new china and glass were sent from Lima. As always, her estimate was precise but as always things outside her control sent costs over budget. By now our hard-gotten UK funds were all but depleted, but we hoped we would recoup from the Bed & Breakfast enterprise. We advertised through all channels available to us and waited expectantly.

As I walked out of the classroom at the Marlborough Summer School in 2010, a text message came through on my mobile. It was *Times* columnist, journalist and broadcaster Matthew Parris, devotee of the Andes, asking if it was worth him and his companion Julian Glover, a leader writer on the *Guardian*, travelling from Bolivia to visit the *Yavari* – was the ship open? I texted back to say that not only was the ship open but we were now offering Bed & Breakfast. They booked in and Matthew subsequently wrote beautifully crafted articles for the London *Times* and the *Spectator* in praise of the experience, which he said had made him feel 'like the luckiest tourist in the world'. Julian wrote in a similar vein for the *Guardian*, 'for my money the best B&B in South America'.

We circulated the articles and, through the web and word of mouth, bookings began coming in, but clearly it would take time to produce enough income to cover our running costs. We had to reduce our overheads. Our night *watchiman*, Manuel, had already left and been replaced by a younger lad on work experience. It was a modest saving. Then, to our great sadness, the gentle giant Teodocio, or Tio Teo (Uncle Teo) as I called him, handed in his notice. He was being cured of arthritis in his hands by a shaman who had prescribed a course of four herbal infusions a day, which was difficult to adhere to while working on board, or so he said. I think, like me, he was weary of the everyday routine and anxious to get back to his plot of land in the *sierra*. Three of his five children had completed their schooling and left Puno, and it was time for a change. However, it was another saving, and because Antonia had had a baby, Yasmine Victoria, and was only working part-time, that meant a further saving.

We were now down to Giselle, Antonia part-time, Henry the night *watchiman* and a skeleton crew, but even so the income from visitors' donations and the B&B were not enough to meet the costs. I injected more funds to help cover the shortfall. Visitor numbers were falling as the global recession bit into people's pockets, and the visitors who came donated less extravagantly and seldom bought souvenirs. The situation was already depressing but became dire when Máximo asked to take three months' leave without pay so that he could go mining gold and make what he needed and what we couldn't afford to pay him. That, too, was a saving but not a reason to rejoice. On the contrary, our longest serving, most resourceful, most experienced and most valuable crew member was leaving us, maybe only temporarily, but nonetheless looking further afield for remuneration and for a change of scene. Máximo and I had started out together so it was particularly painful for me. We had both expected the *Yavarí* to be financed and sailing years before. I had always been optimistic and heard myself telling the crew at the start of each year that 'this was going to be our year'. I believed it, and so did they.

Throughout the latter years, our hopes would be raised and then fall, but I always softened any bad news that I passed on to the crew. Even if I was disappointed each time, I tried not to convey it to them. If this was deception, it was done with the best of all motives, and Carlos concurred. It was important to maintain morale, and yet I couldn't prevent the slow creep of disillusionment. Máximo was disillusioned and his mood aggravated by his dislike for working for a Limeña. He could have given in his notice but thankfully his debts, his loyalty and his love for the *Yavarí* prevented him going that far. Nonetheless, it was a wake-up call for me.

CHAPTER 17

Casting Off

B Y THIS TIME OUR FUNDS IN the UK had dwindled to almost nothing, and Giselle was struggling to cover costs with the income from the B&B and visitors' donations, but postponing drawing her own salary. There had been no apparent action on the part of the *Socios* with regard to future funding. They offered us a number of reasons why not, but it was frustrating from our point of view. We discussed several ideas, among which we favoured *La Asociación Yavarí* setting up a trading company which would charter the ship, fund the modifications, then either operate it or employ a professional operator. This seemed to be the most practical solution, but they pointed out that no-one would be prepared to invest in the *Yavarí* if they could not own the vessel. We had run into this objection before, but felt that the idea, if sold well and supported by our positive business plan showing how such a proposition would make a profit, could be attractive.

But nothing seemed to inspire the Lima team, nor could they devote a lot of time to the problem. They had other commitments, jobs and families to attend to. So, what to do next? We were careering fast towards catastrophe. In London, we called a meeting of the Trustees. It was a grim occasion, alleviated only by the hallowed surroundings in which it was held. Trustee Hallam Murray had invited us to the John Murray publishing house at 50 Albemarle Street. It was uplifting to be overlooked by portraits of Charles Darwin, Jane Austen and Lord Byron, to mention just three luminaries of the many whose manuscripts were pored over in the very room where we sat.

I had put away an emergency fund which was to be the last financial support I was prepared to give to the *Yavarí*. Love her as I do, I couldn't afford to prop her up indefinitely. Now was the time to spend it, but not just to cover daily expenses for another month or two. Better, I thought, to employ someone who could have one last throw of the dice for us. This person needed to be bilingual in Spanish, and to understand business plans, cash flows, tourism, marketing, marine engineering and the Peruvian *modus operandi*. Naturally he had to be a self-starter overflowing with initiative and new ideas. Did such a person exist, I wondered? But then the job specification was a demanding one. This person had first to go to Peru for six months and, working with the *Socios* in Lima, explore every possible potential source of funding from individuals to international funding agencies. This person had first to make an impartial assessment of the situation, then to knock on every door in Peru and Bolivia, to follow up on all ideas and introductions, and to take a fresh look at how to keep the *Yavarí* afloat now and how to finance the modifications required in order for her to sail again with passengers. A challenge indeed, but a challenge with an obvious reward.

A man called Wayne Menary, with a PhD in Geography, was suggested as someone who could tick many of the boxes. He was bilingual, his wife was Peruvian and he had led his own international project in Peru which had involved him in working with local and central government. He was enthusiastic at interview and we took him on.

I had not been to Peru in two years, the longest time away in twenty-five years, so I followed Wayne to Lima in June 2011, intent on introducing him to everyone we knew and a list of hand-picked individuals Giselle had lined up for us in Puno and Bolivia. Peru was two days away from a presidential election run-off between a left-wing former army officer, Ollanta Humala, and Keiko, the daughter of ex-President Alberto Fujimori who had made the fatal mistake of returning to Peru and standing for re-election but who was now in jail for human rights abuses. The polls indicated that Humala had the edge. He professed to have sympathies with the Indians of the *sierra*, which was good from Puno and the *Yavarí*'s point of view, but to be dangerously antipathetic towards capitalism, which was the kiss of death for *Yavarí* funding. The situation was reminiscent of so many setbacks in the *Yavarí*'s saga. Just as we were ready to take full advantage of a thriving economy, capitalism was under threat and the private sector trembling in anticipation of the worst.

More immediately threatening to the *Yavarí*, however, were the demonstrations being held in Puno by the Aymara Indians. I had read about them before leaving London, but over a superb dinner on my first night in Lima (the gourmet heart of Latin America), Giselle gave me a firsthand account. Thirty thousand Aymaras had invaded downtown Puno, throwing stones and smashing banks' windows before setting fire to the tax office. They were protesting against the mining industry and in particular a four-year-old mining concession close to the Bolivian border which, they claimed, was contaminating their water supply and *chacras* (fields). Understandably, the official mining companies do upset the indigenous communities if they despoil the environment and pollute the water. It has become a sensitive and complicated issue that the industry, government and the NGOs are endeavouring to resolve. While they look for solutions, the Indians remain angry, although the irony is that many of the worst offending mines are the informal ones worked by the indigenous people themselves.

On this occasion, possibly politically motivated as well as being genuinely angry, the Aymara had also called a strike throughout the region and blocked all the roads around Puno, so it and the lake became inaccessible to everyone including tourists. Giselle told me how a breakaway group of 300 protestors, in ugly mood, had marched to the Sonesta Posada Hotel. Behind the hotel the *Yavarí* is tied up to her pontoon which is also used by the local tourist launches, and they had ignored the call to strike. The Indians threatened to advance on both the *Yavarí* (which is foreign, like the mining industry) and the tourist launches. Giselle, the *lancheros* (boatmen) and all the lakeside hotels and their guests were truly alarmed. On the principal that the Indians don't like swimming, Giselle had the wisdom to raise the gangplank and hide the dinghy, but she was clearly shaken by the experience. The General of the Frontier Regiment did bring his men out but refused to use force, least of all arms, to quell the uprising in case of spilling blood and creating martyrs. In this he disobeyed orders from Lima and was sacked, but was immediately reinstated by popular demand of the demonstrators.

Publicity of this kind does no end of damage to the tourist industry and many tour operators cancelled itineraries that included Puno, just when the *Yavarí* badly needed visitors.

The *Socios* met in Lima and I introduced Wayne. They were pleased that someone had come to relieve them of their burden of responsibility, although they seemed more or less decided that *La Asociación Yavarí*, as it was, would never attract the right people nor the funding required. As I mentioned before, in Peru it is the people you know who can make the difference between success and failure. Instead, they, but principally Ellie Zúñiga and John Alfredo Davis, had been thinking of forming a National Trust of Peru which would attract the right people, and raise the finance for the *Yavarí* through it. It was an interesting idea and might work, but obviously it would mean my standing down as President, and *La Asociación* severing ties with The Yavari Project. I said that I would like to get some feedback from my UK Trustees, but in principle it would be formalising the 'hand over' we had been discussing in London.

Of this new option and raising the funding through Wayne's efforts in order to get on with the work right away, I still preferred the second, so I suggested that Wayne carry on with the purpose of his engagement and we would see what happened. We began with a visit to the navy in Callao where we were taken out for a fabulous seafood lunch at the officers' club, and I was presented with a brass plaque in recognition of my endeavours for which I warmly thanked our host who was representing the Director General de Capitanías y Guardacostas. There followed visits to our lawyer, our accountant, the chairman of the British Chamber of Commerce and our naval engineer. We then flew up to Puno. I looked down on the brown crumpled moonscape that lies between the ocean and the high *sierra*. It is such inhospitable terrain, yet dotted here and there are shacks, some actually on top of mountains, whose corrugated roofs glint in the sun. I wondered, as I always do, how people exist in such surroundings and why. From my plane window, I could see the thread-like tracks winding up and around the hills, ridges and mountains, but they didn't necessarily connect the shacks with one another or with any settlement.

On board the *Yavarí*, I saw for the first time what Giselle had done to upgrade the accommodation for the B&B service and was impressed. The cabins, shower, heads and galley had been completely transformed. I looked in the Visitors' Book to see what others had thought. The B&B guests were unanimous, bar one, in their appreciation and pleasure. The exception shared with us our dislike of emitting our sewage into the bay. Had I coincided with his visit I would have told him that the whole of Puno does the same, that it is a disgrace, and that as soon as we can afford it we will be installing a sewage treatment plant, or trucking it to a sewage farm which we would first have to create. The matter of treating Puno's sewerage has been under discussion for as long as I've been going there, first with one international agency, then with another. No-one can agree on what to do, so nothing beyond installing a small plant in one corner of the bay gets done.

I also counted up within a few pages some 50 nationalities of visitors, and their comments were heart-warming. It has always been rewarding for me to see what visitors say. '*Magnifique!*' from France. 'I have travelled 14,000 kilometres to see a 4-cylinder Bolinder hot bulb engine,' from New Zealand. 'Superbly restored,' from Norway. And page after page is always the same.

At 8 o'clock the following morning we formed up on deck in the time honoured way to raise and salute the flag before sitting down to breakfast. Wayne wanted to discuss my position in light of the meeting we had had in Lima. I said that I and the Trustees in the UK had already discussed a role reversal, with *La Asociación* taking on full responsibility for the *Yavarí* from The Yavari Project, and that it was encouraging that the *Socios* had had the same idea. For my part, I could see that I would need to stand aside and that I would be very happy to do that as I now felt that the *Yavarí* would, from now on, be in safe hands. I felt a great sense of relief flood over me. It would be agony to walk away, but the decision had been in my mind and had only needed a prod for me to take it. Wayne then went on to talk about removing the Union flag from our logo, indeed removing all vestiges of the *Yavarí*'s British origins. I thought that was absurd. The ship is British and would lose a lot of her *éclat* if anyone tried to disguise the fact.

I realised that this was a big step, and a bitter-sweet step for me. I wanted to think it through but because we had a lot of meetings with the army, navy and regional authorities which Giselle had lined up for us, I didn't immediately have time.

Even on the long bus ride to Bolivia for more meetings, I was distracted from being able to examine the ramifications of the momentous decision I had just agreed to. The Aymaras were still restless, and although we had checked that we would be able to get through to Bolivia, it wasn't long before we came to our first roadblock. We had reached it early and it wasn't yet fully formed. Nonetheless, our young driver was instantly intimidated and announced, '*Amigos!* We are going to have to turn back'. '*Not on your life*', or words to that effect, shouted back a veteran of many roadblocks, to which we all chimed in '*Vamos!*' – 'Let's go'. So the timid youth had no option but to drive on, encouraged by other traffic also driving through. The road runs along between the lake on the left hand side and the mountains on the right. It was harvest time, so the quinoa, kiwicha and barley had been cut and were stacked in stooks, but where it was still standing it made a striking patchwork of colours, dark green, pale green, yellow, gold, maroon and purple, against the dark blue backdrop of the lake. Spectacular! To the right there was farmland in the foreground, scraggy sheep, llamas and donkeys (plastic bottles and bags), and terracing up the dark pink hillsides. Spectacular too!

We hadn't gone far before we ran into our second roadblock, this time of a rather less serious nature. It appeared to have little to do with the protest; indeed, if we paid a toll we could pass. We looked anxiously at one another. *Gringos* are easily spotted. However, for the princely sum of one New Sol each (10p) we were allowed to pass. We eventually got to the rim of the valley 'bowl' in which La Paz lies overlooked by tightly packed shacks clinging to every inch of every hillside. At 12,000 feet, it is the highest administrative capital in the world and capital to the *serrano* Indians of Bolivia, who are invariably at odds with the population of Sucre in the eastern lowlands, which is the country's constitutional capital. Bolivia is a beautiful country but one of everlasting conflict.

We bustled round La Paz, attending the various appointments made for us by Giselle. Among others, we called on the Peruvian Naval Attaché, an engineering company interested in modifying the *Yavarí*'s hull, the British Ambassador, various tour operators, and an agency focused on the bi-national development of Lake Titicaca. It was a whistlestop visit to introduce Wayne to useful contacts, so once done we turned for home.

We got as far as Copacabana, where we picked up rumours that the frontier with Peru was closed. To check for ourselves we took a taxi the 12 miles or so to the border and it was, indeed, closed. The barrier was down and beyond it a hostile mob of Peruvian Indians. We were not alone; there were groups of backpackers and Indian traders, both Bolivian and Peruvian, all wanting to get through. Speculation was rife as to how long the blockade would last, and whether the bus companies would reimburse our money. Was there any truth in the rumour that a launch was coming over from Puno (10 hours by boat away) to fetch us? Was it only one launch, or would there be several? Would it leave immediately that night, or wait until morning? No-one knew the answer to any of these queries, but I put my faith in Giselle, knowing that if anyone would find out what we should do, she would.

We returned to Copacabana in a mini-bus for free on condition that we stayed in the driver's hotel. We did, and it was colder by many degrees than anything I had experienced camping on the *altiplano*. Having had a lacklustre lunch, I went to revisit the sixteenth-century and very beautiful basilica of Santa Maria, the Virgin of Copacabana, while Giselle went off to ferret out some good news. I was in bed by 5 p.m., dressed in all my clothes, under five blankets, beside a portable gas fire spluttering out a feeble flame.

As I knew she would, Giselle returned with three tickets in her hand. We were booked on one of three launches coming from Puno due to arrive at dawn the following morning. We rose at dawn, frozen, and climbed into the same mini-bus which, taking advantage of the situation, toured the town picking up passengers until even a cat couldn't have squeezed in. When we got to the frontier, we found we were only some of many, all of whom were queuing at Passport Control. Eventually the officers turned up and slowly we filed in to have our passports stamped out of Bolivia. We were an international crowd of Argentine, Brazilian, German, Israeli and French backpackers and many Peruvians. It was still uncertain whether the launches would turn up, but we were all intent on getting a ride if they did. A smart *señora* in fluorescent pink, apparently making a fast buck as self-appointed organiser, told us to 'follow her'. So once the passports had been dealt with there was an unseemly race to follow her to the lake.

The shore was a quarter of a mile away down a narrow stony track across rough farmland. I was by far and away the oldest contestant and I had not long recovered from a broken hip. As giant Argentines and Brazilians carrying 50-pound backpacks thundered past me, I was terribly afraid I might get left behind. I hurried as best I could and was relieved when the shoreline and a little stone landing stage came into view. There I saw half a dozen small rowing boats standing by to row people out to the three launches lying 200 yards off. It was cheering to see them; rescue was at hand. I spotted Giselle and Wayne, who sensibly had not waited for me, being rowed out in a very overcrowded boat towards one of the launches. I was keen to get on the same one. There was much jostling and pushing of many people with rucksacks, babies, bundles, baby carriers and bicycles on the slippery rocks which formed the landing stage. Being the *grande dame*, I pushed as well, saying imperiously, '*Dame tu mano*' – 'Give me your hand' – which they kindly did, and I was passed from one hand to the next and finally handled onto the forward thwart of one of the rowing boats. As it happened this was the oarsman's seat, so with more '*Dame tu mano*' I was lifted into a passenger's position. A large *señora* in a bowler hat wanted paying immediately. That was all right by me but not by an Argentine who held an entertaining and loud argument with the *señora* for the entire trip. By 8.30 a.m., I was aboard the same launch as Giselle and Wayne. It was very old with broken windows and just half a dozen life jackets long, long past their sell-by date. They rattled to the touch.

The launch was already crowded. During the next hour we took on more and more boatloads so that eventually we were 47 plus the bundles, bicycles and rucksacks on the roof, in a boat licensed to carry 35 passengers. When Giselle remonstrated, she was told where to go, so we weighed anchor and at six knots headed north to Puno.

I sat between an Italian and an American couple who lived in Delhi, and we wondered what the driver could see since he had covered the windscreen with a blanket against the sun. Thank Goodness the lake was calm, so our greatest threat was an Argentine woman dressed for tango in a sparkly layered skirt and red high heels who insisted on smoking beside the petrol engine which had long since lost its cover. At 6 p.m., two hours away from Puno, the engine stopped. The disagreeable driver, who had threatened Giselle, and his assistant both tinkered with a spanner. The engine coughed into life, but then died again. It was dusk and a dark cloud heavy with rain was moving towards us as we bobbed lifelessly in the lake. Then Providence intervened as a launch heading for Puno from Taquile Island emerged out of the dusk and came alongside. As the drivers of each shouted at one another about fuel and breakdown, Giselle said, 'Quick! Follow me.' We did, and jumped ship. The escape from Bolivia had taken us 12 hours, but once in Puno we celebrated over an excellent alpaca stew and a bottle of fine Chilean red wine.

Wayne left by bus for Lima, which allowed me time alone with Giselle, Antonia, Pacori, and *watchiman* Henry, and time to see dear Teodocio and other friends in Puno.

* * *

When the time came to leave, I stood on the deck of the *Yavarí*, maybe for the last time – how could I tell? – and thought, as I have so often throughout my twenty-five year relationship with the ship, of the words of the very first Englishman to step ashore in Peru, Sir Francis Drake, who later wrote:

> '...there must be a bygynning of any great matter but (it is) the contenewing unto the end untyll it be thoroughly ffynyshed that yields the trew glory.'[14]

These words, better known today in the form of a popular prayer, have encouraged me to keep going through all the vicissitudes of the project. Now I had come to my end but the 'great matter' was not 'thoroughly ffynyshed'. I was sad, but I knew that it was for the best. And if the *Yavarí* had inspired the creation of Peru's National Trust, it made a very fitting launch into the next stage of her life.

* * *

When Giselle and I got to Lima it was time to tie up one or two matters and have the decisive meeting with the *Socios*, including Giselle and Wayne. I had bought in a supply of wine and we sat in my hotel to thrash out the future of the *Yavarí*, of *La Asociación Yavarí* and The Yavari Project. The idea of the National Trust of Peru was first item on the Agenda. I offered to resign as President and said that for the rest of the meeting I would take the Minutes so they could discuss amongst themselves the best way forward in order to get things done as quickly as possible. As both The Yavari Project and *La Asociación* were broke, with ongoing obligations to captain and crew, the situation was critical and the need for short-term funding urgent.

I was strongly reminded of the *Socios*' meeting we had had in 2009, which had resulted in the B&B upgrade but a reluctance to seek immediate donations. I could only hope that this time, if The Yavari Project, which had been 80% responsible for running and financing the *Yavarí* for the last 25 years, moved right out of the picture, *La Asociación* would find the wherewithal to meet the immediate costs.

The meeting closed on a note of high excitement. The outcome was that the Statutes of *La Asociación Yavarí* would be amended. I would become Vice-President, thereby leaving the position of President free for a Peruvian, and the *Socios*, now emboldened by representing the National

Trust of Peru and working for the benefit of Peru's own patrimony, would go forth to recruit high-profile members who, in turn, would attract the funding required to rescue and restore Peru's heritage, of which the *Yavarí* would be the first property to benefit.

I have to admit that I was not entirely convinced. I had heard intentions earnestly expressed before and I remained dubious. I was still optimistic that Wayne would come up with a source of funding so that we could get the work done. The idea of a National Trust sounded complicated and likely to take a long time to establish, and I was worried about the immediate future. I was glad that Wayne was working on preparing a professional proposal and updating our Business Plan to submit to potential investors and international funding agencies, and I had to remain hopeful that he would come up with a short-term solution as well.

The next day, Giselle accompanied me to the airport. Neither she nor I knew what the future held, but we were encouraged. There were two options on the table: either Wayne came up with an investor or benefactor and enabled us to carry out the modifications right away, or the National Trust of Peru was created by the *Socios* and they would find a benefactor and fund the works themselves. Either way the *Yavarí* would win. I boarded the plane for London in something of an emotional daze, but optimistic.

I knew that the time had definitely come, figuratively speaking, to hand the *Yavarí* back to Peru. In fact she already belonged to *La Asociación Yavarí*, a Peruvian-registered not-for-profit organisation, but The Yavari Project had taken full responsibility for her since 1987. I thought of the many generous and kind hearted people who, over the many years, had given so much moral support and encouragement to me and financial support to the project. I hoped they would appreciate how valuable their investment of enthusiasm and funds had been, and that it was only thanks to them that the *Yavarí* had been rescued and is in such fine condition today. She is admired by the thousands who visit her from all around the world, and that would not have been possible without friends and benefactors. I thought again of Saint Paul, and that 'the seed' should now be 'watered' by others. Since the very outset, it had always been the plan that the project would drop the 'Anglo' of the Anglo-Peruvian and become a purely Peruvian enterprise. I had imagined, however, that the *Yavarí* would have been, by then, fully operational and making money from tourism to finance a social programme of education and conservation.

But at least the ship has been saved and will for many years to come, I hope, be recognised as a unique floating legacy of the Industrial Revolution which changed the world, and as a tribute to the vision of Peru's President Ramon Castilla and the Peruvian navy for undertaking the Herculean challenge of transporting her to Lake Titicaca.

* * *

After I got home, there was a pause. We held a Trustees' meeting, again in the salubrious surroundings of 50 Albemarle Street. We knew that if we heard no good news from Wayne, then as a body we might soon have no *raison d'être*. *La Asociación Yavarí*, Peru would take over from The Yavari Project, UK, and our role of funding the *Yavarí* would become extinct. I thought back to how optimistic I had been of copying the Cusichaca Project in involving young people, and of operating an exchange between the Thames and Titicaca of young 'mariners', but none of that would happen now, particularly in today's economic climate. When Wayne's final report arrived offering possibilities but nothing we could count on, our options were reduced to one. My Trustees were, as always, gentle with me as I faced the facts.

When the first draft of the amended Statutes appeared, there were points to be argued and negotiated which I did with my Trustee Robert Munro, but essentially we were witnessing, in black and white, the birth of the National Trust of Peru, inspired by the *Yavarí* and, indeed to be called *La Asociación Yavarí*. I felt a frisson of pride. If our beloved ship had inspired the creation of such a potentially august institution as Peru's National Trust, and was to be its first acquisition to be funded, then we could raise a hearty cheer and say 'Bravo Zulu' – 'Well Done'.

There followed another pause, then one day the new Statutes in their final form slipped through my letter box and, having paid a visit to the Peruvian Consulate to legalise my signature, I signed them. It was 19 December 2011.

It was the end of one era and the beginning of another.

* * *

The *Yavarí* arrived in Peru in 1862, one hundred and fifty years ago, as a fine example of Victorian ingenuity and shipbuilding prowess. Notwithstanding her various incarnations, she has endured, and as grandmother of the lake fleet has now earned her rightful place in maritime history.

She has survived a life of triumphs and disasters, a story which resonates loudly with the story of her rescue and restoration. Over the years, I have known ecstasy and despair, exasperation and gratification, glee one moment, gloom the next, but at the time of writing this book I have real hope for her future. Everything points to more and many years of sailing around her lake, Lake Titicaca, the highest navigable lake in the world, giving pleasure to visitors, encouraging education and conservation and serving the lakeside communities.

Her Anglo-Peruvian history is an integral part of her background, which I hope will never be overlooked.

No matter where she goes, the *Yavarí* will always carry a small part of me with her. From my heart I wish her a fair wind. May God bless all those who are now responsible for her, those who crew and maintain her, all those in the United Kingdom and around the world who know and admire her, and finally – May God bless all who sail in her.

Reference Notes

1. *Travels Amongst the Great Andes of the Equator.*

2. 'The Anvil', *Norman Conquest 1066*, written for C.R.L. Fletcher's *History of England*, 1911.

3. The Agrarian Reform Act 1964 was introduced by President Fernando Belaúnde Terry's *Acción Popular* party, but radically reformed and imposed in 1969 (Law No. 1776) by General Juan Velasco Alvarado's military regime.

4. Sir Clements Markham, who attempted to collect the cinchona tree (the source of the anti-malarial quinine) to transplant to India, was a self-confessed Peruphile. He wrote about Peru with such affection that the Peruvian Government erected a statue to him at the Royal Geographical Society in London.

5. According to the Bank of England's Inflation Chart.

6. Acosta, José de (2002), *Historia natural e moral de las Indias*, Seville, 1590.

7. Tome VIII, Volumen 3, by Dr Fernando Romero Pintado.

8. A.F. Tschiffely's bestselling account of this journey with two horses named Mancho and Gata was published by Heinemann in 1933 under

the title *From Southern Cross to Pole Star*; it was later re-titled *Tschiffely's Ride*, and was most recently re-issued by Pallas Athene in 2002.

9. In *The Andes and the Amazons*, Harper and Brothers, 1875.

10. In *Around and About South America, Twenty Years of Quest and Query*, published in 1897 by D. Appleton and Company, New York, 1890.

11. From *A Journey Across South America from the Pacific Ocean to the Atlantic*, Vol. IV, Blackie and Son, London, 1873.

12. From *Peru, Incidents of Travel and Exploration in the Land of the Incas*, Harper and Brothers, 1877.

13. 'The Llama', from *More Beasts for Worse Children*.

14. In a letter to Sir Francis Walsingham written from Cape Sagres, Portugal (15 May, 1587), while carrying out a pre-emptive raid on the Spanish fleet as it was preparing for the Armada.

Bibliography

Acosta, José de (2002), *Historia natural e moral de las Indias,* Seville, 1590

Banbury, Philip, *Shipbuilders of the Thames and Medway*, David & Charles, 1971

Bankes, George, *Peru before Pizarro*, Phaidon, 1977

Barnes, Eleanor C, *Alfred Yarrow and His Work*, Edward Arnold, London, 1924

Bingham, Hiram, *The Lost City of the Incas*, Atheneum, New York, 1973

Blanchard, Peter, *Markham in Peru*, University of Texas Press, 1991

Briggs, Asa et al, *The Nineteenth Century*, Thames & Hudson Ltd., 1970

Brower, Norman, *International Register of Historic Ships* © World Ship
    Trust, Anthony Nelson, 1993

Burger, Richard L, *Chavín and the Origins of Andean Civilization*, Thames
    & Hudson, 1995

Cambridge Encyclopædia of Latin America, Cambridge University Press, 1985

Cameron, Ian, *Kingdom of the Sun God*, Random Century, 1990

Clayton, A Lawrence, *Grace, W.R. Grace & Co., The Formative Years 1850-1930*,
    Jameson Books, Ottawa 1985

Dorst, Jean, *South America and Central America – A Natural History*, Random
    House, 1967

Espinar, Humberto, *A History of the Building of Steamers "Yavarí" and Yapurá"*,
    Puno, Peru, 1949 (by kind permission of the National Records of Scotland and
    University of Glasgow Archive Services. Alexander Stephen & Sons Ltd.
    Collection GB0248 UCS 3/1/227).

Farbrother, Robina (Ed.), *Ships*, Paul Hamlyn, London, 1963

Fawcett, Brian, *Railways of the Andes*, George Allen & Unwin, London, 1963

Fincham, John, *A History of Naval Architecture*, Scolar Press, London, 1979

Goreinstein, Shirley et al, *Prehispanic America*, Thames & Hudson Ltd, 1974

Haws, Duncan & Hurst, Alex, *The Maritime History of the World*, Vol. II, Teredo
    Books Ltd., Brighton 1985

Hemming, John, *The Conquest of the Incas*, Macmillan, 1970

Herring, Hubert, *A History of Latin America*, Alfred A. Knopf, New York, 1967

James, Lawrence, *The Rise and Fall of the British Empire*, Little, Brown & Company, 1994; Abacus, 1995

Kendall, Ann, *The Everyday Life of the Incas*, Dorset Press, 1973

Lobely, Douglas, *Ships through the Ages*, Galley Press, 1979

Marcoy, Paul, *A Journey Across South America: from the Pacific Ocean to the Atlantic*, Vol. IV, Blackie and Son, London, 1873

Marett, Sir Robert, *Peru*, Ernest Benn, London, 1965

Markham, Sir Clements, *History of Peru*, Charles H. Sergel & Company, 1895

Mason, J Alden, *The Ancient Civilizations of Peru*, Penguin Books, 1957

Morris, James, *Pax Britannica* trilogy, Faber & Faber, 1968

Morrison, Tony, *Land Above the Clouds*, Andre Deutsch Ltd., 1974

Moseley, Michael E, *The Incas and their Ancestors*, Thames & Hudson, London, 1992

Orton, James, *The Andes and the Amazons*, Harper & Brothers, New York, 1875

Robinson, Arthur RB, *The Magnificent Field of Enterprise, Britons in Peru 1815-1915*, Lima, 1997

Rodman, Selden, *The Peru Traveller*, Ward Lock & Co. Ltd., 1967

Romero Pintado, Fernando, *Historia Marítima del Perú*, Tomo VIII, Volumen 3, 1850-1870, Instituto de Estudios, Lima, 1985

Server, Dean, *The Golden Age of Steam*, Todtri Productions Ltd., 1996

Smith, EC, *A Short History of Marine Engineering*, Babcock & Wilcox, London, 1937

Squier, E George, *Peru, Incidents of Travel and Exploration in the Land of the Incas*, Harper & Brothers, New York, 1877

Trevelyan, GM, *British History in the Nineteenth Century*, Longmans, Green & Co. Ltd., 1922

Tristan, Flora, *Peregrinations of a Pariah* (first published in French, 1838), English translation Virago Press Ltd., London, 1986

Tschiffely, Aimé Felix, *From Southern Cross to Pole Star*, Heinemann, 1933 (later *Tschiffely's Ride*, Pallas Athene, 2002)

Vega, Garcilaso de la, *Royal Commentaries of the Yncas*, Librerías ABC, S.A., Lima, 1979

Vincent, Frank, *Around and About South America, Twenty Years of Quest and Query*, D. Appleton & Company, New York, 1890

Von Hagen, Adriana & Morris, Craig, *The Cities of the Ancient Andes*, Thames & Hudson, New York, 1998

Ward, DR, *Foreign Affairs 1815-1865*, Collins, 1972

Warder, Arthur C, *Steam Conquers the Pacific*, Hodder & Stoughton, London, 1940

Weiner, Charles, *Perou et Bolivie*, Universidad Nacional Mayor de San Marcos, 1880

Whymper, Edward, *Travels Amongst the Great Andes of the Equator*, John Murray, London, 1892

Wu Brading, Celia, *Testimonios Británicos de la Ocupación Chilena de Lima*, Editorial Milla Batres, 1986

Acknowledgements

A great many people have contributed to the success of The Yavari Project with financial, professional, material and/or moral support. To each I owe my deepest thanks, and if I have missed anyone I apologise but my gratitude is no less. Indeed, it is impossible to list the tens of thousands of visitors from around the world who have signed the *Yavari*'s Visitors' Book and added heart-warming comments; their encouragement has meant a great deal.

My one sadness is that some very dear supporters died before this book was written (†); I hope they realised my appreciation.

My special thanks must go to:

HRH The Duke of Edinburgh KG, KT. for honouring The Yavari Project with his foreword and for his interest and support since I received his goodwill message in 1986.

Mr Ian Biles, Mr Frank Carr CBE†, Mr Adrian Chapman†, Mr John L.M. Denham, Mr Per Fonser, Técnico Julian González, Mr Christopher Hobson CSD BIDA, Dr† and Mrs Philip Hugh-Jones, Mr John Kusner†, my mother Billy Larken†, Sir Brian McGrath GCVO, The Mercers Company, Mrs Marjorie Michell†, The John Murray Trust, Mr Michael Palin CBE, Mr M.R.C (Tim) Parr C.Eng. MRINA, Sir John Smith CH CBE† (The Manifold Trust).

Vice Presidents
Mr Ralph Hammond Innes CBE†, Sir William Harding KCMG CVO, Dr Roger Knight, Viscount Montgomery of Alamein CMG CBE, Mr Peter Stanford (USA), Admiral Sir Frank Twiss KCB KCVO DSC†, Captain John Wells CBE DSC RN†, Sir Eric Yarrow MBE.

Trustees and Treasurers in UK
Mrs Lesley Alexander, Mr Colin Armstrong, Mr Simon Cole, Mr Adrian Evans†, Commander David Harris MBE RN†, Dr John Hemming CMG, Miss Morven Hutchison MBE, Mr John Illman CMG†, Mr Peter Lea FCA, Mr Tony Morrison, Mr Robert Munro and Mr Hallam Murray.

Trustees and Advisers in Peru
Sr Victor Salas Bartra, Sr John Alfredo Davis, Sra Martha Giraldo, Mr Gareth Hughes, Srta Yasmine Martin, Sr Cristian Nonis, Sr Juan Palao, Sr Aldo Passano, Sra Teresa Quesada, Dr Alfredo Quintanilla, Ing Mauricio de Romaña, Sr Eduardo (Teddy) Ronalds† and Sra Ellie Zúñiga.

Captain & Crew
Cápitan Carlos Saavedra, Administrator & Interregnum Cápitan Giselle Guldentops, Sr Máximo Flores, Sr Teodocio Cahuana, Srta Antonia Quispe, Sr Manuel Quispe, Dr Ricardo Roca, Sr Basilio Pacori, Sr Tatu Zapana†, Sr Freddy Cahuana, Sr Henry Lerma, Srta Cecilia Zona, and all our student guides.

Volunteers, Benefactors in kind and Participants

In UK
Mr John Benn, Ms Anna Benson-Gyles, Mr Rory Bowen, Mr Trevor Chambers, Mr Roland Craven, Ms Ann Dunkley, Mr Jonathan Gillespie-Payne, Ms Pam Harkness, Mr David Henshall, Mr Chris Jones, Mr Nigel Kenyon (USA), Mrs Christine Lea, Mr Richard Lee, Ms Anne Lewis, Dr Alan P. McGowan, Sr Miguel Palomares, Mr and Mrs Geoff Peel, Ms Clare Porter, Mr Steve Pullen C.Eng MRINA, Mrs Eve Scott, Silverline Press, Mr Ben Wade, Mr Tony Waller, Mr Ken Williams, Mr John White.

In Peru
Dr Andrés Aramburú†, Mrs Anna Bailetti, Ms Katarina Bovin, Mrs Sally

Bowen, Dr Barbara Burns, Sr Rogelio Cahuana, Sr Percy Calisaya, Mr Rodrigo Carrillo, Almirante AP Fernando Casaretto, Dr Carlos Deustua, Sr Luis Dienderas, Captain John Effey, Sr Coco Gutierrez, Mrs Amy Griffis†, Srta Adriana von Hagen, Mr Roger Hart CMG, Dra Patricia Huareg, Ms Jo Kendall, Sr José la Jara, Ms Alice Jenkins, Sr Gaston Larco, Sr Rafael Leon, Srta Esperanza Navarro, Mr Fred Parker†, Ing Carlos Paz, Sra Lucha Porras†, Mlle Françoise Pohu, Mr Matt Powell, Ms Mary Powers†, Mr Richard Ralph CMG CVO, Sr Charles Ricketts, Sr Ernesto de Romaña, Mrs Michie Searles, Ing Manuel Suarez†, Ing Helia Tapia, Sr Amauri Valls, Ing Pedro Vasquez, Sr Romulo de la Vega, Mrs Yolanda Williams, Mr Paul Wright and Sr Walter Wust.

Those who have made various contributions to the publication of this book: Ms Jane Ades, Mrs Caroline Beagley, Mrs Jane Conway-Gordon, Ms Fiona Lesley, Mr Iain Finlayson, Mrs Prue Fox, Ms Denise Heywood, Mrs Hilary Hugh-Jones, Mr Robert Munro, Ms Juliet Simpkins, and Ms Mary Sandys for the final edit. I especially thank my publisher, Anthony Weldon.

Contributors
Mr Bill Addis
Mrs Bill Addison
Ms Jane Ades
Mr and Mrs Peter Afford
Mrs B.J.G. Allen
Mr Michael Amphlett
General de Brigada Willman Andia
Mr John Antony
Mr Mark Arena
Mr Sven Arnegärd
Mrs V.M. Armitage
Mr Peter Ashton
Mr Michael Atkinson
Ms Diana Back
Mr Stuart Badger
Mr Tim Baker
Sr y Sra Hernán Balcazar
Sr Juan Balcazar
Ms Tessa Bamford
Mr Alan Barber
Mr and Mrs John Barnett†
Lady Pamela Barnett†

Mr and Mrs Andrew Barrett
Miss Beth Barrington-Haynes LVO
Mr D.R. Barthrop
Dr G. Bates
Sr Dietrich Bauer
Mrs Caroline Beagley
Mr Chris Beale
Mr W. Beckett
Captain Eric Beetham
Ms Suzannah J. Bell
Mr and Mrs Clifford Bentley
Mr Simon Berthon
Mr Chris Binnie
Mrs Audrey Binyon
Mr and Mrs G.R. Birchall
Mr and Mrs Bob Bleasby†
Mr Patrick Blow
Mr Peter Bolton
Mr W. David Bouch
Mr Andrew Bowcock
Mr Ben Box
Mrs Margaret Bradshaw

Mr M.I. Bromfield
Miss I. Brotherton-Ratcliffe
Mr Douglas Brown
Mrs Luz Burnett
Mrs Lydia Burnet
Mr Alistair Burns
Mr Richard D. Cacchione
Mr Robert Capurro
Mr John Carey
Mrs Anne Carter
Mr Tim Carter
Ms Caroline Carver
Mr Wyndham Carver
Sra Maria Fé Cassinelli
Mr Denholm Christie
Mr Michael Clark
Mr Ron Clark
Mrs Christine Clarke
Mr W.D. Cleaver
Ms Elizabeth Clyne
Mr David Coates
Mr and Mrs Michael Coates
Mr B.T. Colling

Mr T.W. Collins
Mr Nigel Coombes
Mr and Mrs Christopher Cotterell
Sr y Sra Hernán Couturier
Mr L.R. Cox
Mr Roland Craven
Mr† and Mrs John Cunningham
Mrs Carolinda Dacres Russell†
Mr and Mrs John Dallas
Mr Hywel Davies
Mr J. Davies
Miss Esther M. Dean
Mr David Dell CB
Mr N.J. Dennis
The 11th Duke of Devonshire KG MC†
Mr and Mrs Iain Dewar
Mr Robert Dick
Dr A.J.G. Dickens
Mr Denis Doble
Mr and Mrs Bruce Douglas
Mr Simon Duckworth
Commander Dan Duff DSC RN Retd.
Mr F. Dyer
Mrs Hugh Eaton
Mr D.E. Edney
Mr Harvey Edser
Mr John Eldred
Mr Peter Elphick
Ms L. Farleigh
Mr and Mrs John Fairbairn
Ms Norah Farnham
Major and Mrs Robert Ferguson†
Mr Martin Foreman
Mr and Mrs Ian Fosten
Mr John Foster
Mrs Julie Frampton
Mrs Peter Francis
Mr and Mrs Nigel Gallop†
Mr Barry Gardiner
Admiral Sir John and Lady Garnier

Mr Alan Gaskell
Mr David Gilmour
Mr Julian Glover
Mr Julian Glyn-Owen
Mr David Gobbit
Mr Richard Goble
Mr B. Godfrey
Sra Elena González
Mrs Cecilia Goodall
Dr Richard Gorski
Mr and Mrs Paul Goulder
Ms Angela Graham
Mr Ian Grant
Mr John Greaves
Sir Robert Green-Price
Ms Mary Greenwell
Mr Errol Gregory
Mr David Griffith
Dr Michael Grimes
Mr Alan Grundy
Mr and Mrs Charles M. Hale
Mr David Hall
Mr Donald Hall†
Mr Frank Hall
Mrs Kathryn Hall
Mr Nick Harris
Mr and Mrs Iain Harrison
Captain George Hart
Mr Bruce Harvey
Mr and Mrs Alan Harvey
Mr Robert Harwood
Contralmirante Guillermo Hasembank
Ms Julie Heathcote
Mr Martin Hedley
Mrs Margaret Henderson-Tew
Mr Simon Heyes
Mr Simon Higginson
Mr Robin Higgs OBE
Mr Bryan Hird
The Baroness Hooper CMG
Mr and Mrs Frank Hopkins
Mr James Hopley
Mr John C. Horn
Mr Jeremy Horner†
Mr and Mrs John Hoskin

Mr Jason Howard
Mrs Margaret Hoy
Mr R.L. Hudson
Mr David Hughes
Mrs Vanessa Hurran
Mr John Illingworth
Ms Leticia Jack
Mr Stuart Jackman
Mr Michael Jacobs
Mrs Karen Jankel
Sr Alfredo Jochamowitz
Sra Beryl Jochamowitz
Ing Sune Jonsson
Mr B. Johnson
Mrs L.A. Jones
Mr Siv Juhlin
Mrs Penelope Kellie
Mr and Mrs David Kellie-Smith
Mr Nick Kelly
Mr John Kempton
Dr Ann Kendall OBE
Mr Ian Kilgour
Mr and Mrs Laurie King
Mr Anwer Kirmani
Mr Timothy Labrum
Sr Carlos Landa
Ms Jane Lane
Mr Robert Langton
Miss Beryl Larken
Mr† and Mrs Jasper Larken
Mrs Peggy Larken†
Captain and Mrs Wyatt Larken†
Mr Eric D Lawson
Mr David Lewis
Mr E.W. Lewis
Mr and Mrs John Lewis
Mr Paul Lewis
Mr Douglas J. Lindsay
Mr Stuart Little†
Ms Lis Long
Mr and Mrs P.J. Lowden
Mr David Lumsden†
His Honour Judge and Mrs Shaun Lyons
Captain and Mrs Colin Macgregor
Mr Rory Mackean

Mr Niall MacNeill
Mr and Mrs Eric Malcolm
Mr and Mrs Marsh
Mr and Mrs A.C.
Marshall
Mr Jeremy Martin
Mr David Marwood
Mr and Mrs Robert
Maund
Mr Ken D'Maurney
Gibbons
Mr Hugh McCoy
Mr Peter McFarren
Mr Brian Mears
Sra Liliana Merino
Mr and Mrs Tony Merrick
Mr Charles Miller
Ms Carolyn K. Millhiser
Dr Alexandra Morgan
Mr and Mrs David
Morgan
Professor Arthur S. Morris
Mr and Mrs Tony Morris
Sra Mariana Mujica
Mr and Mrs Charles
Muller
Mr Philip Munn†
Mr D. Murray
Mr Brian Nash
Mr Keith Newlands OBE†
Mrs Gordon Nicholson
Mr W.D. Nicholson
Mr and Mrs Noble
John Julius Norwich
Mr and Mrs David Orr
Mr Ian Orr
Ms Sophie Orr
Mrs Joanna Oswin
Mrs Elizabeth Owen
Mr Robin Owen
Mr John Owens
Mr and Mrs Gavin
Owston
Mr Gary Parfoot
Mrs Eileen Parker
Mr Matthew Parris
Mr Rob Partis
Mr Robert Pasley-Tyler
Mrs J.S. Penfold
Mr and Mrs John Perrin

Sr y Sra Maurik Pino
Miss E. Margaret Potts
Mr and Mrs John Pratt
Mr Robin Price
Mr Arthur Prothero†
Mr Paul Quinn
Mr Rob Rachowiecki
Srta Cecilia Raffo
Mr Francis Rainsford
Dr Stewart D. Redwood
FIMMM
Mr and Mrs John Reeve
Dipl.Ing Udo Renger
Mr Michael Reupke
Mr George Rew
Mr Peter Roberts
Ms Isla Robertson
Mr Arthur Robinson
Mr John Robinson
Cápitan Cleto Rodriguez
Srta Gladys Rodriguez
Sr Alejandro Rojas
Mr R.E. Ross
Mr and Mrs R. Ross
Mr Stanley B. Rudge
Mr Brian Saunders
Mr Robin Scales
Mr Tom Schrecker
Mrs Marcia Schultz
Sra Maria Seipt
Ms Rosita Sherrard
Mrs Ann Savours Shirley
Ms Stephanie Simmonds
Mr J.M.W. Simpson
Mr Christopher Singer
Mrs John Slocock
Mrs Gillian Smith
Ms Helena M.F. Smith
Mr Michael Smith
Miss Decima Snell†
Mr and Mrs Wagdy
Soliman
Mr M.J. Soutar
Mr and Mrs Jeremy
Spencer
Ms Anne Spurgeon
Mr Trevor H. Stephenson
Sr Juan Stoessel
Mr Oliver Stonehouse
Mr and Mrs Simon St.

Leger-Harris
Dr Michael Straiton
Mr Howard Strongitharm
Ms Mandy Sugrue
Mr Bob Sutton
Mr M.J. Tapper
Mr and Mrs Nick Tarling
Mr and Mrs Jonathan
Taylor
Mr Stephen Teather
Mr Joseph Teesdale
Ing e Sig.ra P.L.Tesei†
Mrs Diana Tinson
Mr Sean Tooth
Mrs Lyn Traves
Mr John N. Tyacke
Sr Jean-Jacques y Sra
Hortensia Valleton
Mr David Vermont
Mr Norman Vigars†
Sr Eduardo Ponce-Vivanco
Mr Jim Walton
Miss Elizabeth Ward
MBE†
Mr Peter Warwick
Mrs Dorothy E. Watson
Mr Peter Warwick
Mr Philippe Weisshaar
Mr Anthony Westnedge
OBE
Rear Admiral Anthony
Wheatley
Mr Rhodes Wheatley
Mr Paul Wignall
Mr and Mrs Willie Wilks
Mr Colin Wilson DipTP
RIBA
Mr and Mrs Ken Wight
Mr and Mrs John
Woodvine
Srta Penelope Wrightson
Mr A. Yeoman
Mr and Mrs Michael
Younger
Srta Eliane Zilberman
Srta Diana Zileri

Sponsors
Anglo-Peruvian Society
The G.C. Armitage

Charitable Trust
Asociación Cultural Peruano-Británica
Atlas Copco Peruana S.A.
Batchelor Foods
The Marjorie J. Bainton Foundation
Berg Kaprow Lewis Accountants
The British Embassy, Lima
Black & Decker, Perú
The Box Trust
Braillard S.A.
Burness Corlett & Partners
Cámera de Comercio Peruano-Británica
Castrol del Perú
Centro de Estudios Histórico-Militares
The Chiron Trust
Hotel Colón Inn, Puno
Colwyn Bay Model Boat Club
Cooper Dale (Mr Roger Pring)
Hotel Eco Inn, Puno
The Duke of Edinburgh's Trust
Ely Fund Managers
The Embassy of Bolivia, London
The Embassy of Peru, London
The Esmé Fairbairn Trust
Hotel Ferrocarril, Puno
The Fitton Trust
Fundación Telefónica del Perú
Nigel Dewar Gibb & Co
The ss Great Britain Trust
Grupo de Deseño
The Hadley Shipping Company Ltd
The Henhurst Charitable Trust
The J & C Hilton Trust
Hispanic and Luso Brazilian Council (Canning House)

Inca Trail/HERO Car Rally
Institution of Mechanical Engineers (for their Heritage Award 2011)
Journey Latin America
Latin American Travel Association (LATA)
Lloyds Register of Shipping (MARSPEC)
Mabey & Johnson Ltd
MacAlister Elliott & Partners
La Marina de Guerra del Perú:
  Dirección de Control de Intereses Acuáticos de la Dirección General de Capitanías y Guardacostas del Perú
  Dirección de Intereses Marítimos e Información de la Marina de Guerra del Perú
  Dirección General de Capitanías y Guardacostas del Perú (DICAPI)
  Fuerza de Aviación Naval
  Museo Naval del Perú
  Servicios Industriales de la Marina de Guerra del Perú (SIMA)
  Instituto de Estudios Histórico-Marítimos del Perú
  Capitanía de Puerto, Puno
Marine Society & Sea Cadets
Munketellmuseet (Bolinder), Eskilstuna, Sweden
National Maritime Museum
National Maritime Historical Society (USA)
Leisure Property

Part Time Careers Ltd.
PeruRail/Orient Express
Prom Perú Ramblers Holidays Ltd.
Rathbone's
Robert Fleming & Co. Ltd.
Royal Geographical Society + IBG
Royal Institute of Naval Architects (Mr Trevor Blakely MRINA)
Royal & SunAlliance – Seguros Fenix
Ruffer LLP
Sayer Vincent Accountants
Scanda Sportswear
Scottish Maritime Museum
Sider-Perú S.A.
Hotel Sonesta Posada del Inca, Puno
Banco Standard Chartered
Star Communications Consultants Ltd
Teknoquimica S.A.
Volvo S.A. (Sr Enrique Ruiz†)
The Warrior Preservation Trust
Western Ferries (Clyde) Ltd.
Wimbledon Copy Bureau
The Winston Churchill Memorial Trust
World Ship Society
World Ship Trust
The Sir Alfred Yarrow Trust

I would also express my appreciation for the guide books which highlight the *Yavarí*, the many journalists who have written about the ship, and the tour operators and guides who direct visitors to her.

Index